DESIGN WITH THE OTHER 90% CITIES

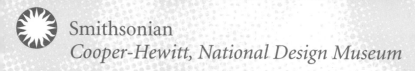

Smithsonian
Cooper-Hewitt, National Design Museum

NEW YORK

CONTENTS

FOREWORD
04

Bill Moggridge, Director
Caroline Baumann, Associate Director
Cooper-Hewitt, National Design Museum

FOREWORD: INNOVATION IN THE AGE OF CITIES
06

Judith Rodin, President, The Rockefeller Foundation

INTRODUCTION
08

Cara McCarty, Curatorial Director
Cooper-Hewitt, National Design Museum

DESIGNING INCLUSIVE CITIES
12

Cynthia E. Smith, Curator of Socially Responsible Design
Cooper-Hewitt, National Design Museum

SHACK/SLUM DWELLERS INTERNATIONAL
32

Interview with Sheela Patel, Founder, Society for Promotion of Area Resource Centers,
and Chair, Shack/Slum Dwellers International, and Jockin Arputham, Founder, National
Slum Dwellers Federation and Shack/Slum Dwellers International

BUILDING NEW WORLDS: DESIGN AND THE SECOND URBAN TRANSITION
40

Edgar Pieterse, Director, African Centre for Cities, University of Cape Town

URBANISM MANUAL 54
Interview with Gabriela Sorda, Co-coordinator, Secretariat of Community Action,
Faculty of Architecture, Design, and Urbanism, University of Buenos Aires

TRUSTING THAT PEOPLE CAN DO IT 60
Somsook Boonyabancha, Founding Director, Asian Coalition for Housing Rights

USHAHIDI 72
Interview with Juliana Rotich, Environment Editor, Global Voices Online,
Cofounder and Program Director, Ushahidi

DIRTY WORK: LANDSCAPE AND INFRASTRUCTURE 78
IN NONFORMAL CITIES
Christian Werthmann, Associate Professor of Landscape Architecture,
Harvard Graduate School of Design

ABALIMI BEZEKHAYA 94
Interview with Christina Kaba, Field Operations Director, and
Robert Small, Resource Mobilization Leader, Abalimi Bezekhaya

DIGITAL DRUM 100
Interview with Sharad Sapra, Uganda Representative and former
Director of Division of Communication, UNICEF

PROFILES 108
Selected by Cynthia E. Smith with Andrea Lipps

SELECTED BIBLIOGRAPHY 224

SELECTED INDEX 226

ACKNOWLEDGMENTS 229

Foreword

Bill Moggridge, Director
Caroline Baumann, Associate Director
Cooper-Hewitt, National Design Museum

Ahmedabad, Bangkok, Buenos Aires, Cape Town, Caracas, Dakar, Delhi, Dhaka, Kampala, Manila, Mexico City, Mumbai, Nairobi, Rio de Janeiro, São Paulo—they are all huge cities in hot countries not too far from the equator, full of bustling humanity and the hubbub of people and machines, rich with the complex aromas of food and perfume as well as pollution and decay. These fast-growing cities share a common element: informal settlements, also called barrios, favelas, shantytowns, slums, or self-made cities. These settlements lack many basic services, but they are also places where people are creating ingenious solutions to the problems they face, collaborating and designing in unexpected ways to make something from almost nothing.

Cynthia E. Smith, Cooper-Hewitt's Curator of Socially Responsible Design, has been on the road for over a year, visiting these cities and seeking out the most interesting examples of resourceful design emerging from the dramatic pressures and needs of their rapidly growing populations. Almost one billion people already live in informal settlements around the world, and this population is expected to double in the next twenty years as people continue to move to the cities in search of work and opportunity. In her essay, Cynthia describes her fascinating journeys of discovery, showcasing hybrid solutions connecting the formal and informal city. She, with the help of Curatorial Assistant Andrea Lipps, has assembled sixty projects for this exhibition, with many more included in the Design Other 90 Network, developed for the exhibition's Web site. Featured projects include a kit of locally manufactured bicycle parts which Africans are using to create customized carts and trailers. In Chile, "incremental housing" provides the essential structure and utilities, but leaves the customized build-out to the locals. An answer to rising sea levels is provided in Bangladesh by a flotilla of modified river boats, equipped to become schools, libraries, clinics, and community centers with solar-powered computers and communication technology. A community cooker in Kenya uses local trash for fuel, with an oven that provides hot water and baked goods. A rapid-transit system in China carries close to a million passengers a day, using dedicated bus lanes and design details such as bicycle storage and elevated platforms to make the system effective and easy to use. These and other projects demonstrate that local talent combined with global resources can provide a glimmer of hope for a better life for the residents of informal settlements.

Design with the Other 90%: CITIES builds on the first exhibition in this series, *Design for the Other 90%*, mounted by Cooper-Hewitt in 2007, which explored the critical issue of poverty and demonstrated how designers are developing solutions to meet the needs of underserved communities around the world. We are gratified to report that *Design for the Other 90%* generated such interest that it has been traveling continuously to venues around the country for four years and is slated to go abroad next year.

We are hugely grateful to the Rockefeller Foundation, especially its President, Dr. Judith Rodin, along with Benjamin de la Peña and Edwin Torres, Joan Shigekawa and Darren Walker (both formerly of the Foundation), who were all early supporters, for recognizing the value of this series and sponsoring the research to develop a second exhibition, which examines the challenges and opportunities encountered at the scale of the city.

We also thank Citi, in particular Susan Avarde, immensely for providing lead support for the exhibition. We are grateful for additional support provided by Procter & Gamble, Deutsche Bank, the Smithsonian 2.0 Fund, the Albert Kunstadter Family Foundation, and the Smithsonian Institution's Research Opportunity Fund. Finally, thanks are due to our colleagues at the United Nations, in particular Michael Adlerstein, Jan Arneson, Ramu Damodaran, Nathalie Leroy, Renata Morteo, Ambassador Joseph Verner Reed, Maria Felisa Wichmann, and Zaw Win. This exhibition is presented at the United Nations in the context of the United Nations Academic Impact initiative, while Cooper-Hewitt's galleries in the Carnegie Mansion are under renovation.

Foreword: Innovation in the Age of Cities

Judith Rodin
President, The Rockefeller Foundation

To say that this groundbreaking exhibition is timely is an understatement. The statistics may be quoted often enough, but they are nevertheless staggering: more than half of the world's population, close to 3.5 billion people, now lives in cities. That number will swell to more than three-quarters of the total global population by the middle of the century.

This incredible growth is at once confounding and promising: while cities aggregate poverty, they also multiply opportunities. As Ed Glaeser puts it, "Cities don't make poor people; cities attract poor people." The very density of the population—the interwoven webs of social networks and myriad communities—creates more possibilities for livelihood per square meter for any single individual than they might have otherwise. But while necessity is the mother of invention, intensity breeds innovation. In the teeming communities of the world's cities, the "adjacent possible" opens up rapidly and new ideas fuse with others to create opportunity.

The innovations that *Design with the Other 90%: CITIES* highlights are not about the big "eureka" moments, which present a false image of invention. Rather, it is, as Edgar Pieterse puts it, "about knitting together a number of small ideas that make sense in a particular context." From housing strategies produced by slum dwellers themselves in Pune, India, to the M-PESA money-transfer system in Kenya and the T*ubig Para sa Barangay* (Water for Low-income Communities) program in Manila—these innovations are marked by small changes that profoundly impact the lives of the households and cities that produced the innovations.

At the core of *Design with the Other 90%: CITIES* is an amazing spirit, the human ability to continually improve. As Sheela Patel and the Slum Dwellers have taught us, when people living in informal settlements operate at survival levels, they produce remarkable innovations to create the communities in which they live.

We are proud to support Cooper-Hewitt, National Design Museum's *Design with the Other 90%: CITIES* exhibition and book. Innovation has been the hallmark and driving force of the Rockefeller Foundation's century of impactful work. From the development of a vaccine for yellow fever to the foundation of the Red Cross, finding innovative solutions to humanity's most pressing problems has been our core focus. We are convinced that helping communities find their own solutions brings not only innovation, but ultimately builds resilience. Grassroots advances are both indicators and generators of community empowerment. As we look forward to this century of the city, we also look forward to the momentous ideas that will emerge from this urban planet and the innovations that will define the next one hundred years.

Our congratulations to Bill Moggridge for his excellent leadership of our nation's national design museum, to Cynthia Smith for her outstanding work scouring the globe for these gems of community-led design, and to the rest of the team at Cooper-Hewitt for continuing to educate us all on the impact of design on our daily life.

Introduction

Cara McCarty
Curatorial Director, Cooper-Hewitt, National Design Museum

Museum exhibitions are public arenas that bring together under one roof works and ideas that often encourage discussion and new ways of thinking. One of the important missions of the Smithsonian's Cooper-Hewitt, National Design Museum is to create an awareness of the way design affects the lives of people remote from everyday life in this country. Such an understanding can come from experiencing different cultures firsthand, yet most visitors never see the excluded parts of cities. I was fortunate to visit Diadema in São Paulo and the Morro da Providência *favela* (informal settlement) in Rio de Janeiro, Brazil, as well as the Khayelitsha and Crossroads townships in Cape Town, South Africa, as part of my travels to those cities. Those experiences left powerful and enduring impressions on me, including the realization that many of the challenges faced by people living in informal settlements are also global challenges.

Cities have become the world's central places for people to live, and in some of the poorer parts of the globe, they are growing faster than ever before. This urbanization is due not only to overall population growth, but because cities are now seen as providing the only possible opportunity to emerge from poverty and assume a path to a full economic and social life. There is no more important design challenge today than the need to create sustainable means of survival for these urban poor.

In 2007, Cooper-Hewitt organized *Design for the Other 90%*, a groundbreaking exhibition that demonstrated how designers are developing workable solutions to improve the lives of populations in need across the globe. *Design with the Other 90%: CITIES*, the second exhibition in the series, focuses on a range of projects responding to urban migration and informal settlements. They are increasingly originated and built by local communities in reciprocal collaboration with designers and architects, underscoring the systemic shift taking place to address the problems associated with rapid urbanization. This emphasis on "designing with" expands the traditional definition of design to include the creative activity of marginalized populations, who are harnessing their energy and skill in ambitious and communal ways to build a better world for themselves and the city they live in. A significant proportion of the world's people now lives in informal settlements, often referred to as slums, and their numbers are continuing to soar at an unprecedented rate. They lack the most basic necessities, and until recently, many of them were invisible, not even recognized by their own governments.

Designers, particularly architects, have long admired the aesthetic qualities of indigenous building and the morphology of squatter settlements. What is now required is an enlarged design perspective that involves questions of land security, affordable economics, clean water and sanitation, overall site design, energy use, and climate change on the one hand; and healthcare, education, and community organization on the other. Citizens cannot achieve this vision on their own. It requires the contributions of design specialists educated not only in the theory and practice of the economically endowed cities of the world, but also in the experience, ingenuity, and lessons of the cities of the Global South. It is time these metropolises were added to the world's urban knowledge base.

This exhibition is a promise of a new idea in design. While this catalogue features sixty examples of the extraordinary capacity of people to innovate, it is also a reminder of how much more could be achieved if local and state governments could reduce the barriers to such innovation and fuse their policies with the efforts of their poorer constituents. With unprecedented population growth and urbanization, it is only through such collaboration that a good, inclusive public infrastructure will be achieved.

There are many questions still to be answered as to how the efforts shown in this exhibition can be scaled up to meet much larger demand. Despite the well-publicized difficulties often associated with the places where economies are still emerging, recent efforts by organizations in these countries to develop effective participation and communal enterprise among poor people and to share these experiences internationally give reason for optimism. Such knowledge exchange and networking are building a new consciousness about informal cities and their transformation. *Design with the Other 90%: CITIES* is not only a recognition of the advent of this good news, it is also an invitation to designers from all over to join in this global enterprise.

Almost one billion people are living in informal settlements, commonly called slums. This population is projected to swell to two billion by 2030.

"We are poor, but not hopeless."

—Melanie Manuel, Backyarders Network,
Manenberg, Cape Flats, South Africa

1

Designing Inclusive Cities

Cynthia E. Smith

Curator of Socially Responsible Design, Cooper-Hewitt, National Design Museum

Hybrid Innovations

I was on my third liter of water; dirt and sand covered me as I walked in blowing wind next to the largest dumpsite in Dakar, Senegal. I had just come from seeing the efforts of a team of Senegalese and Canadian architecture students,[1] who designed and built with local artisans a series of mosaic-clad community wells for the growing peri-urban settlement of Malika (fig. 2). We took an hour's journey back to the center of the city, passing building after building under construction, emblematic of this city's rapid growth.

This would be my last interview after a year of field research in fifteen different cities in Asia, Africa, and Latin America. "What have you discovered in your travels?" asked Oumar Cissé, Executive Director of the African Institute for Urban Management. I told him I had set out to find successful design solutions to rapidly expanding informal settlements, and had found that the most innovative were hybrid solutions that bridge the formal and informal city.[2] Oumar affirmed, "Formal mechanisms are not adequate to tackle this rapid informalization of the city. We are not able to make services available as quickly as the growth. We should make our process more appropriate for this

new reality by creating an interface between the formal and informal."

Clogged streets and overloaded public transport are typical in many of the cities I visited, and Dakar was no exception. A sea of motorbike taxis wove in and out of traffic. Often illegal and unregulated, motor-taxis, with minimal start-up costs, meet the growing demand[3] for cheap transport in many cities in the Global South. Rather than banning these illegal taxis, Oumar described an alternative system in which local governments register the drivers and provide brightly colored and numbered vests to identify them (fig. 3). Through this low-cost solution, motorbikes require no alterations, and their new visibility improves their perception and value within the city.[4] In Bangkok, Thailand, the government is going one step further with Prachawiwat, meaning "Progress of the People," a new evolving program where drivers and other informal workers get benefits like Social Security and bank loans.[5]

Designing with People

In 2007, the first exhibition in Cooper-Hewitt's series on humanitarian design, *Design for the Other 90%*, helped spark an international dialogue

1. Community residents prepare building materials for manufacture, Kaputiei New Town, Kisaju, Kajiado District, Kenya.

about how design could improve the lives of poor and marginalized communities around the world. Professional designers have traditionally focused on the 10% of the world's population that can afford their goods and services, but that has dramatically changed in this new millennium. This new wave of designers, architects, engineers, NGOs, and philanthropists is working directly with people with limited resources, collaborating across sectors to find solutions, and utilizing emerging technology that "leapfrogs" poorer communities into the twenty-first century. They are proving that design can play a significant role in solving the world's most critical problems.

For the first time in history, more of us are living in cities than ever before. This massive urban migration into crowded, unhealthy informal settlements is the leading challenge of this century pushing beyond the capacity of many local institutions to cope. *Design with the Other*

90%: CITIES was conceived to broaden exchanges of knowledge among the people living in our growing cities and architects, engineers, designers, planners, policy-makers, and nongovernmental and funding organizations to generate healthier, inclusive cities. Placing people at the center of the solution is paramount to gaining the required insight to meet this challenge. In his *Triumph of the City*, Edward Glaeser remarks, "Cities don't

2. A local artisan creates a mosaic on a community well, Diamalye informal settlement of Malika area, Dakar, Senegal.
3. Registered Prachawiwat motorbike taxi, Bangkok, Thailand.

The United Nations Habitat Program defines informal settlements as "residential areas where a group of housing units has been constructed on land to which the occupants have no legal claim, or which they occupy illegally; or unplanned settlements and areas where housing is not in compliance with current planning and building regulations (unauthorized housing)."

Naval Settlement, Diadema, Brazil, 2008

UN-HABITAT'S SLUM INDICATORS[61]

UN-Habitat has developed a definition of a slum household in order to use existing household-level surveys and censuses to identify slum dwellers among the urban population. A slum household is defined as one which lacks any one of the following five elements:

Access to sufficient water (for family use, at an affordable price, available without extreme effort)

Access to sanitation (access to an excreta-disposal system, either a private toilet or a public toilet shared with a reasonable number of people)

Security of tenure (documentation to prove secure tenure status or de facto/perceived protection from evictions)

Durability of housing (permanent, adequate structure in nonhazardous location)

Sufficient living area (no more than two people sharing the same room)

make people poor; they attract poor people. The flow of less advantaged people into cities from Rio to Rotterdam demonstrates urban strength, not weakness."[6] The participation of slum dwellers and the urban poor is changing the dynamics of design at all levels.

Migrant Cities

Almost one billion people live in informal settlements, commonly called slums, around the world.[7] That number is projected to double by 2030. Most of the growth will be in emerging and developing countries of the Global South, in an increasingly climate-challenged world.[8] This massive urban migration signals a historic shift in our civilization. There are over 400 cities with one million inhabitants, more than twenty cities with ten million inhabitants, and three cities with at least twenty million.[9] In Latin America, close to 80% of the population live in urban areas,[10] and in Brazil, 90% are city dwellers. By 2030, all "majority world countries"[11] will have more people living in cities than in rural villages.[12] There are an estimated 200,000 slums around the world,[13] with dense living conditions; in Dhaka, Bangladesh, for example, 70% of the population live on only 20% of the city's land.[14] (fig. 4)

Close to 200,000 people are pulled to cities each day,[15] enticed by the possibility of finding work, greater social mobility and freedom, and a better life for their families. They are also pushed from their villages by rising waters, expanding deserts, and refugees from local conflicts. These migrants

erect housing from the materials at hand in leftover, often precarious space. They arrive to divided cities typified by "inclusion and exclusion, integration and marginalization, wealth and poverty, equality and inequality."[16]

Adaptive Solutions

According to John Beardsley of Harvard University, "Slums are now the dominant form of urban land use in much of the developing world."[17] Under constant transformation, cities are complex, with distinct physical features, geographies, cultures, and histories, whose social, economic, and political structures evolve over time. Successful designs adapt to existing conditions. Amidst the extreme geography of Caracas, Venezuela, settlements were built in the vertical mountains that surround the central city. The architecture firm Proyectos Arqui5, working with the San Rafael Unido community in Caracas's La Vega settlement, designed a network of stairs and public landings that incorporate water and sewage systems throughout the settlement. Families were able to remain in their homes, which was critical to maintaining social cohesion.

Coastal cities throughout Asia, with large populations of urban poor, which face changing temperatures, rainfall declines, rising sea levels and flooding, erosion, and salt intrusion, are piloting long-term, citywide measures.[18] India's Surat City engages a range of stakeholders, including industry, academia, and government, via online resources to increase climate-change resilience among poor and vulnerable communities. In the Philippines, My Shelter Foundation solicited designs for a multiuse structure that could withstand typhoons. The winning structure is engineered so that high winds easily pass through it. Located on a hill above the flood line and constructed from locally grown, sustainable bamboo, it doubles as a public school and emergency shelter for the surrounding community (fig. 5).Understanding and utilizing local knowledge are critical for successful design. In Diadema, once one of Brazil's most violent cities, the murder rate dropped from a high of 140 per 100,000 in 1999 to 14 per 100,000 by 2009. In 1983, three out of ten people lived in squatter communities, or *favelas*; by 2010, only three out of every one hundred dwellers lived in them.[19] Using participatory planning and budgeting, the

4. Residents of the dense Korail informal settlement, Dhaka, Bangladesh, access their community via boats.

5

citizens of Diadema drew up plans and allocated the resources necessary to achieve these results. Certificates of tenure,[20] based on right of access for ninety years, were delivered so people could feel secure enough to invest in their future. In contrast, the Savola Ghevra slum-resettlement scheme I visited, twenty-five miles (approx. 40 km) from the center of New Delhi, India, was an isolated urban island. Longstanding poor communities were moved from the center of the city and given small plots of land (less than 18 square meters, or 200 square feet, per resident), dismissing the importance of their established socioeconomic networks and physical proximity to their places of work. In response to this dire situation, the Center for Urban and Regional Excellence (CURE) develops new income-generating solutions such as sewing cooperatives and waste-collection enterprises with residents, especially women and youth (fig. 6). They also share safer design and construction solutions to vastly improve the quality of these families' lives.

In Medellín, Colombia, city plans integrate a cable public-transportation system that links the poorest neighborhoods with the rest of the city. Its Integral Urban Plan introduced safe public spaces, world-class libraries, business centers, and improved schools and medical facilities. This long-term design vision, in direct collaboration with citizens, reduced poverty and violence and improved local capacity and environmental sustainability. As such, it is a replicable model for other cities facing similar conditions.

Right to the City

Anna Kajumulo Tibaijuka, UN-Habitat's former Executive Director, states, "Urban inequality has a direct impact on all aspects of human development, including health, nutrition, gender equality and education."[21] The largest slum in Southeast Asia, Dharavi, in Mumbai, India, is often referred to as "a city within a city." A fishing village in the 1960s, it was transformed into a

5. The Millennium School Bamboo Project design is low-cost, uses local, sustainable materials, can withstand 150-kph (93-mph) winds, and incorporates natural light and ventilation, Camarines-Sur, Philippines.

6

diverse slum of migrants with a vibrant informal economy of globalized exports. In *Urban Revolution*, Jeb Brugmann describes Dharavi as an "engine of urban poverty reduction" for several reasons: high density; low transportation costs, since most workers in Dharavi also live there; high property usage, as buildings are used twenty-four hours a day for housing and workshops. Moreover, manufacturers, suppliers, and retailers are next door to each other, and there is a strong migrant affiliation within micro-industries.[22] Once outside the city, Dharavi now sits on valuable land as the formal city has expanded around it. Families face eviction, either to the periphery of Mumbai or to alternative housing they cannot afford, where they confront a new poverty, moved far from their means of livelihood, where the cost of living outpaces any potential benefits. Local residents formed Shack/Slum Dwellers International to bring attention to their and others' plight in cities around the world. Renowned anthropologist David Harvey calls for "another type of human right, that of the right to the city"[23] for all citizens via new modes of

urbanization that do not dispossess the poor when the land they have settled on increases in value.

Current versions of "world-class cities" consume land at a social, economic, cultural and ecological cost, displacing the urban poor in order to compete in the global marketplace, building airports, technology hubs, highways, golf courses, malls, high-end hotels, and gated communities.[24] Laila Iskander of CID Consulting proposes an alternative approach which draws on traditional methods and culture rather than importing systems more suited for the more economically developed Global North cities. In Cairo, Egypt, CID cooperates with the Zabaleen, a community of minority Coptic Christians who are the primary waste pickers, to maintain an effective pro-poor system of waste management. Daily door-to-door retrieval and sorting recycle 80% of the collected waste while providing income for the pickers. CID has developed innovative partnerships with the Zabaleen to meet the demand for plastic among local and international industries. This system of waste

6. In Savola Ghevra, Delhi, India, a resident cleans the streets and generates income, one local livelihood solution developed by CURE.

removal has spread to other countries, including Peru, Colombia, and Brazil.[25]

In Asia, particularly India, migration is accelerating due to reduced rural economic activity. Rather than occurring at a slower generational pace—in which the first generation moves to a nearby town, the second to a large city, and the third to an international network of cities—all three movements will occur simultaneously.[26] Urban sociologist Saskia Sassen notes that cities are systems of power and laws, suggesting we need to change our systems of authority to meet this challenge.[27] Land-use reforms and securing tenure for informal settlers require cooperation from local authorities and private owners. In Cape Town, South Africa, the government provides public land for urban agriculture next to squatter settlements. An architect in Bangkok designed an equitable tenure solution called "land sharing," in which private land is shared with urban squatters. Reflecting Thai customs of compromise and sharing, the owners develop the street front for commercial use while slum dwellers receive legal tenure and improved housing.[28]

Rather than pushing the poor to the outskirts of the city, policy makers in São Paulo have devised a "compact city" strategy that builds support capacities and infrastructure, mixed-use housing closer to work opportunities, and increased social inclusion and diversity.[29] The São Paulo Municipal Housing Secretariat (SEHAB) was the first city agency in Brazil to publish a public central database, HABISP, with information and statistics about the city's settlements. Architect Elisabete França, SEHAB's Social Housing Director, coordinates programs addressing slum upgrading, water sourcing, and land-tenure regularization.[30] By providing tenure titles (as opposed to property titles)[31] the city has created "planning laws that give the social function of land priority."[32] In an effort to create common ground between top-down planning and bottom-up initiatives, the housing agency partnered with Venezuelan-based Urban Think Tank on the São Paulo Architecture Experiment, inviting Brazilian and international universities to design and implement new housing types and construction technologies in a dozen of the city's settlements.[33]

New Urban Strategies and Practices

New inclusive urbanism approaches respond to subtleties of local culture. URBZ's Mathias Echanove and Rahul Srivastava's action-based urbanology places local users' experience above the trained expert.[34] In their Urban Typhoon workshops from Tokyo to New Delhi, local residents collectively author their urban visions with small multidisciplinary teams. The Indian Institute for Human Settlements (IIHS), in consultation with MIT, Stanford, and Harvard Universities and design firms Arup and IDEO, is creating a new profession. "Urban practitioners," grounded in practice, are taught a set of interdisciplinary skills enabling them to deal with rapid and complex urban growth—just in time, as India's 5,000 urban centers are projected to quadruple to a staggering 20,000 cities by 2050.[35] In Mumbai, Partners for Urban Knowledge's (PUKAR) Youth Fellowship Project democratizes research by bringing together international students with local youth, with the philosophy that "MBAs can learn much from rag pickers." Using research as a transformative tool for advocacy and education, PUKAR's "barefoot researchers" explore their own communities while breaking down class and gender barriers through the student partnerships.[36] A number of international collaborations and initiatives are tackling sustainable urban development. A global coalition of cities called City Alliance is providing investment, planning, and support for poverty reduction, slum urbanization, and future growth, partnering with multilateral organizations like UN-Habitat and the World Bank, nongovernmental groups such as Slum Dwellers International, and ten countries, including the United States, Sweden, South Africa, and the Philippines. C40 Cities is a network that shares solutions for reducing emissions and energy use in urban areas, which produce 70% of the world's CO_2 emissions and consume two-thirds of its energy. In 1992, the

United Nations set Agenda 21, and participating countries agreed to a set of common goals for sustainable development in the twenty-first century. The long-term plan called for local actions that support the environment, social inclusion, and poverty reduction via a broad participatory planning process.[37]

Sustainable and Resilient Cities

As the world's population expands and resources diminish, we need our cities to become more sustainable and resilient, especially in response to increased climate-related activity. For millennia, people have settled along river deltas due to their fertile land and their strategic locations for transport. TU Delft's Room for the River project adapts to river overflows within a densely populated delta region by creating park areas and new building typologies for controlled flooding. Working with local farmers, it designed a "calamity polder," in which cows graze in a green area, and when the water rises, the animals are moved to new artificial "hills" until it recedes. These ideas

have implication on a larger scale since dense informal settlements are the most vulnerable to rising water and changing weather. TU Delft's urban-design students are mapping vulnerable deltas around the world[38] to observe evolving urban ecological systems and formulate more resilient city strategies.[39]

The world's urban centers play a decisive role in reducing our carbon output. The challenge of the twenty-first century—and the third wave of globalization—will be to design effective systems of production, consumption, and habitation. The economic systems set up during the first two waves of global migration—in the nineteenth century as a result of the Industrial Revolution, when the world's population was only one billion; the second at the end of the twentieth century—ran first on coal, then on coal and oil. As these sources of energy become less viable, renewable energy will be needed. Delhi's IIHS is designing an Atlas of Urban Transformation that visualizes global expansion in relation to economic growth

7. Children play on the Platform of Hope, above Gulshan Lake, Dhaka, Bangladesh.

8

and ecological footprint. Dynamic visuals help compare trends: China currently imports natural resources from around the globe to match its rapid growth; Brazil is utilizing local sugarcane for energy; Europe is designing more compact cities; American cities are testing smart technologies to reduce consumption; and India, due to its unique settlement structure, may be able to "tunnel through" this transition period. Even though it may quadruple its urban population, India's carbon footprint may not increase due to its dispersed urban landscape of many cities (rather than just a few large ones) and the availability of rural food supplies near its urban centers.[40]

Insights and Ingenuity
Gulshan Lake separates Dhaka, Bangladesh, from Korail, its largest slum. It lies directly across from the twenty-story headquarters of BRAC, the world's largest development NGO. While living with a local family, architect Khondaker Kabir

constructed the bamboo Platform of Hope above the water. Local children gather on it to play and share the fruits and vegetables from the thriving compact garden Khondaker planted between squatter shacks. We arrived in Korail by bike rickshaw to visit the platform. We walked once the street turned to narrow paths dense with people and vibrant markets, passed small schoolrooms, stepped over open sewage, and made our way to where the slum met the water. Standing on the platform, we realized it created a quiet, open urban space floating between two cities. The low, dense informal city fell away behind us, and the formal city's skyscrapers rose in the distance across the stagnant water (fig. 7).

Other architects, designers, journalists, and artists have resided in informal settlements, and the experience provides them with firsthand insight and changes how they come up with potential solutions. Robert Neuwirth, author of *Shadow*

8. A mural by community youth and artists Haas&Hahn, Vila Cruzeiro favela, Rio de Janeiro, Brazil.

Cities, lived for a time in four sprawling squatter communities in Brazil, Kenya, India, and Turkey, and found them to be thriving centers of ingenuity. Dutch artists Jeroen Koolhaas and Dre Urhahn of Haas&Hahn took me to the gang-controlled favela Vila Cruzeiro, in Rio de Janeiro, where they lived for a year while painting a series of public murals (fig. 8) in an effort to bring international attention to the favelas' living conditions. Bullet holes riddled nearly all of the youth center's walls except for its impenetrable granite-walled stairwell, a safe harbor designed by Dutch architects for children during the frequent gun battles between Rio's police and gangs.

Journalist Steven Otter moved into a makeshift shack in a dense informal settlement miles from the center of Cape Town to confront his own perceptions of race and culture in post-apartheid South Africa. The resulting book, *Khayelitsha, uMlungu in a Township*, exposed the adverse living conditions and, more important, the resourcefulness and strong social fabric of the million people who reside in Khayelitsha, just one of the many slums surrounding Cape Town.[41]

Collective Voices

In Buenos Aires, Argentina, I met with squatter families who mobilized, after being evicted from their homes, to form the Movimiento Territorial de Liberación (MTL) cooperative. Rosa Batalla of MTL described a sort of epiphany, when she "started to realize the answer is not an individual, but a collective solution."[42] The 326 families designed and constructed their own housing with the help of a prominent architect. The group has been so successful that it now builds social housing for similar cooperatives, employing construction workers and its own architects.

Reimagining a settlement or *villas de emergencia* (emergency dwellings) on the southern side of Buenos Aires, architect Flavio Janches used games to gain youth participation for the design of a new public space. A starting point for the revitalization of the community, a playground features on one

INFORMAL HUMAN SETTLEMENTS: NAMES AND TERMS[59]

Informal squatter settlements and slums occur in many countries around the world, and different cultures use different words to describe these precarious settlements. Some terms are used by authorities, others by the community. Terms change and evolve over time, as do attitudes.

Inadequate housing

Informal settlement

Marginal settlements

Non-permanent structures (definition varies from country to country)

Precarious settlements

Squatter town

Unconventional dwellings (inappropriate for human habitation)

Unplanned settlements

Villas de emergencia: "emergency dwellings" (Argentina)

Villa miseria: "poor city" (Argentina)

Ukumbashi: "squatters, people without shelter" (Bangladesh)

Sukumbashi basti: "homeless people's settlement" (Bangladesh)

Favela (Brazil)

Sahakhum: "poor settlement" (Cambodia)

Campamento (Chile)

Barrio marginal (Ecuador)

Dambo muro: "underground cardboard settlements" (Japan)

Huho sengkyo: "illegal occupation" (Japan)

Tento muro: "tent village," i.e., temporary vinyl houses built by homeless construction laborers (Japan)

Sweepers' colonies, butchers' colonies, etc., named for inhabitants' traditional tasks (Nepal)

side large wall murals painted in memory of those lost to violence by local youths with earlier records of violence, artists, and social workers, giving expression to the socially and spatially isolated Villa Tranquila neighborhood.[43] (fig. 9)

Trash and pollution cause many social and health problems in the Kibera settlement in Nairobi, Kenya. The Community Cooker (*Jiko ya Jamii*), designed and engineered by the Nairobi architectural firm Planning Systems, is a large-scale oven that uses trash, collected by local youth for income, to power a neighborhood cooking facility (fig. 10). Community members bring collected trash in exchange for use of the cooker, one hour or less to cook a meal, or twenty liters of hot water. Elsewhere in Kibera, a collective of local artisans and groups, landscape designers, architects, and engineers has reclaimed a dumping site next to a stream that runs through the slum. The Kibera Public Space Project incorporates a variety of uses, including micro-enterprises, a community pavilion, youth playground, and gardens for composting.

9. A new playground and mural by local youth commemorate those lost to violence, Villa Tranquila neighborhood, Buenos Aires, Argentina.

Muhoga Chongchakji: "settlement without permission," city planners' legal and technical term (Korea)

Daldongne: "moon village," settlement on undevelopable hilltop (Korea)

Sandongne: "mountain village," settlements built on the steep hill slopes (Korea)

Amchi wasti: "for our settlement" (India)

Kampong kumuh: kampong ("village") with legal tenure but bad living conditions (Malaysia, Indonesia)

Kampong liar: "illegal settlement" (Malaysia, Indonesia)

Hak milik: "rights owned by the people," a new term for informal settlements (Malaysia)

Asentamiento irregular (Mexico)

Chapro: shack or poor-quality house (Nepal)

Squatter settlement: Official term for illegal settlement (Nepal)

Slum: official term for poor settlement with legal tenure (Nepal)

Katchi abadi (Pakistan)

Basti: "small settlement" (Pakistan)

Colony (big settlement, Pakistan)

Barriada (Peru)

Bidonville (Tunisia)

Turgurios (San Salvador)

UmKhuku: "chicken coop" in Zulu, describing shacks and shack settlements (South Africa)

uMjondolo: "shack" in Zulu (South Africa)

Shack settlements (South Africa)

Palpath: "shanty settlement," official term emphasizing illegality; not used by community (Sri Lanka)

Watta: "garden," euphemism for shanty or squatter settlement (Sri Lanka)

Chumchon bukberk or chumchon: "pioneering community" (Thailand)

Chumchon Aai-aat: "crowded community," official government term (Thailand)

Barrio (Venezuela)

Khu nha o chuot: "settlement of rat's houses" (Vietnam)

Nhaa tam bo: "temporary house," legal term (Vietnam)

Nhaa lup xup: "precarious house," legal term (Vietnam)

Visible Settlements

A fundamental step in gaining better living conditions in an informal settlement is to understand its circumstances. In Nairobi, no one could tell me exactly how many people lived in Kibera—anywhere from 750,000 to 1.5 million. The slum is roughly two-thirds the size of New York City's Central Park, making it one of the largest informal settlements in eastern Africa.[44] But technology is helping to visualize what actually exists in these blank spots on the official map. In Bangladesh, Venezuela, and Kenya, Google Map satellite images help display the density of settlements. Using open-source mapping software, GroundTruth works with local youth to pinpoint water and sanitation locations, security problems, and health clinics via Map Kibera.[45] Other slum dwellers use enumeration and mapping in an effort to understand who lives in the settlement and what services are lacking, an early step in upgrading. In Cape Town, I interviewed women community leaders from Manenberg's Federation of the Urban Poor and SDI, who had been invisible to the municipality but now live in improved housing. In the townships (the South African term for slums), families often rent out their backyards to the newest squatters, the "hidden backyarders," who were revealed in a new survey of the overcrowded neighborhood (fig. 11). A new organization formed the West Cape Backyarders Network to improve the conditions of these families living without water, electricity, and toilets, often sleeping four to a bed in makeshift shacks.

Informal Exchanges and Incremental Design

Denied the basic services, proper shelter, jobs, and other advantages cities offer, informal settlers are discovering new forms of exchanges and collaboration to meet their needs. In Manila, I met with the Payatas Scavenger Association, mostly women that are "no longer waiting for the government."[46] An affiliate of Shack/Slum Dwellers International, it formed a micro-saving group and pooled money to move its members away from Payatas's mountain of garbage, which had killed close to 2,000 people when a landslide

12

SHACK/SLUM DWELLERS EXCHANGES[60]

When professionals are the agents of change, the focus of learning is taken away from the community. Most rituals of "participation" actually seek to ensure the consensus of the group to the ideas suggested by the professionals. As a result, three problems arise:

Communities are unable to advance their own strategies and approaches to their own problems.

The ability to create genuine federations and networks of poor urban communities is denied.

Solutions driven by professionals are often too expensive and inappropriate to the needs of the poor.

engulfed a section of the slum after heavy rains. Purchasing land, they designed housing with help from volunteer architects and learned the skills to purchase materials and construct new homes themselves. They are currently turning the new community, Miraculous Hills, into a sustainable "eco-village". This innovative approach to building a pro-poor city started in Mumbai, India, and has spread to thirty-four countries in Asia, Africa, and Latin America via Shack and Slum Dwellers International exchanges (fig. 12). Fundamental to this process is the belief that people deserve the information to choose where to go and how to live safely.

Alternatively, a group of families who used to beg on the streets of Nairobi saved enough money to purchase land 43.5 miles (70 km) outside the city and are manufacturing their own building

10. Kibera residents make use of the Community Cooker, Nairobi, Kenya.
11. Squatters in Manenberg settle in the backyards of other families, Cape Flats, Cape Town, South Africa.
12. Mahila Milan discusses saving as a group to a local community in the slum settlement of Pune, India.

13. A bicycle fabricated using the Design With Africa bicycle modules, Rustenburg, South Africa.

materials (fig. 1). They formed the Jamii Bora Trust and worked with architects to erect Kaputiei New Town, a safer, cleaner village with over 700 houses and temporary storefronts, primary and secondary schools, churches, factories, and a town generator.[47]

Basic urban planning and design knowledge are shared with newly arriving squatters in Argentina. Architects from the University of Buenos Aires' Secretary of Community Action program designed, produced, and distribute a free workbook, *Manual de Urbanismo para Asentamientos Precarios* (*Urbanism Manual for Precarious Settlements*), on how to build in safer, more strategic locations that anticipate their future. Other initiatives overcome limited available resources to find a solution. In South Africa, industrial design group ...XYZ[48] demonstrated to me the Design With Africa initiative, which uses local context and culture to design products for Africa. Rather than deliver a highly specialized, fully made product, they conceived a minimal, low-cost armature, which includes parts local artisans can easily manufacture, and can be transformed for many uses—in this case, a bike, cart, or taxi (fig. 13).

To meet the exploding demand for housing, Chilean architects Elemental designed half-built "incremental houses," which include the basics such as the roof, kitchen, and bathroom, leaving the occupants to build the rest.

Equal Access
Mzonke Poni, organizer of Abahlali baseMjondolo, a grassroots movement fighting for better conditions in South Africa, walked me through narrow passages between small shelters in QQ Section Site B of Khayelitsha. As we turned a corner past outdoor hair salons and makeshift saloons, the air filled with the smell of frying chicken feet and sounds of vuvuzelas blowing in the distance in anticipation of the soccer World Cup. Mzonke showed me where the small shacks, built on land much lower than the road, flood regularly. He explained that the local electrical company refused to provide electricity—a necessity, not merely an option, for residents of informal settlements around the world if they are to participate in the world economy. In Manila, the local utility, Meralco, electrified dense settlements by bringing distribution lines to the edge of the slums and creating "elevated meter centers" that provide power and protect lines from unsafe connections.

Slipping and sliding at times, stepping over open sewage, we made our way to several shower and latrine blocks constructed by local NGO Maji na Ufanisi, whose motto is "Water is life; sanitation is dignity." Part of K-WATSAN (Kibera Integrated Water, Sanitation & Waste Management Project), in Soweto East, one of the twelve villages in Kibera, it worked with the UN-Habitat/World Bank Cities Alliance and the Government of Kenya to build eight such sanitation blocks. Users pay a small fee to the community-based organization, which runs the sanitation block and maintains the clean water, showers, and toilets. Also in Nairobi, Ecotact has created Ikotoilet Malls, which provide similar services for the urban poor and business community. Users' nominal costs are offset by local enterprises, such shoeshine booths, mobile-phone services, newspaper vendors, barbers, and

snack shops, and by advertising. Biogas from human waste is used to generate light and hot water. Unmade Trust designed fourteen BioCentre community latrine blocks in Kibera. Three stories high, they feature toilets and showers accessible to the disabled and free "child-only" toilets; kiosks selling affordable clean water; and a community center and offices on the top two floors (fig. 14). A biogas-generating latrine block treats human waste in situ without requiring sanitation infrastructure. Built with locally available technology and unskilled labor, it requires minimal maintenance and has no movable parts.

In Kampala, Uganda, I met merchants from the Kalarwe Market, who formed a micro-savings group, Zibulaatudde Savings and Development, which is unusual in that it formed around a market rather than a neighborhood. When asked what they were saving for, most responded, "Proper education for our children." In Mumbai's slums, the organization Pratham, working with UNICEF, runs schools in nontraditional spaces such as temples and homes, helping first-generation learners gain basic literacy and numeracy skills. It targets poor urban communities, or *bastis*, for universal elementary education, and has thus far established programs in 4,000 bastis. Their learning-by-doing method was designed to significantly impact the students in four to eight weeks.[49]

Using the neighborhood streets of Villa Madalena in São Paulo, Gilberto Dimenstein and *Bairro Escola* (Neighborhood as School) engage the community by forming a network of resources, such as a theater, school, cultural centers, and businesses. At school, children hone their creativity and skills by designing books, stools, and media.[50] (fig. 15)

14. BioCentre community latrine block, constructed by Umande Trust, in Kibera, Nairobi, Kenya.

This innovative model has spread to five hundred Brazilian cities in partnership with local and federal agencies.[51] To improve access to transportation, the new Janmarg Bus Rapid Transit system in the growing city of Ahmedabad, India, raised platforms for at-grade boarding and pre-ticketing, greatly reducing boarding time. We easily entered the bus and quickly moved through the congestion of motorbikes, cars, bicycles, and rickshaws on either side of us. Our fellow passengers were a cross-section of the population: the elderly and disabled, people heading to work, young students. Abhijit Lokre from the Centre for Excellence in Urban Transport at CEPT University explained how one poor minority community far from the center is now connected to the rest of the city via this initial BRT route.[52] The city, which expects its population to double from five to ten million by 2030, plans to create a fifty-five-mile network of Janmarg ("the people's way") BRT lines linked to different modes of transport.[53] Another Indian city, Chennai, is working on an integrated regional transportation plan that accommodates growth in surrounding cities. In rapidly urbanizing China, Guangzhou's high-capacity BRT system comes close to what Sue Zielinski of SMART (Sustainable Mobility & Accessibility Research & Transformation) calls "multi-modal forms of transport, commuter trains linked to bus rapid transit and bike lanes that provide a door-to-door, seamless system enhanced by information technology."[54] Handling one million passenger trips a day, Guangzhou's dedicated BRT corridor connects to the subway at six stations and 8,000 bikes via 150 bike-sharing stations; information technology is still on the horizon.[55] (fig. 16)

15. The Bairro Escola in the Villa Madalena neighborhood, São Paulo, Brazil.
16. The Guangzhou Bus Rapid Transit system serves 8,500 passengers an hour and helps cut carbon emissions and reduce congestion, Guangzhou, China.

Innovative Urban Solutions

Urbanization is perceived by some to be the problem; paradoxically, it can be the solution because it can provide "pathways out of destitution"[56] and opportunities for a better future. Rather than disrupt, ignore, or neglect the poor, cities should build their capacity, pulling all segments of the city together toward improving their lives. Design is giving form to ideas generated in partnership with all of the cities' stakeholders. Yet more is needed to meet this growing challenge.

For those still living or migrating to precarious settlements in the next decades, innovative measures to improve security of tenure, basic amenities, and livelihoods will be required, such as CODI's land-sharing in Thailand, ENDA's sustainable wastewater system in Senegal, and the COOPA ROCA collective's entrepreneurial efforts in Brazil. This will require creating new systems for sharing successful models like these, adapted for local culture and place; scaling up for wider implementation; helping authorities at the local level improve infrastructure; redefining what constitutes a sustainable, inclusive, competitive, world-class city; preparing for increased climate activity; and developing a "knowledge web for urban infrastructure."[57]

Countries' economies are linked to cities; in the United States, 90% of the GDP comes from urban areas.[58] Establishing thriving, sustainable cities in the Global North as well as in the Global South is imperative during this period of urban migration, climate change, and economic expansion. We need to show a new generation of practitioners how to design for density, mixed use, and social inclusion through mixed-income cohabitation, long-term investment in multi-modal public transportation, and collaborative regional approaches. We can all learn directly from developing and emerging economies how to create innovative solutions from limited resources and challenging environmental requirements. Urban Think Tank's Vertical Gym, designed for the violent slums of Caracas, can easily be translated for the dense borough of Queens in New York City; and Planning System's Community Cooker can serve those in remote locations in Canada.

It will be difficult to meet the extraordinary challenges that our urban areas face from the massive population shift from villages to cities. We need to plan for transformative change, include people in the planning, and educate for urban

complexity. The projects included in *Design with the Other 90%: CITIES* explore new social, spatial, and economic structures. It is critical we find ways to share this information—the urban success stories, ways to implement and sustain these efforts, and their impact over time. This will require a more inclusive urban design; responsible economic and environmental policies; establishing new institutions; transparent governance; improved equity and security; and land reform for a more just and humane urban world.

Notes

1. Field research with design/build team of students and Denise Piché and André Causult, Professors of Architecture, University of Laval, Quebec City, Canada, and students from the Collège d'Architecture de Dakar, in the peri-urban area of Malika in Dakar, Senegal, June 24, 2010.

2. Carlos Brillembourg, "José Castillo," in *BOMB* 94 (winter 2005–6).

3. Meeting with Oumar Cissé, African Institute for Urban Management, Dakar, Senegal, June 24, 2010.

4. Ibid.

5. "Thailand's Motor-bike Taxis: Enter the Orange Shirts," in *The Economist* (February 17, 2011): 42–43.

6. Edward Glaeser, *Triumph of the City: How Our Greatest Invention Makes Us Richer, Smarter, Greener, Healthier, and Happier* (New York: The Penguin Press, 2011): 9.

7. Pietro Garau, Elliott D. Sclar, and Gabriella Y. Carolina, *A Home in the City: UN Millennium Project, Task Force on Improving the Lives of Slum Dwellers* (London: Earthscan, 2005): 12.

8. "Slum Dwellers to Double by 2030: Millennium Development Goal Could Fall Short," in UN-HABITAT: Twenty-first Session of the Governing Council, April 16–20, 2007, http://www.unhabitat.org/downloads/docs/4631_46759_GC%2021%20Slum%20dwellers%20to%20double.pdf (accessed 3/15/11).

9. 2009 statistics: 376 cities between 1–5 million; 32 cities 5–10 million; 21 cities with at least 10 million; 3 cities with at least 20 million (Tokyo, Delhi, SãoPaulo). "Urban Agglomerations 2009," in United Nations, Department of Economic and Social Affairs, Population Division, http://esa.un.org/unpd/wup/Documents/WUP2009_Wallchart_Urban-Agglomerations_Final.pdf (accessed 5/3/11).

10. "World Urbanization Prospects: The 2009 Revision," in United Nations Department of Economic and Social Affairs/Population Division 9, 9–10, http://esa.un.org/unpd/wup/Documents/WUP2009_Highlights_Final.pdf (accessed 5/3/11).

11. Less economically developed countries where most people of the world live.

12. UN Habitat, *State of World's Cities 2010/2011: Bridging the Urban Divide* (London: Earthscan, 2008): viii.

13. Mike Davis, *Planet of Slums* (London: Verso, 2006): 26.

14. Ibid., p. 95.

15. "Every year, close to 70 million people leave their rural homes and head for the cities. That's around 1.4 million per week, 200,000 a day, 8,000 each hour, 130 every minute." Robert Neuwirth, in *Shadow Cities: A Billion Squatters, a New Urban World* (New York: Routledge, 2006): xiii.

16. UN-Habitat, *State of the World Cities 2010/2011*, back cover.

17. John Beardsley, "A Billion Slum Dwellers and Counting," in *Harvard Design Magazine*, no. 27 (fall 2007–winter 2008).

18. Sarah Opitz-Stapleton et al., eds., *Asian Cities Climate Change Resilience Network (ACCCRN): Responding to the Urban Climate Challenge* (Boulder: Institute for Social and Environmental Transition, 2009).

19. José de Filippi, "Diadema, SP, Brazil: Housing, Urban Design and Citizenship," in *ReVista, Harvard Review of Latin America* IX, no. 2 (spring/summer 2010): 25–26.

20. Mário Realie and Sérgio Alli, "The City of Diadema and the City Statute," in *The City Statute of Brazil: A Commentary*, 38 (São Paulo: Cities Alliance and Ministry of Cities, 2010).

21. Eduardo Lopez Moreno, "UN-Habitat: State of the World's Cities Report 2008/9," http://www.un-ngls.org/site/article.php?id article=590 (accessed 4/26/11).

22. Jeb Brugmann, *Welcome to the Urban Revolution: How Cities Are Changing the World* (New York: Bloomsbury Press, 2009): 98, 99.

23. David Harvey, "The Right to the City," in *New Left Review* 53 (September–October 2008), http://www.newleftreview.org/?view=2740 (accessed 4/26/11).

24. "IIHS in Conversation with Prof. Yves Cabannes, Development Planning Unit, University College of London," in Indian Institute for Human Settlements, https://sites.google.com/a/iihs.co.in/iihs/interviews-and-videos/yves-cabannes (accessed 5/1/11).

25. E-mail correspondence with Laila Iskandar, CID Consulting, December 14, 2010.

26. Brugmann, pp. 41, 42.

27. Saskia Sassen, "Bridging Cities: Social and Ecological Systems," lecture at Cities and Eco-crises Conference, Columbia University, New York, NY, October 1, 2010.

28. Meeting with Somsook Boonyabancha, Asian Coalition for Housing Rights, Bangkok, Thailand, January 14, 2010.

29. Remarks by Domingo Pires, Secretary of Housing of São Paulo and SP Urbanismo, at "Debating Poverty Reduction (II), Design and Planning Strategies" panel, organized by Columbia University, New York, NY, April 12, 2011.

30. E-mail correspondence with Gabriella Carolini, Edward J. Bloustein School of Public Planning, Rutgers, the State University of New Jersey, February 13, 2010.

31. Edesio Fernandes, "Regularising informal settlements in Brazil: By Legalization, Security of Tenure and City Management," paper presented at the ESF/N-Aerus Annual Workshop, Leuven, Brussels, May 23–26, 2001).

32. E-mail correspondence with Gabriella Carolini, February 13, 2010.

33. Alfredo Brillembourg, Elisabete Franca, Elton Santa Fe Zacarias, and Hubert Klumper, "São Paulo - Projeto de Urbanização de Favelas (Sao Paulo Architecture Experiment)" (São Paulo: HABI - Superintendencia de Habitação Popular/Secretaria Municipal de Habitação; New York: Columbia University Graduate School of Architecture, Planning and Preservation SLUM Lab, 2010): 6.

34. E-mail correspondence with Matias Sendoa Echanove, March 09, 2011.

35. Meeting with Aromar Revi, Indian Institute for Human Settlements, New Delhi, India, January 22, 2010.

36. Meeting with Anita Patil Deshmukh, PUKAR, Mumbai, India, January 29, 2010.

37. Agenda 21 was formulated at the United Nations Conference on Environment and Development (UNCED), held in Rio de Janeiro, Brazil, June 3–14, 1992. "Agenda 21," UN Department of Economic and Social Affairs, Division of Sustainable Development, http://www.un.org/esa/dsd/agenda21/index.shtml (accessed 4/18/11).

38. TU Delft U-Lab's Urban Delta program: Rhine-Meuse Delta (Netherlands), Mississippi Delta (US), Yangtze Delta (China), Pearl River Delta (China), Parana River Delta (Argentina), Mekong Delta (Vietnam), Kaoshiung Delta (Taiwan); email correspondence with Han Meyer, TU Delft, August 17, 2011.

39. Meeting with Han Meyer, Urban Design Department, TU Delft, Delft, Netherlands, January 7, 2010.

40. Meeting with Aromar Revi, January 22, 2010.

41. Steve Otter, *Khayelitsha: uMlungu in a Township* (South Africa: Penguin, 2007).

42. Meeting with Rosa Batalla, Movimiento Territorial Liberación, Buenos Aires, Argentina, April 1, 2010.

43. Meeting with Flavio Janches, B&J Architecture, Buenos Aires, Argentina, April 2010. See also "Designing Urban Opportunities," in *ReVista, Harvard Review of Latin America* IX, no. 2 (spring/summer 2010): 24.

44. Adam W. Parsons, *Megaslumming: A Journey Through Sub-Saharan Africa's Largest Shantytown* (UK: Share the World's Resources, 2009): 28.

45. Meeting with Erica Hagen, GroundTruth Initiative, Nairobi, Kenya, June 14, 2010.

46. Meeting with Philippine Action for Community-Led Shelter Initiatives and Homeless People's Federation Philippines, Manila, Philippines, January 10, 2010.

47. E-mail correspondence with Elector Atieno, Jamii Bora Trust, May 23, 2011.

48. Meeting with Roelf Mulder and Byron Qually, ...XYZ Design, Cape Town, South Africa, June 8, 2010.

49. "Pratham: Every Child in School and Learning Well: History," http://www.pratham.org/M-13-2-History.aspx (accessed 4/30/11).

50. Meeting with Gilberto Dimenstein, Apprendiz, São Paulo, Brazil, March 30, 2010.

51. Gilberto Dimenstein, "The City as School," in Harvard Business Review Blog (April 22, 2011), http://blogs.hbr.org/revitalizing-cities/2011/04/the-city-as-school.html (accessed 4/30/11).

52. Meeting with Abhijit Lokre, Centre for Excellence in Urban Transport, CEPT University, Ahmedabad, India, January 25, 2010.

53. Meena Kadri, "People's Way: Urban Mobility in Ahmedabad," in *Design Observer* (April 19, 2010), http://places.designobserver.com/feature/peoples-way-urban-mobility-in-ahmedabad/12918/ (accessed 5/3/11).

54. Cooper-Hewitt public program: "Food and Transportation: New Systems Approach to Transforming Cities Sustainably," New York, NY, October 19, 2010.

55. E-mail correspondence with Stephanie Lotshaw, Institute for Transportation & Development Policy, May 24, 2011.

56. Glaeser, p. 90.

57. Meeting with Michael Lindfield, Asian Development Bank, Manila, Philippines, January 11, 2010.

58. Statement by Derek Douglas, Special Assistant to the President for Urban Affairs, White House, at the 2011 Regional Assembly "Innovation and the Global City," New York, NY, April 15, 2011.

59. Asian Coalition for Housing Rights, "Housing by People in Asia," in *Newsletter of ACHR* no. 12 (April 1999): 22. See also "The Slums of Asia: An Etymological Tour around Asia," in Asia Society, http://asiasociety.org/policy-politics/social-issues/human-rights/slums-asia (accessed 4/30/11).

60. "Exchange Programmes," in Shack/Slum Dwellers International, http://sdinet.org/rituals/ritual5.htm (accessed 4/4/11).

61. "The UN Millennium Declaration and Its Goals: UN-Habitat's Slum Indicators," in UN-Habitat, http://ww2.unhabitat.org/mdg/ (accessed 3/15/11).

1. A record of Mahila Milan member savings is kept, Mumbai, India.
2. Residents discuss Sheffield Road settlement enumeration and community mapping, Philippi Township, Cape Town, South Africa.

Shack/Slum Dwellers International

Interview with
Sheela Patel, Founder, Society for Promotion of Area Resource Centers, and Chair,
Shack/Slum Dwellers International
Jockin Arputham, Founder, National Slum Dwellers Federation and Shack/Slum Dwellers
International

By Cynthia E. Smith

What are the Society for Promotion of Area Resource Centers and Mahila Milan, and what are their missions? How do SPARC, Mahila Milan, and the National Slum Dwellers Federation work together? How many members make up this coalition?
Sheela Patel: SPARC was set up in 1985 by a group of professionals seeking to develop an institutional framework that would allow them to collaborate and establish longstanding partnerships with slum organizations. It began to work with a women's collective called Mahila Milan to address the issue of evictions of slum dwellers by municipalities. NSDF, a national organization of slum dwellers set up in 1974, sought to form a partnership with SPARC and Mahila Milan, and this has been in existence since 1986–87.

NSDF membership is comprised of communities rather than individuals, and its present membership is about 750,000 households in seventy cities in nine states in India. Mahila Milan is a network of collectives from those neighborhoods which, through savings groups, seeks to train women to manage community processes and work with male leadership to address challenges faced by slum dwellers.

SPARC, NSDF, and Mahila Milan have a symbiotic relationship in which all legal agreements of state and grant-making institutions as well as all forms of contracts are made with SPARC. However, almost all areas of work, projects, and activities are developed through priorities set by the federations. Together, they seek to instill the slum communities with leadership capacities and the ability to represent their issues and problems with city, state, and national agencies. They seek to demonstrate that their solutions not only work for dwellers, but also help resolve other challenges the cities face (fig. 2).

3. The Municipal Commissioner reviews housing designs for Yerwada slum upgrade, Pune, India.
4. Houses are numbered as part of the enumeration of informal settlements, Kenya.

Shack/Slum Dwellers International is described as a grassroots network of organized squatter groups on three continents. How many slum dwellers' lives has SDI reached throughout the world? What is SDI's vision for the urban poor? What strategies does SDI employ to build an urban safety net?

SP: SDI believes that secure shelter and basic amenities are crucial safety nets for the poor in cities. It works to build the capacity of its member communities to seek out these basic human rights and for all urban poor. SDI was formed in 1992 after an initial interaction between the Indian alliance and township leaders of South Africa, who developed the South African Homeless People's Federation along the lines of NSDF and Mahila Milan. SDI then found other African and Asian countries also exploring what it called the "federation model." Today, this federation model is being adapted in thirty-four countries, where organizations are operating at different levels of maturity and for local contexts.

At SDI, we believe that, for a few decades to come, governments and cities will have neither the capacity nor the strategy to deal with existing slum dwellers. Nor will they be able to deal with the growing numbers of the poor who will move to cities as their countries urbanize. They will need to develop and scale up various strategies, policies, and investments to accommodate the slums and the poor who live there, and SDI's role is to help build member-based networks of slum dwellers as well as work with officials to explore these challenges in a spirit of collaboration, rather than fear, neglect, and hostility. SDI also seeks to bring slum dwellers' voices directly into global discourses as global agencies debate these challenges. We at SDI believe that the largest number of migrants coming to cities will be poor and unskilled. Municipalities and neighborhoods that have thus far neglected existing informal settlements will have to anticipate future urban migrants. SDI will facilitate national dialogues between government, public, private, and civil society agencies, academia, and the general public (fig. 3).

In the 1960s, you began organizing against forced evictions after officials bulldozed your home in the Janata colony, even after assurances it would not be destroyed. You then founded the National Slum Dwellers Federation, resisting an order of eviction of 70,000 slum dwellers in Dharavi, Mumbai, India. What were the early years like? What is NSDF's mission?
Jockin Arputham: I started the slum-dweller movement in 1974. This movement is completely managed, run, and designed by slum dwellers. Why should we keep on putting out our hand? Why can't we put our heads together, collect information, and change our lives? Why should somebody else determine what we do and how we eat, sleep, earn, and build? These are things we are capable of doing.

For the first ten to fifteen years, we were a movement of activists, and I myself got into agitation, fighting, and other such activities. We were notorious. The government and policy makers were not delivering anything. We asked for water, we did not get water; so we decided to find out how to get it. But in 1985, we changed our way of thinking and started doing things. We started building toilets and houses and improving the environment. That is when we started working with SPARC.

How have SDI's efforts improved secure tenure, basic amenities, and livelihoods for people living in the informal city? Explain SDI's community-to-community exchanges. Why are local savings and credit collectives important in taking pro-poor development to scale? Why is the participation of women, especially

the poor, illiterate or pavement dwelling women, critical to making this happen?

SP: The value and contribution of women in informal settlements are often very important and yet very invisible. Women tend to abdicate their leadership roles in managing settlements when external agencies, be they state-run or NGOs, get involved. SDI seeks to acknowledge women, network them, and integrate them into the mainstream leadership process (fig. 4).

Savings and loan programs are one way by which women's collectives learn to build relationships through their community. Through daily savings, which ensure contact with all families, they learn to manage money and create rules for lending to each other. At SDI, we say we collect people, not just money. Often, the savings book is a sign of a family's membership in the federation and shows how long it has been associated with the organization (fig. 1).

Male members of the federation acknowledge that the issues of habilitation, land, and amenities require patience and perseverance. In our experience, many more women than men have shown these qualities because they seek these for their families. Their persistence and energy are channeled to seek ongoing and persistent pressure on city and state agencies to address their needs. SDI's women members also ensure that when resources come they are equitably distributed.

5

5. Sheffield Road residents identify areas of need on self-produced map, Philippi Township.
6. Housing under construction in Mother Theresa Nagar, Yerwada slum.

What happened that prompted NSDF's shift from mostly male-dominated street resistance to an organization led by women working to improve living conditions and the built environment?

JA: We had been a male-dominated organization, but in 1984, we realized that we were not delivering anything. That is when we changed the whole concept to women's leadership. If you want to bring any quality to change in life, you need to include women's leadership to bring a change in values.

It started with all of our demonstrations for access to water. Who takes care of supplying and carrying the water? It's the women. Men do not care if there is water or not. From day one, at any demonstration, it was mostly women.

But they were not yet the leaders. Then I thought, Who has the money at the lower levels, among the urban poor? Who runs the home and the family? I realized it was very clearly the women who ran the household from morning to evening. They are the ones responsible for the money, who take out the loans; they collect because they are responsible for repaying the loan. For me, in Indian and Asian culture, money means women.

For any development, you need three things: money, information, and communication. And in our society, women control all three. All of the issues surrounding poverty are connected directly to the women. So I realized they should be the leaders, and in my way of working, women comprise 60% and men 40%. We trust the women. We give our life to them. And women can affect real change if you give them the means to do so.

I traveled widely in India from 1967 to 1975, trying to gather support for my movement. Mostly men attended the community meetings. When they went home, they did not tell their wives about the meetings, and it was hard to build momentum. But when women attended the meetings, they would communicate what had been discussed to other women, adding and articulating information as necessary. This is what brought about the growth of our movement. And so it is with many issues among the urban poor (fig. 10).

In 1984, we aligned with SPARC, whose focus from the beginning was working with women. Because SPARC started with women and NSDF started with men, I always joke that SPARC and NSDF got married. In India, there is a saying that if your first child is female, you'll be prosperous. That is what happened to SPARC and NSDF. Our first baby was Mahila Milan. So that is how our

7. Residents at a Yerwada slum community workshop.
8. Byanapalli children's toilet block, Bangalore, India.

SDI pioneered a people-driven approach to water and sanitation by designing, building, and maintaining local community toilet blocks. SDI affiliates utilize enumeration, vacant-land surveying, full-size house models, and community labor to design and build adequate and affordable housing. Why have these participatory methods been successful in numerous cities around the world?

SP: In each instance, federation members identified priorities and developed strategies to accomplish their goals. They took ownership of the process and represented themselves in dialogues with the cities. They inspired others who saw what they were doing and sought to learn from them, because seeing truly is believing. As they began scaling these projects in cities, they now had champions in the city and state who saw value in these partnerships and began to share this with their counterparts in other cities and countries. As the innovations spread, their legitimacy and logic became more and more self-evident, and this led to further invitations by government for SDI to design solutions in their countries (figs. 5–8).

How is SDI's innovative approach to building pro-poor cities and communities changing the field of urban development? How does the organization work with professionally trained architects and engineers and with government officials? What lessons can designers and architects learn from SDI's pro-poor methods and solutions?

SP: SDI's successes demonstrate the value of organizing the urban poor, who can become partners, rather than adversaries, in addressing challenges. They are also reminders that urbanization is here to stay, and in the Global South, more poor

movement began, and now it is working in more than 750,000 households in seventy cities throughout India. We have also spread out in thirty-three countries, using the same model, in eastern or southern Africa, Brazil, or other parts of Asia, under the name Shack/Slum Dwellers International.

than non-poor will come to cities. SDI-affiliated federations always have NGO partners with which they work. By and large, NGOs who work in cities tended to stay away from habitat issues, as they viewed them as contentious, political, and time-consuming, taking decades rather than neat three-year project periods to produce tangible results. However, they, along with professional academics and government officials, have begun to see value in these long-term relationships and now facilitate others to explore them as well. A critical ingredient is to accept and acknowledge the urban poor and their leadership in a spirit of collaboration (fig. 9).

9. Mahila Milan and Jockin Arputham, cofounder of SDI, speak with community members, Dharavi, Mumbai, India.
10. A savings group collects and records savings, Dharavi.

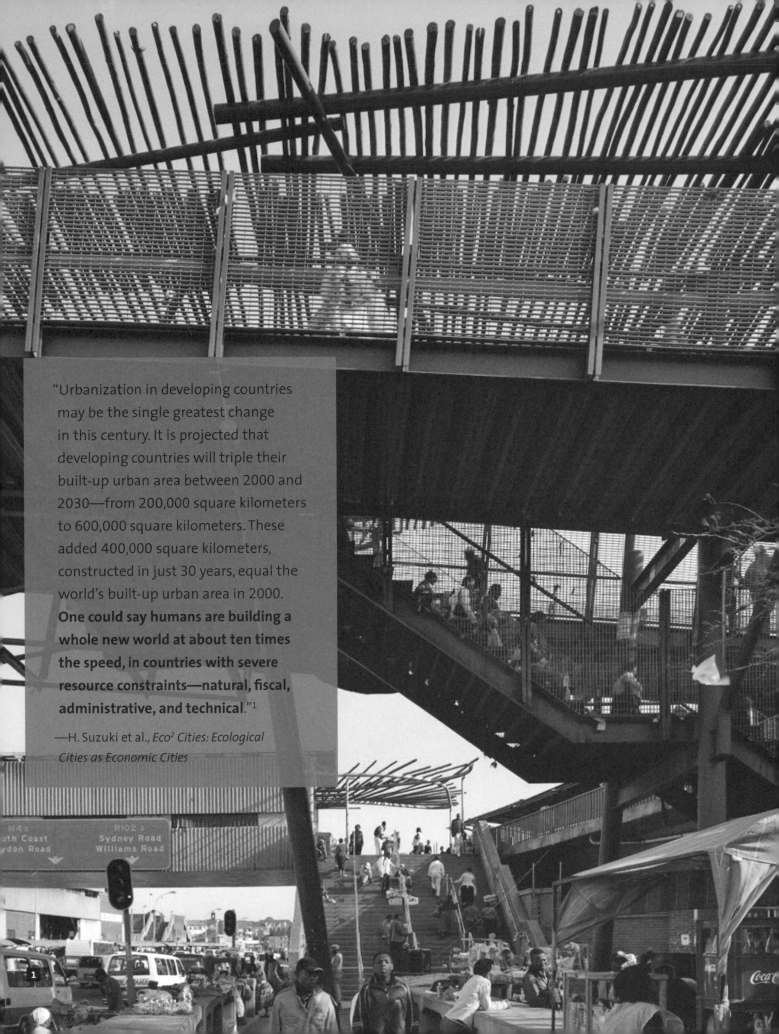

"Urbanization in developing countries may be the single greatest change in this century. It is projected that developing countries will triple their built-up urban area between 2000 and 2030—from 200,000 square kilometers to 600,000 square kilometers. These added 400,000 square kilometers, constructed in just 30 years, equal the world's built-up urban area in 2000. **One could say humans are building a whole new world at about ten times the speed, in countries with severe resource constraints—natural, fiscal, administrative, and technical.**"[1]

—H. Suzuki et al., *Eco² Cities: Ecological Cities as Economic Cities*

Building New Worlds:
Design and the Second Urban Transition

Edgar Pieterse

Director, African Centre for Cities, University of Cape Town

Design with the Other 90%: CITIES is being published amid the second urban transition, a sweeping demographic shift from 300 million people living in urban areas in 1950 swelling to 3.9 billion people in the Global South alone by 2030.[2] We find ourselves poorly equipped to come to terms with the ecological, social, and economic implications of this shift. Various development trends and indicators, reflected in various overview reports by the World Bank, United Nations Environment Program, and United Nations Development Program, remind us that radical changes in our quality of life and in our ecosystem are not forthcoming.[3] If anything, our capacity to live with large-scale impoverishment, marginalization, insecurity, violence, and hunger seems endless.

Almost half the global population lives on less than $2.50 a day. That is more than three billion people, almost all in developing countries. Even more shocking, the proportion of people below the $2.50-per-day poverty line has remained more or less constant between 1981 and 2005, if one takes China out the equation.[4] Furthermore, the gap between rich and poor is widening. According to the World Bank, the richest 20% of the world's population accounts for 76.6% of all consumption; the bottom 40% accounts for only 1.5%.[5]

Compounding these trends is spatial inequality— the unequal access that different groups of people in a city have to a range of opportunities and resources. UN-Habitat suggests that the dynamics of land markets and various barriers between the rich and the poor often aggravate urban poverty, creating "a spatial poverty trap marked by six distinct challenges: (a) severe job restrictions; (b) high rates of gender disparities; (c)

1. The iTRUMP project has improved the efficiency and safety of street trading in Warwick Junction, Durban, South Africa.

deteriorated living conditions; (d) social exclusion and marginalization; (e) lack of social interaction; and (f) high incidence of crime."[6] Unsurprisingly, the report finds that in cities with a prevalence of slums, the prospects are very slim indeed for new entrants into the labor market to find formal jobs. In fact, about 85% of all new employment opportunities around the world occur in informal economies, and young people in slums are more likely to settle for informal-sector work than their non-slum peers.[7]

Since these dynamics are concentrated in urban areas, our cities are where the struggle for alternative futures will be fought—and hopefully won—through the efforts of ordinary people as they take control of their lives, neighborhoods, and resources. This essay attempts to map out the anchors for a cultural transition toward a more just and sustainable society, especially in the Global South. My aim is to provide a larger conceptual canvas for the movements, interventions, and innovations featured in the *Design with the Other 90%: CITIES* exhibition. I hope these diverse, ethically connected projects will help readers appreciate their larger significance, and that the seeds of structural transformation of our cities can be gleaned from them.

Ethical Touchstone

If we are to make a dent in the amount of deprivation and suffering in the world, especially amidst the rampant consumerism that dominates popular media and culture, it is important to start

**2. The Northeast Integral Urban Project upgraded public spaces and walkways in the Balcones del Ajedrez neighborhood, Medellín, Colombia.
3. Balcones del Ajedrez before the upgrade.**

with our shared ethical horizon. It seems to me that a sufficiently far-reaching response to the perfect storm anticipated by prominent urbanist Mike Davis (see his quote later in this essay), as we enlarge our built world depends on a broad-based agreement on the following four key principles:

1. Resource efficiency through decoupling: Find more efficient and waste-free means of increasing economic output while decreasing the rate and intensity of non-renewable resource extraction and consumption.

2. Inclusivity: Provide every resident in a settlement a fundamental set of rights to healthcare, education, land, and social space to exercise cultural freedoms— a bundle of rights that UN-Habitat invoked, in its 2010 development report on cities, as the "Right to the City."

3. Economic opportunity: Pursue more inclusive and fulfilling forms of economic development and growth to address the labor "excess" of two billion people in the contemporary global economy.

4. Human flourishing: Offer a safe and nurturing context within which citizens and social collectives can come into their own cultural fullness—the magic vitality that makes all cities and places unique and connected. Social networks and identities are always simultaneously irreplaceable and trans-local.

These four principles are indivisible. In other words, if a policy or action violates any one of these principles, it damages the long-term effectiveness of the other principles. If trade-offs need to be struck between these principles, they must be subject to impartial scrutiny and oversight as well as time limits.

A compelling example of a city working hard to address these principles in tandem is Medellín, Colombia. Between 2004 and 2008, the city government drove a four-part program of radical urban intervention that dramatically improved the

lives of the urban poor living in crowded barrios on the slopes of the city (figs. 2, 3). The first line of intervention focused on education by vastly improving the area's libraries and parks—a clear sign of the city's placing its youth as a priority. The second line of intervention, Proyectos Urbanos Integrales (PUI), reconnected the isolated barrios to the city center through a cable-car system, which in turn created opportunities to create high-quality public spaces at the system's anchor points. The third line of intervention targeted social housing in communities located in hazardous locations. These various actions were then glued together by the fourth line of intervention: the Walkways plan, which included the Emblematic Streets program and the *Lineal Sistemsto*, aimed at connecting the city across its various lines of division and segregation.[8] *Design with the Other 90%: CITIES* provides further insights into this visionary program, a concrete example of the four key principles mentioned above in action.

To fully appreciate the potential power and relevance of these principles for reimagining the functioning of cities, it is essential to understand that a city's residents construct it in their own unique way every day through a constant negotiation of aesthetic and functional considerations. Aestheticism signals the ineluctable demands of beauty, desire, and transgression that bubble up from the collective subconscious, regardless of class or location or age, to orient engagement with the world, the city, and its myths. Functionalism denotes the pragmatic requirements of nutrition, dwelling, mobility, sociality, and economy that require urbanites to pursue their livelihood and well-being. These impulses intertwine our interior and exterior worlds. As can be seen in many of the examples cited in this exhibition and book, innovation arises when activists and entrepreneurs respond to very practical needs in ways that allow people to bring their own creativity, cultural ownership, and sweat to the endeavor. (The striking design and building response of communities in Chile to the half-finished houses of Elemental is one

obvious example; fig. 4.) Until we can come to terms with the fact that the poor—with all of their contradictory cultural attachments and desires, who are in most need of urban justice and systemic transformation—are the key to appropriate design solutions, we will miss the unprecedented design opportunity that the second urban transition presents.

Systemic Transformation

However, culturally resonant design responses for particular households or neighborhoods will not add up to much unless we can also envisage large-scale systemic transformation. In the next thirty to fifty years, a change will need to occur in how we understand the nature of cities and smaller urban settlements. One entry point for this thought experiment is the need to build and retrofit new and existing infrastructures (fig. 5). Various estimates suggest that somewhere in the order of $40 trillion is required to address the infrastructure of the world over the next twenty to twenty-five years.[9] The past few years have been a watershed in terms of mainstream thinking on urban development, planning, and design premised on the realization that infrastructure imperatives

hold the most promise to advance a fundamentally different approach to city building. This is most clearly manifest in the various development reports of international development agencies such as the Organization for Economic Cooperation and Development, the United Nations Environment Program, UN-Habitat, and the World Bank.[10]

A central trope that arises from these standard setting reports is the link between cities and climate change. For example, the Organization for Economic Cooperation and Development, typically known for its focus on economic competitiveness and state efficiency, published a major report on the pivotal role of cities in achieving the dramatic targets to reduce CO_2 emissions by 2050.[11] This movement was clearly reinforced by the United Nations Environment Program's *Green Economy Report*, published in 2011, which features a special chapter on cities to demonstrate how urban centers anchor and link together the emerging green-economy agendas. Urban-policy considerations such as density, compaction, and energy efficiency are in many ways directly tied to concerns about climate change.

4. Incremental Housing allows residents to expand spaces as resources become available to them, Iquique, Chile.

5

These momentous policy shifts in mainstream urban development approaches hold important implications for thinking about the design nexus between development, planning, management, and sustainability.[12] Keeping in mind the gap between policy intent and actual practice, it is possible to envisage a much more radical urban development and design agenda that can use the imperative for more sustainable lives, livelihoods, urban systems, and outcomes as a coherence point.

My optimism stems from a reading of the "yet-to-be-designed" instruments at the intersection of ecological, infrastructural, and technological imperatives to achieve more efficient systems and ensure more sustainable urban metabolisms, such as from a resource-consumption point of view. I believe that this broader design imperative is as important as the specific innovations catalogued in this publication. But what we need now is the bringing together of the macro and the micro dimensions of sustainable and inclusive urbanism.

This requires a fresh and adaptive conceptual framing.

A robust conceptual framework must tie together three critical meta-domains of urban transition that need to be pursued simultaneously if we are serious about advancing sustainable human

5. The Janmarg Bus Rapid Transit system provides access to improved urban transportation, Ahmedabad, India.

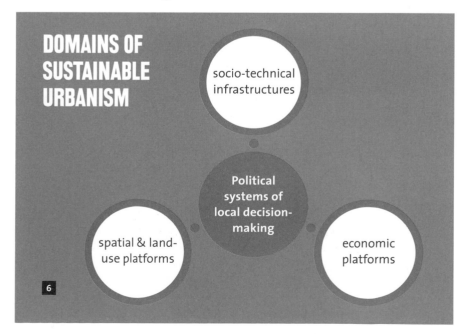

DOMAINS OF SUSTAINABLE URBANISM

socio-technical infrastructures

Political systems of local decision-making

spatial & land-use platforms

economic platforms

6

settlements and cities. These domains are: sustainable infrastructure, the inclusive economy, and efficient spatial form, glued by processes of democratic political decision-making (fig. 6).

One way of thinking about cities is that they require various "operating systems," much as computers or mobile phones do. The diagram highlights three critical operating systems for all cities: i) infrastructural, ii) economic, and iii) spatial form, or land-use. The infrastructural system can be further delineated between social and biophysical infrastructures. The former refers to the social development investments that forge identity and community, such as cultural services, education, health, public space, housing, and the arts; the latter refers to roads, transportation, information/ communication technology, energy, water and sanitation, food, and ecological services that make urban life and movement possible. By definition, social infrastructures need to be tailored to local community-scale dynamics, which implies a substantial degree of community involvement and control in their execution and maintenance. The Kibera Public Space Projects (fig. 7) in Nairobi and the *Gimnasio Vertical* (fig. 8) in Caracas are both examples of vital social infrastructures.

9

The economic operating system involves production, consumption, and market systems that underpin the exchange of goods and services. It is important to note that they span formal and informal institutions, and often involve an entanglement of the two, especially in our era of globalization. However, one of the most challenging problems confronting cities in the developing world is that the formal economy absorbs less than half of the labor force; the rest have to eke out an existence in the informal economy or be completely disconnected from any gainful activity.[13] (fig. 9) Those "lucky" enough to engage in informal work have to put up with extremely low, often irregular income, which puts them in the category of the working poor. In a broader context of deepening global integration of economies and value chains, it is becoming more

difficult for national governments to protect jobs, provide support to the working poor, and induce employment, because such actions are, ironically, perceived as undermining competitiveness. And as long as the monetization of economic value generation continues apace, it will be difficult to promote labor-absorptive and equalizing economic policies.

In the face of these trends, it is essential that cities find creative ways of redefining and boosting local economies in order to broaden the base of those who are included in economic life. A powerful example of this is the Warwick Junction initiative, part of the iTRUMP (Inner Thekwini Regeneration & Urban Management Program) in Durban, South Africa.[14] (figs. 1, 10) In other words, the challenge is not just about generating more formal jobs. On

7. Kibera residents congregate in the Kibera Public Space Project pavilion, Nairobi, Kenya.
8. The Vertical Gym, designed by Urban Think Tank, converted a rundown sports field in Barrio La Cruz into a four-story sports facility, Chacao, Caracas, Venezuela.
9. A handmade trowel handle made from discarded plastic bags, one of the many informal enterprises in Kibera informal settlement, Nairobi, Kenya.

47

10

the contrary, the biggest, most urgent challenge is to absorb young adults between the ages of fifteen and twenty-nine in activities that can reconnect them to society, nature, and their surroundings. Amongst South Africa's youth demographic, more than 50% cannot access formal jobs, even though they may have completed primary and portions of secondary schooling. At the same time, South Africa has the largest HIV/AIDS rate in the world. In order to contain and manage the scale of the AIDS pandemic, it is vital that a national network of home-based care workers be established. These service workers need formal medical training and must work with affected households to ensure that anti-retroviral medications are taken in conjunction with sufficient nutritional intake, as well as provide psychological support to help sufferers and their families deal with stigma and shame (fig. 11). Another pertinent example relates to various kinds of labor-intensive activities to restore ecosystem services. For example, rivers and canals

in developing countries are often highly degraded because of upstream pollution and downstream neglect, sometimes combined with invasions by alien species. Restoring these systems is a vital part of improving the overall well-being of cities and communities. Also, if done cleverly, it can also be a gateway to reconnect young people in more positive and enriching ways with nature and their peers. There are literally hundreds of examples that one can dream up if this logic is pursued. Until governments and civil groups begin to pay attention to these alternative kinds of economic pathways and identities, we will remain within the deeply unequal and unjust conditions offered by mainstream approaches.

Economies and infrastructures fundamentally depend on land and, more pertinent, land-use systems. The patterns of infrastructural and economic distribution add up to the spatial form of cities. If the spatial form is expansive, marked

10. Street traders in the improved Bead Market, Warwick Junction, Durban, South Africa.

48

by sharp divisions between uses, functions, and population groups, it is likely to be inefficient and exclusionary (fig. 12).

In the vast majority of cities in the developing world, land-use systems further marginalize the urban poor and reinforce privilege for those who control them. It is essential that land use address the imperatives of greater efficiency and access. Ideally, greater density through compaction should be linked with a much stronger emphasis on mixed usage. A public-oriented approach such as those seen in Bogotá, Curitiba, and Medellín is encouraged in the recalibration of land use, which informs a broader agenda to foster greater cultural and social integration.[15] (fig. 13) Many of the projects featured in *Design with the Other 90%: CITIES* illustrate how efficiently the urban poor utilize land, as well as the importance of reclaiming land for greater public use. Since poor people live predominantly in public arenas in order to move about, access services, enjoy cultural practices, and trade, offering them safety, security, and control is vital. However, such a vision often goes against the conventions and rules. It is vital that land-use norms be redefined to support their aspirations and livelihood practices to make our cities more inclusive and resilient. For instance, social-zoning provisions, set up through the "Special Zones of Social Interest" instruments in master plans of municipalities in Brazil, delimit underutilized land and designate it for use by the poor.[16] (fig. 14) In other words, its gets isolated from speculative activity and potentially allows for better urban integration and class mixing.

Finally, these three operating systems depend fundamentally on how power is distributed in society and mediated in political institutions.

11. As part of reurbanization, community health workers deliver services directly to residents, Diadema, São Paulo, Brazil.
12. Poor favela communities formed next to wealthier neighborhoods, Paraisópolis, São Paulo, Brazil.

13

If local governments are beholden to national government for revenue and resources, they will struggle to be responsive to local needs.[17] If local governments act unilaterally, or isolate themselves from the voice and actions of the organizations that represent slum dwellers, such as Slum Dwellers International and its affiliates (fig. 15), they are unlikely to recognize or understand the innovations that come from the citizens themselves. However, although there has been an unmistakable trend towards democracy and decentralization across the world over the past two decades, there are still very few examples where participatory local governance is a vibrant reality. This suggests that political reform and institutional retooling are necessary precursors to systemic change in cities.

Design Sensibilities for Building New Worlds

At the heart of the challenges facing contemporary design vis-à-vis urbanization is a complex set of sensibilities. On the one hand, for it to be effective, design work has to be done deliberately and cumulatively by organizations and communities working inside the settlements and urban spaces. At the same time, designers in the broadest sense of the term have to be able to connect work being done locally to larger system transitions. This involves a finely honed capacity that can only come from practice—to articulate the sensibilities of art, craft, and science. Management theorist Henry Mintzberg suggests that agents of effective change can discern when they need to draw on and advance scientific knowledge and frames to solve a problem.[18] However, in the real world, with complexities shot through with unpredictable factors, intuition is also critical. One has to draw

13. Medellín's Metrocable and Integral Urban Project provide new public buildings and transportation systems for the poorest parts of city, Santa Domingo Library and Park, Medellín, Colombia.
14. Tá Bonito upgraded housing, Vila Olinda neighborhood, Diadema, São Paulo.

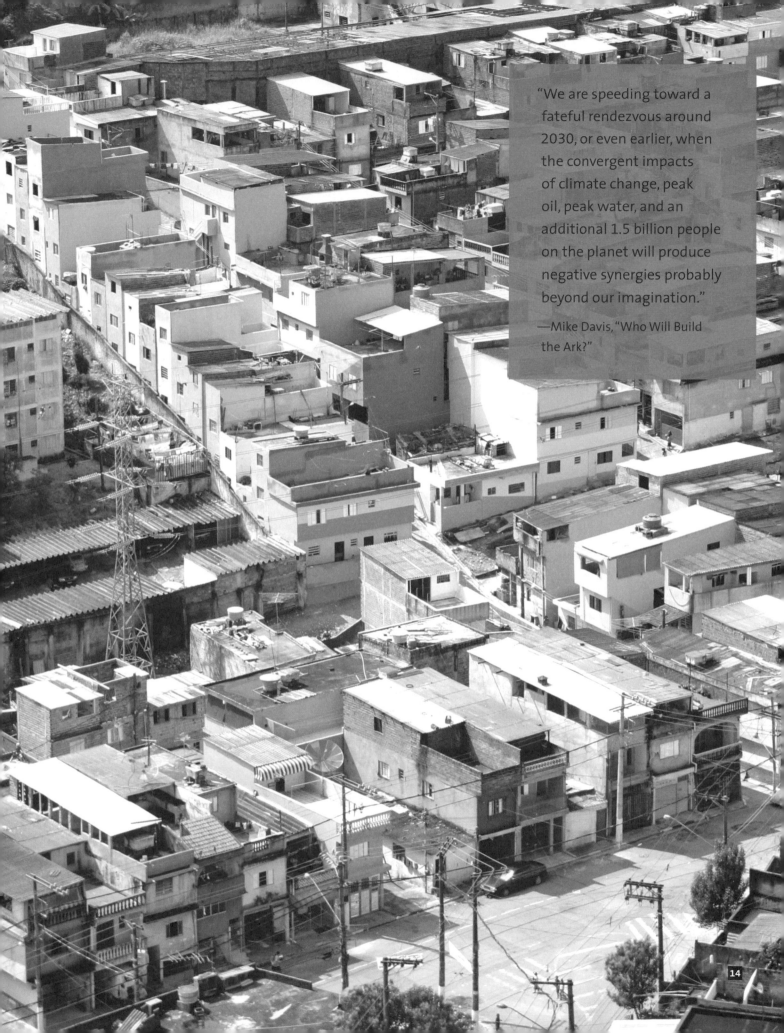

"We are speeding toward a fateful rendezvous around 2030, or even earlier, when the convergent impacts of climate change, peak oil, peak water, and an additional 1.5 billion people on the planet will produce negative synergies probably beyond our imagination."

—Mike Davis, "Who Will Build the Ark?"

14

on expertise in reading and responding to an emerging situation or context. Finally, complex and intractable solutions often require the passion and determination of the artist, who offers access to creativity that cannot come from either science or craft-based expertise (fig. 16). It seems to me that urbanists of all stripes—politicians, activists, engineers, architects, planners, sociologists, entrepreneurs, ecologists, et al.—need to inhabit this dynamic triad of science, craft, and art to rise to the challenge of building new worlds that are beautiful, just, and exhilarating for all the opportunity they offer everyone, regardless of geography, identity, age, or gender. It may just be that those pioneers celebrated in this exhibition and book may have glimpsed these worlds, and it will serve us well to take them seriously.

The research and editorial support of Kim Gurney and the editorial team at Cooper-Hewitt, National Design Museum is gratefully acknowledged.

Notes

1. 100,000 sq. km = 38,610.22 sq. miles. Emphasis is the author's.

2. The first transition unfolded in the Global North between 1750 and 1950, when the percentage of urban inhabitants increased from 10% to 52%; see UNFPA (2007): 7–8. The Global North refers to Western Europe, North America, and Japan, in the northern hemisphere. The rest of the world, predominantly in the southern hemisphere, denotes the Global South, or what used to be known as the second, third, and fourth worlds in earlier parlance.

3. Examples of such reports are Hassan, Scholes, and Ash, 2005; UNDP 2010; UN-Habitat 2010.

4. Chen and Ravallion, 2009: 41.

5. Source: Shah, 2010.

6. UN-Habitat, 2010: xiii.

7. Ibid., xiv.

15. Mahila Milan architects discuss slum improvements and upgraded housing with the Yerwada community, Pune, India.

8. Echeverri, 2010.

9. BCG, 2010.

10. Kamal-Chaoui and Robert, 2009; Suzuki, Dastur, Moffatt, and Yabuki, 2009; UNEP 2011; UN-Habitat, 2009 and 2011.

11. Kamal-Chaoui and Robert, 2009.

12. Even though these shifts are a positive signal, it would be naïve to ignore a number concomitant risks: One, these could simply be passing development fashions that achieve little more than becoming "buzz words" in development policies and programs without much regard for their fundamental implications (Cornwall & Brock, 2005). Two, almost of all these new policy agendas are inherently multidimensional and complex, which may mean they are indigestible and essentially not implementable for most governments, marked by capacity limitations and insufficient funds, and often captured by elite interests (Manor, 2004). Three, the mainstream deployment of these overlapping policy discourses could produce a sterilization of transformative ideas and practices, especially once they have been swallowed and regurgitated by government institutions.

13. Renowned observer of informal economic dynamics Marty Chen (2008: 6) points out that "informal employment broadly defined, including self-employment in informal enterprises and wage employment in informal jobs, comprises two-quarters of total employment in development countries; three-quarters or more in South Asia and sub-Saharan Africa; and around 60% in the Middle East, North Africa, and Latin America."

14. For a full account of this fascinating case study, see Dobson and Skinner, 2009.

15. UN-Habitat, 2009.

16. Rolnik et al., 2008.

17. Manor, 2004.

18. Mintzberg, 2004.

16. As the train, covered with images of the eyes of local women, passes through Kibera, it aligns with portraits on the slope beneath the train. These portraits by artist JR call attention to the central role played by women in informal settlements, Kibera, Nairobi, Kenya.

1. New settlement laid out using *Urbanism Manual* as a guide, Barrio Los Eucaliptus, José León Suárez, San Martín, Buenos Aires, Argentina.
2. Manual illustration of the new settlement, a hopeful image of the future.

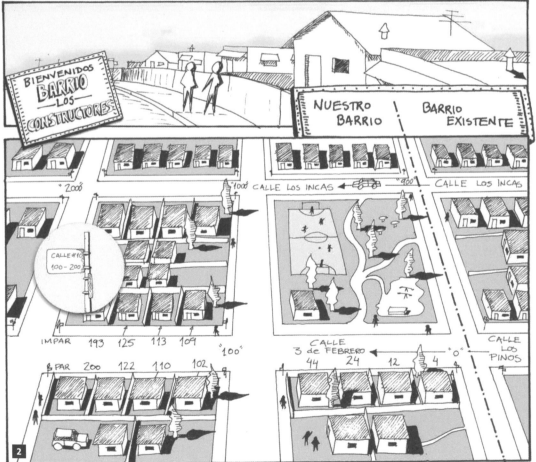

54

Urbanism Manual

Interview with
Gabriela Sorda, Co-coordinator, Secretariat of Community Action,
Faculty of Architecture, Design, and Urbanism, University of Buenos Aires

By Cynthia E. Smith

What is the *Urbanism Manual for Precarious Settlements*?
Gabriela Sorda: The *Urbanism Manual for Precarious Settlements* is a short, practical compilation of urban principles for slum settlers. Its aim is to provide them with urban tools so they can build a "neighborhood" instead of a "slum." By following urban principles and local laws, settlers can improve their quality of life and increase the possibilities of legalizing land tenure at the same time. The manual also provides some information about dynamics of groups and presents tools to develop an urban design participatory process.

Why did the University of Buenos Aires decide to make this manual? What circumstances led up to its development?
GS: The Faculty of Architecture, Design, and Urbanism decided to increase its ties with the community. The Secretariat of Community Actions had organized several counseling, teaching, and research actions in different neighborhoods. During our work in slums, dwellers asked us some questions that we could not answer, and

we discovered that no practical literature existed at that point; there was research describing slums, but nothing on how to "build" a neighborhood properly. Also there was no compilation of urban rights and laws focused on slums, nor a directory of state agencies that deal with slum settlements.

Academia teaches us how to make an urban plan in a bare lot; but slums grow quickly, without any plan, most of the time in lots unsuitable for building. There is a gap between academic knowledge and actual slum dwellers' practices. On the other hand, we discovered that our weekly visits to neighbors were insufficient. In between our visits, new people occupied land and there was no one to give them any advice. Thus we decided to write some documents for local leaders so they could use them when we are not there. Those documents were the origin of the manual.

Why was the guide developed using an interdisciplinary approach? Was this limited to the design disciplines or also

to other fields? How did each discipline contribute?
GS: During our field work, we found that some slum dwellers knew about urban-generation principles, other communities had good group dynamics, and still others had some understanding of legal matters. But the knowledge was fragmented and incomplete. We needed urban designers, social workers, and legal advisers to create the contents of the guide. However, the manual had to be a clear, useful tool, so we needed communication specialists, graphic designers, and illustrators. We invited teachers, researchers, and students to work pro bono, and they visited several slums to try to comprehend the dwellers' wishes, knowledge, and visions. We had wanted to give the volunteers tasks according to their specialties; but everyone wanted to go back to the neighborhoods and conduct interviews, look for further information, and, later on, test our drafts by showing them to the dwellers.

We met twice a month to discuss the upgrading and the next tasks. Everyone

GUIA DE ICONOS

GLOSARIO. Se refiere a palabras cuyas definiciones o explicaciones se pueden encontrar desde la página 87.

TESTIMONIO. La voz de los vecinos contando sus experiencias en primera persona.

BUENA PRÁCTICA. Indica que en la página 85 se pueden ver imágenes y testimonios sobre esas prácticas.

LEY o CÓDIGO. Identifican los aspectos legales que es necesario tener en cuenta a la hora de buscar y construir nuestro nuevo barrio.

ADVERTENCIA. Situaciones a tener especial cuidado. Se recomienda leerlas antes de continuar.

3

bono, long-term work, it's difficult to keep participating; but the creation of deep relationships between the fellow participants, and with the neighbors, fortified the engagement to finish the manual.

The design of the manual is very simple. Was this intentional? How is the book meant to be used? Whom is the manual meant for? How is it distributed?
GS: Its simplicity was intentional—and very difficult to achieve. The manual is meant to be used by slum dwellers, most of whom are not used to reading long, complex, technical texts. Thus the book had to translate as much text into graphics as possible. To divide and clarify the remaining text we created a system of icons that shows when we are writing about laws, presenting a testimony, pointing out a "good practice," and so on. We added a glossary for technical terms, as well as empty pages for exercises presented at the Urban Design Participatory Process meetings.

To demystify the manual as an object, we created a dynamic and "dirty" design, using handwriting and typography that resembles handwriting. Many of the visuals were taken from our field work, because we wanted to create empathy: the simulation of stencil drawing or of a wallboard where dwellers stick communal news, the feel of writing in a spiral-bound notebook.

The manual is also meant for social scientists working in slums. Like the slum dwellers, they are not used to abstract architectural language, so we had to be figurative. That led us to consider ethics along with design: How do we draw human figures without stereotyping? How can we be clear without being

3. The icon system used in the manual translates complex text into graphics: Glossary – definitions or explanations; Testimony – neighbors recount their experiences; Good Practice – images and testimonials; Law and Code – legal aspects in the construction of a new neighborhood; Warning – situations that require special attention.
4. Guidelines for laying out new sidewalks and streets, including minimum distances.
5. A resident begins construction on a newly laid-out settlement street, Luján, Buenos Aires, Argentina.

added graphic and contents ideas, and many conducted research. Thus everybody learned a little bit from a different discipline. In the process of explaining the ideas to persons from another discipline, we learned to overcome communication obstacles before we tested the sketches in the neighborhoods. Discussion also led to better, bolder ideas; and in a personal way, we learned to listen, to delegate, and to trust.

Sharing the work and the outputs consolidated us as a group. In pro-

patronizing? We also used graphic design to prompt changes in attitude. One of the biggest problems among the poor is that they are frequently unable to envision a positive future for themselves—because in the slums, anyone can be killed for 50 cents. Another problem is that many hold a stubborn belief in unrealistic or "magical" solutions, such as winning the lottery, because dwellers often feel powerless to come up with them on their own. So we wanted to work with a hopeful image of the future and of progressive development, without being naïve. One graphic idea to achieve that goal was the design of the cover of the manual, which presents an orderly, "nice" neighborhood, to show a possible realization.

To emphasize that improving is a process, we created a graphic index for each chapter that shows how the neighborhood on the cover is changing. There are "tricks" to help dwellers achieve the self-esteem necessary for the difficult task of self-management, such as an exercise from the Urban Design Participatory Process, in which people are invited to write not what "their neighborhood lacks," but "what would they like for their neighborhood," in order to empower dwellers by emphasizing their right to wish instead of stressing that they are "needy."

This also led to ethical considerations, as many slum dwellers believe that slums which look like legal neighborhoods allow them to better integrate into society and avoid stigmatization. As middle-class scholars, we did not agree; we wanted slum dwellers to be proud of their picturesque vernacular production, and that the people who stigmatize them are the ones that needed to change.

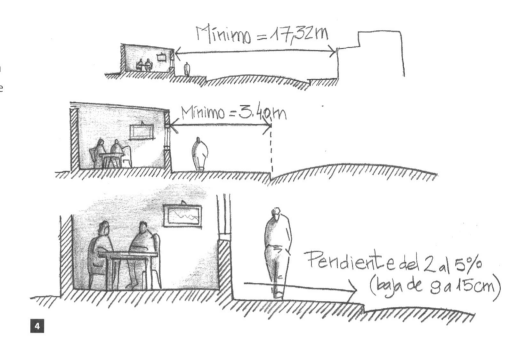

4

5

6. Graffiti announcing "Housing for All," Los Eucaliptus, José León Suarez, Buenos Aires.
7. New residents using the *Urbanism Manual*, Frenta Popular Darío Santillán grassroots movement, Barrio Villa del Parque, Luján, Buenos Aires.

But slum dwellers were not nearly as romantic; they did not want to change society, they simply wanted to be included in society. We printed a thousand copies of the manual to be distributed for free, and designed it to be in a common A4 size format for easy photocopying and to prevent paper waste. We also avoided grayscales in the text boxes to further facilitate the reading of photocopies.

Why did you see the need to provide basic urban-planning and design principles to the new settlers but not to the municipal governments? What are your goals for providing this kind of information?
GS: In terms of economic turnover and massive migration, traditional planning tools to deal with slums were failing. The reality of quick, unexpected change had overcome urban planners' ideals of anticipating and fully controlling human settlements. In recent years, there has been consensus among scholars that we cannot eradicate slums due to the high social costs of evictions. It has also become clear that the main problem in slums is not the construction of houses—slum dwellers know how to build, and a lot of construction workers live in slums— but access to credit and to specialized knowledge. State and municipal programs, such as the Favela Bairrio in Rio de Janeiro, tried to integrate slums into the formal city. But the economic and social costs of turning slums into neighborhoods are also high, because many slums are already consolidated in ways that make it virtually impossible to fix them. Often it is cheaper, easier, and healthier to tear them down.

The lack of synchronicity between social practices and state actions occurs because local politics have a different sense of time than the slums. Politicians consider slums in their agenda only when they become big or important enough to be weighed up as a problem to solve. In the meantime, the logic of the people in slums is to consolidate with as many people as you can, and to build houses and infrastructure as fast as you can, in order to prevent eviction.

The manual tries to be a tool to articulate social and political timing. If people have access to technical knowledge and build their neighborhoods according to urban principles and laws, they can achieve a better quality of life, prevent evictions, integrate better into the rest of the city, and facilitate land-tenure processes. Dwellers invest a lot of money and time in providing urban infrastructure for themselves; those efforts should be capitalized, not thrown out only to be built (and paid for) again. The state also spends fewer resources legalizing slums if they are well designed from the beginning, and social and spatial integration becomes more sustainable— economically, socially, and ecologically.

Where do you see it being implemented?
GS: We did not formally evaluate implementation because our work

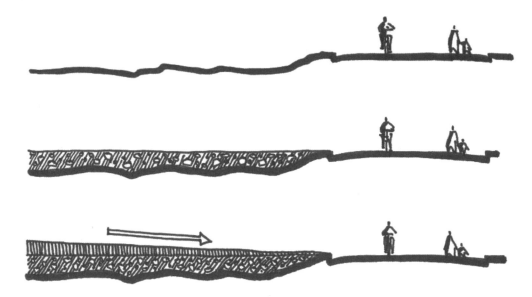

at the university had finished. But we were notified of at least fourteen neighborhoods constructed using the manual; one of them, the Movimiento de Trabajadores Comunitarios de Luján, from the Frente Popular Darío Santillán, is already consolidated. Ninety-four organizations and NGOs, including Red Hábitat, Tierra para Vivir, and Un Techo para Mi País, have asked for it. We have also had a lot of positive feedback from academics, the media, and specialized publications; and the Senators Chamber of the Provincia de Buenos Aires has proposed to declare the manual as "being of cultural interest."

What has been the reaction of new informal settlers when you give them the book?

GS: It has been a resounding success. During an annual meeting for Habitat Day, we had slum dwellers literally pulling the books out of our hands. We distributed the manual through social organizations because they had asked for it and because it made dissemination more efficient. It has been very satisfying to meet slum dwellers who have used the manual and praised it to us without knowing we had published it. We encountered a man in the street reading it carefully, saying he was using it in his neighborhood. The book was in the streets, where it belonged.

As for the neighbors with whom we worked, they were so proud because their voices and practices, usually unheard, were printed in the testimonies and the Good Practices chapter of the manual. Their experience now transcends them and can be used by other people.

Do you have plans to share this information with other cities and regions experiencing the same rapid, informal expansion?

GS: The manual is especially useful for Buenos Aires's slums because it was prepared with local codes and context in mind. But we did not copyright the book, and would be glad if other teams wanted to take the torch and adapt the manual for their local conditions. The book can be downloaded for free from our blog (www.urbanismopopular. blogspot.com); from the Web pages of the Habitants International Coalition (http://www.hic-al.org/index.cfm), or the Web page of Infohabitat (http://www.

8. The dynamic book design includes hand-drawn diagrams to help new residents determine safe locations of water resources, high-tension wire, and soil types.
9. Residents filling in a new street for proper drainage, Barrio Los Eucaliptus, José León Suárez, Buenos Aires.

infohabitat.com.ar/web/cnt/es/notas/9/recursos/otras_publicaciones_de_interes/_01042009010820/).

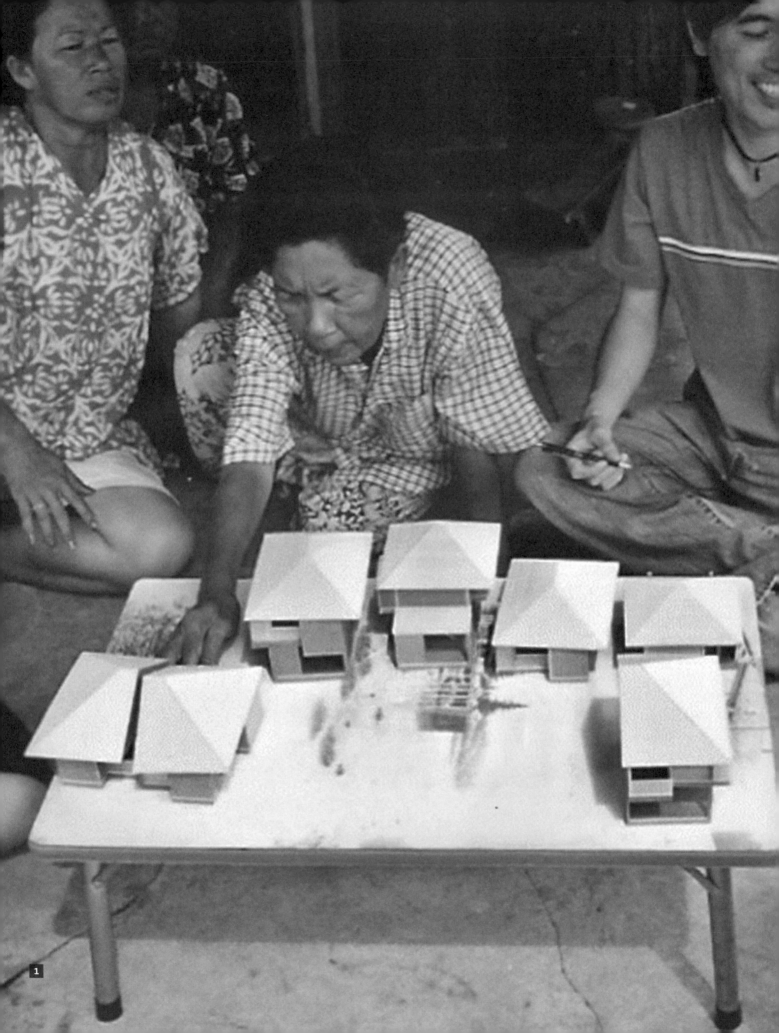

Trusting that People Can Do It

Somsook Boonyabancha
Founding Director, Asian Coalition for Housing Rights

There is a notion going around that the poor are helpless, lazy, ignorant, and untrustworthy, that they do not have resources or ideas, and that they cannot think for themselves or manage money. So it follows that they need to be helped, trained, organized, spoken for, and made aware. This assumption infects the policies of a great deal of the world's development agencies and of housing-activism, shelter-delivery, and poverty-reduction programs, where solutions are conceived and carried out on the poor's behalf by professionals, bureaucrats, activists, and social organizers.

But if we look at the situations of poverty which define the reality for so many human beings around the world, helpless is just about the last word you would choose to describe the energy, resourcefulness, and creativity with which people manage to feed, clothe, and house their families, without help from almost anyone. In fact, the poor are the creators and implementers of the most comprehensive and far-reaching systems for solving problems of poverty, housing, and basic services. Their systems reach down to rock bottom and cover more ground and more lives than any government program or development intervention can ever do. Informal settlements grow and flourish around an established quantum of practical understanding about *how to survive*: how to get a house, how to get water, how to find work, how to borrow money.

These systems are a long way from perfect. They're almost entirely illegal, and can be exploitive, inequitable, and substandard. But they represent the best people can do with extremely limited resources: a reasonable and ordered response to urgent necessity, where no legal or accessible alternatives exist. In this evidence of human creativity in ragged clothes, there is remarkable independence, a self-generating vitality that is one of the great, unchanneled sources of energy in Asia. Imagine if this huge force were marshaled in such a way to allow communities of the poor to refashion themselves? What if their efforts were legitimized and supported, and they were given room to experiment, innovate, and scale up their own solutions? And what if development interventions could nurture those solutions with injections of assistance and a light touch grounded in trust?

Unfortunately, trust is seldom part of the formula. Governments tend to view all this energy as misbehavior on a colossal scale that they

1. Members of the Bang Bua Canal Network discuss the different housing typologies available through the Baan Mankong Community Upgrading Program, Bangkok, Thailand.

2

need to punish or contain, while development interventions usually ignore it or shackle it within the condescending parameters of "community participation" or somebody else's idea of what the poor need. This top-down version of development, in which the professionals call the shots and handle the money, remains the predominant development model today. And it is so thick with mistrust that the most vital and simple truth is obscured: the poor are the ones most eager to bring about change, and the ones whose numbers and energy are sufficient to do it.

I am a believer in the trust system, and the work I have been involved with over the past thirty years, in Thailand and other Asian countries, has put trust in people at the center of a process of large-scale development alternatives, conceived and carried out by the poor themselves. I trace my faith back to my mother, who never learned to read or write, and worked hard to raise several children with care and responsibility all her life. Yet this woman understood the depth of life, in all its aspects. When I work with people from poor communities, I do not see strangers, with lives that are different and incomprehensible to me, but rather a thousand versions of my mother, on whom I can rely to know what is best and to take care of things with honesty and common sense.

Learning to Work with People

My generation came of age amid great political and social upheaval in Thailand—a period of military regimes, new democratic changes, elections, coups d'état, and student uprisings. All these changes were part of the "real-world" training society was

2. Community planning session, Poo Pok Community, in Pattani, Bangkok. House plots (blue pieces of paper) are in clusters of five or six houses, each with a small shared courtyard. The coffee cup at center represents the mosque that will be the heart of their new community.

giving us, and it infected our professional training with idealism and a sense of responsibility toward our country. After finishing architecture and planning studies at university, I joined the National Housing Authority. Back then, the NHA constructed blocks of social housing, and started to upgrade the infrastructure in slums—mostly in Bangkok, which was in the early stages of explosive urbanization and economic boom. Housing tends to be looked at in commercial or industrial terms—a technical matter of densities, unit costs, budget subsidies, finance terms, and profit margins—and I found the NHA's approach no different. But during my second year there, I had a chance to take part in a training course in Denmark which looked at housing in a very different way, as something not separate from society, but a product of social, economic, political, and human realities. That course helped confirm for me a growing notion that housing was much more than a consumer product; it could be a process that helped build communities and be the root of a more just and healthy society. Back in Thailand, I joined the NHA's slum-upgrading program. It was run realistically, operating in communities that already existed, and the residents of the settlements had to be involved in the upgrades and agree to the improvements. I took it as a challenge because we—the professionals and the community—had to learn how to do that upgrading work together, and this two-way process was a revelation for me (fig. 2).

Rights versus Solutions

The NHA program was an important early endeavor, but it had its weak points. Because the drains and walkways were planned by engineers and constructed by contractors according to fixed standards, there was not much room for community people to participate in the process. Plus, many informal settlements never got on the NHA's list because of land tenure and eviction problems. But more seriously, because the program did not touch the difficult issue of tenure security, many of the upgraded settlements were still targeted for eviction. Activists and human-rights groups were understandably outraged by

the growing tally of evictions to make way for the shopping malls and expressways going up all over Bangkok. As I started getting involved in land-conflict cases, I found that activists and professionals responded quite differently to the crisis. Activists encouraged communities to confront and to demand their rights. While their efforts may have helped stall demolitions, shame nasty developers, and bring the eviction issue into the public eye, ultimately, the people in those settlements were still as powerless as ever and living in miserable conditions, waiting for the government to solve their problems for them. As a professional, on the other hand, I tried to use the tools of planning and design to develop pragmatic alternatives to eviction, acceptable to both the landowners and the people who occupied their land (fig. 3). Our efforts yielded a number of pioneering land-sharing projects. With proactive intervention, negotiation, and sensitive planning, compromise agreements were reached in several conflict situations, in which parts of the land were returned to the landowners to develop, and others were sold or rented to the communities to develop new projects with better housing and secure tenure.

Those early land-sharing projects, in which slum communities transformed themselves into legal, secure, and decent neighborhoods, were an immersion course. We found ways to bring all of the complex elements of these people's lives into concrete physical plans: the diverse array of informal jobs; the varying shades of tenure status; the different-sized plots and the many ways of using houses; the wildly divergent opinions and expectations; the heroes, cranks, and trouble-makers. Helping people develop affordable, fair housing plans and new community layouts was difficult and messy, but I began to understand the real meaning of a people's housing process: those vulnerable communities were creating a new social system, in which they protected and supported each other (figs. 4, 5).

AREA FOR HOUSING

AREA FOR COMMERCIAL DEVELOPMENT

ORIGINAL SETTLEMENT

3 (after)

3 (before)

Setting Up the Country's First Community-development Fund

In 1992, after twelve years at the NHA, I joined a team to study the possibility of setting up a community-development fund that would offer financial tools to poor communities and support a more community-driven development process at a national scale. With initial capital of $40 million provided by the government, the Urban Community Development Office was Thailand's first such fund. From the start, the clear idea was that this was to be the poor people's fund, and we created some very unconventional systems for running it with as much flexibility and as little bureaucracy as possible, all over the country. The UCDO helped poor communities organize and implement a variety of initiatives and projects. With UCDO's support, community-savings groups were set up in cities throughout Thailand, and the groups began to link together into citywide networks. Several housing-relocation projects were developed by communities facing eviction and supported with land and housing loans from UCDO. It was a people-initiated and people-

4 (after)

3. Manangkasila, in central Bangkok, was one of Thailand's first land-sharing initiatives, carried out in the early 1980s. The community negotiated a long-term lease and rebuilt its housing on half the site, returning the rest to the Treasury Department. At the core of a process like this is the ability to compromise and find a "win-win" solution, acceptable to all parties involved. The poor become legal owners or tenants of their land, and the landlord finally gets to develop the land.

4. Trok Kanom Toay after an upgraded walkway, Bangkok, Thailand.

5. Trok Kanom Toay before the upgraded walkway.

5 (before)

6

managed process, and UCDO acted as its catalyst, supporter, and finance department (fig. 6).

Of course, there were problems and crises along the way: savings groups collapsing, loans not being repaid, corrupt leaders, political meddling. But those hard lessons helped refine a new kind of development support through the mechanism of people-managed finance. Adjustments made constantly by communities and UCDO staff and real progress allowed everyone to see new possibilities. And the UCDO's revolving-fund model yielded unmistakable results: after financing projects around the country, investing in

communities and networks, and building all kinds of new assets in poor areas, the original $40 million was not only still there—it had grown.

Unleashing the Problem-solving Force of Poor People

One of the most important things the UCDO experience showed us was that people must learn to manage their finances if they are to manage their own development. Being poor means never having enough money—to build a house, to buy land, to start a business, or to invest in education. What poor people need is a financial resource which trusts them and can mesh with the realities of their lives. But the capacity for people to manage their finances has to be developed collectively, beginning with community savings and credit groups that people administer themselves. As individuals, the poor do not stand a chance in this competitive, market-driven world; their only strength comes from pooling their resources into a larger, stronger force.

But being poor also means not having enough power, and that creates insidious side effects in poor communities: people lack confidence, they do not believe they can change their lives, they do not trust their neighbors. If you deal with different aspects of poverty in isolation—an education program, a microcredit initiative, a water-supply project—without addressing this fundamental question of power, you are only treating the symptoms, not the underlying causes. Real change in relationships and in power equations gives the poor a greater chance to make decisions and negotiate better deals for themselves. I believe that one of UCDO's most essential tasks was to open up the possibility for the impoverished to reclaim their role as legitimate members of society.

When people live in a slum, they are often fooled into believing they are somehow different from other people who have better houses or educations. It is crucial for the poor—and for those of us who work with them—to believe that the poor are no different than anyone else. In the conventional approach to development, we are encouraged to look at poverty as a long list of awful and terrible problems, which the poor have to endure and somebody else has to fix. But all those "problems" can distract us from seeing the flip side of poverty—the problem-solving side.

Through my work with poor communities and in managing institutions to support their initiatives, I have come to the conclusion that there are really only two systems by which things in this world are managed: management that is based on *distrust*, in which people are assumed to be incapable or untrustworthy, and must therefore be controlled

and policed with rules, checks, timelines, and quotas; and management based on *trust*, in which people are assumed to be creative and capable of solving their own problems, with the right kind of support. Sadly, it is the systems of distrust that rule the world we live in. But what is clear to me now is that development driven by poor communities can only thrive within systems of trust. If professionals like us can trust in people and try to understand their ways, then we will find the right ways to assist them. And the more people find space to learn and develop, the more we professionals learn also. It is a two-way process between equal partners.

I also believe that if the poor are to bring about lasting changes in the lopsided and inequitable structures which consign them to poverty, landlessness, and marginality in the first place, those changes have to be grounded in concrete action, in projects and initiatives that they do themselves. The politics of poor people's development is not one of abstract concepts and policy debates, but of doing things right away— things that prove change is possible and can show what change looks like. When a poor community paves a walkway or lays a water-supply system in its settlement, it becomes a doer, a solver of its own problems. And it negotiates support for its solutions along the way.

Baan Mankong: Citywide Slum Upgrading
In 2000, UCDO merged with a rural-development fund to become the Community Organizations Development Institute, a new type of public-development institution which enjoyed greater autonomy, a larger government budget, and a broader mandate to support community-driven development processes in both rural and urban areas across the country. One of CODI's most important programs was the Baan Mankong ("Secure Housing" in Thai) Community Upgrading Program. Launched in 2003, it channels infrastructure subsidies and soft housing and land loans directly to poor communities, which plan and carry out improvements to their housing,

6. A late-night planning session with the Jabang Dhigor community, in the southern Thai city of Pattani—one of Thailand's many community housing projects supported by the Baan Mankong Community Upgrading Program. In the photo, they are working with the Open Space team of young community architects to see how their preliminary housing models fit on the new land they have bought collectively on the outskirts of town with a loan from CODI.

7 (after)

environment, basic services, and tenure security, as well as manage the budgets themselves. The Baan Mankong Program is putting the management-by-trust principle to its greatest test yet, with Thailand's poor communities at the center of a highly decentralized process of developing long-term, comprehensive solutions in their cities (figs. 7, 8).

This program is the distillation of years of experience, and the largest-yet application of the belief that housing projects can be planned, implemented, and owned entirely by poor communities. It draws on decades of experience dealing with the financial aspects of community-driven development, and is being facilitated by

professionals and activists who have been working with and learning from communities for twenty to thirty years. But several new ingredients have been added to the recipe as well. Architects and architecture schools around the country have been invited to apply their professional skills to projects in which the residents are the planners and the architects become the facilitators (fig. 1). The program has also introduced new concepts of cooperative land tenure to help communities use their group power to solve difficult problems that come up during the upgrading process—delays, negotiation setbacks, difficulties getting permits, internal disagreements, dueling factions, lack of participation, corrupt leaders, disappearing budgets—and during the vulnerable period

7. Ruam Samakee community after participating in the Baan Mankong Community Upgrading Program. Soi Ramkhamhaeng, Bangkok, Thailand.

8 (before)

afterwards, when they are repaying their loans. Another key aspect of the program is that communities work together with their local governments as much as possible to develop upgrade plans citywide, carried out in partnership with stakeholders in each city. This collaboration can be a powerful way to transform antagonistic relationships into productive partnerships and bring about genuine structural change in cities.

The Baan Mankong Program is now being implemented in 260 cities in Thailand. Projects like the ones along the Bang Bua Canal in Bangkok, featured in this exhibition and book (figs. 9, 10), have either been completed or are being carried out in more than 860 sites around the country, covering over 1,500 poor communities and about 90,000 households. Each one of these projects has its own story and cast of characters. But in

all of them, the funds for grants and loans are transferred directly to the communities, which own and implement the projects. After seven years, Baan Mankong has proven that change on a large scale is definitely possible if people can be the key actors and leaders of that change—a new kind of democracy (fig. 11).

Postscript: the Trust System Goes Regional
Many groups have visited Thailand over the years and taken back ideas from CODI, the community networks, and the Baan Mankong Program about network-building, flexible housing finance, and community upgrading. The process in Thailand has likewise been enriched by ideas and innovations from other countries, which have brought new dimensions into the work. For example, the Mahila Milan women's savings collectives in Bombay are like older sisters to the Thai savings

8. Ruam Samakee community before it began upgrading. Soi Ramkhamhaeng, Bangkok, Thailand.

9 (before)

10 (after)

groups. The Kampung Improvement Program in Surabaya, Indonesia; the Community Mortgage Program in the Philippines; and the Orangi Pilot Project in Karachi, Pakistan, have also contributed knowledge and helped shape Baan Mankong and the Thai community process it is part of. Since the late 1980s, many of these pockets of innovation in Asian countries have been brought into the spotlight and linked together into a large, friendly pool of inspiration, ideas, and mutual learning and assistance through the work of the Asian Coalition for Housing Rights. The ACHR's formation and evolution, which have occurred in tandem with the work I have described in Thailand, are a parallel story we unfortunately do not have the space to tell here. But I conclude by reporting that the community-driven, citywide slum upgrading being implemented in Thailand has spread to more than one hundred cities in fourteen Asian countries, with support from ACHR's new Asian Coalition for Community Action Program.

9. Bang Bua Canal community before it began upgrading. Bang Bua, Bangkok, Thailand.
10. New housing, Bang Bua Canal, after upgrading.
11. Bang Bua Canal community upgrade construction.

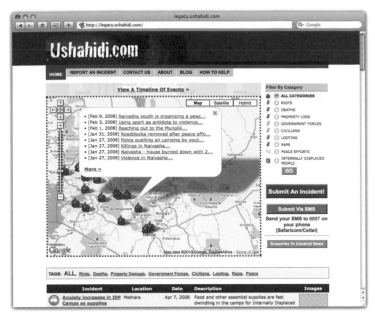

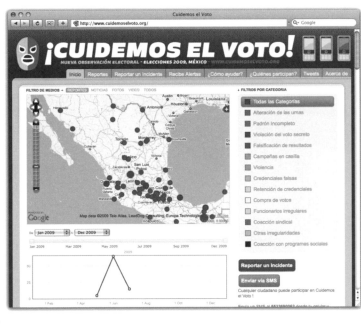

1

Ushahidi

Interview with
Juliana Rotich, Environment Editor, Global Voices Online,
Cofounder and Program Director, Ushahidi

By Cynthia E. Smith

You have written that Africa is experiencing a renaissance that has led to innovations which could be used worldwide. Can you elaborate?
Juliana Rotich: I see the African renaissance through the eyes of a different generation—what Dr. George Ayittey, the noted African economist and intellectual, calls the "Cheetah Generation": a fast-moving crop of Africans who do not accept the status quo; and who are rooted in their heritage, but choose to find alternative ways of changing the state of affairs in their countries. The African renaissance is multifold, from the cultural reawakenings that can be glimpsed through African digital art, music, social change, and, most of all, technology. I have witnessed it mostly though the prisms of technology and how African people have interacted with mobile phones, computers, and the Internet. This renaissance is also powered by a highly connected generation that is transnational and at times multicultural.

Trickle-up innovation: This is the type of innovation coming out of various parts of Africa that also has global relevance.

One example is the mobile-money concept embodied by M-PESA, a wildly successful money-transfer service. Started by Safaricom and Vodafone in 2007 with about 50,000 customers, it now has more than eight million customers, and 20% of Kenya's GDP is processed through mobile money. This innovation has been exported to many other countries, including Afghanistan, Germany, and Nigeria. Another example is Ushahidi interactive mapping software, made in Africa but currently used in various parts of the world.

As one of its cofounders, can you explain what Ushahidi is? How was it conceived? What was the inspiration?
JR: Ushahidi started as an ad-hoc group of technologists and bloggers hammering out software in a couple days, trying to figure out a way to gather more and better information about the post-election violence in Kenya in January 2008.

Ushahidi now refers to two things: the organization, Ushahidi Inc., formed to continue the work that began in 2008; and an open-source platform available

1. Organizations worldwide have used the Ushahidi platform for their own crowd-sourcing and mapping projects.

for free to individuals and organizations, now being utilized by organizations big and small all over the world to crowd-source information from multiple sources—SMS (short message service), email, Web reports, Twitter, and phone calls. The Ushahidi platform not only collects data, but also visualizes and maps them interactively. The cloud-based version of the Ushahidi platform is called Crowdmap.

How is Ushahidi being used? In what ways does this type of platform inform communication design?
JR: To date, Ushahidi and Crowdmap have been deployed in a wide variety of scenarios, such as monitoring and observing elections, tracking crime and civil unrest as well as natural disasters, promoting peace initiatives, documenting the impact of the Deepwater Horizon oil spill, visualizing urban development in Prague, and mapping disruptions caused by the London Tube strike. We have seen

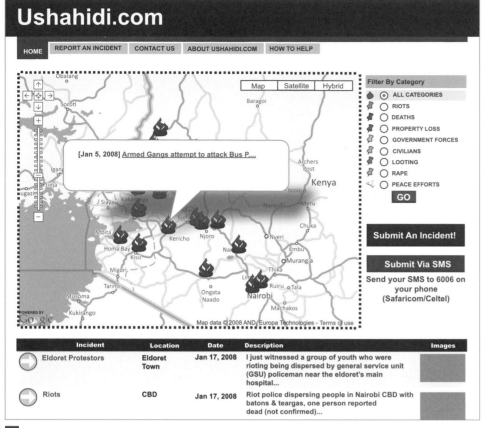

Ushahidi.com

HOME | REPORT AN INCIDENT | CONTACT US | ABOUT USHAHIDI.COM | HOW TO HELP

[Jan 5, 2008] Armed Gangs attempt to attack Bus P....

Filter By Category

- ● ALL CATEGORIES
- ○ RIOTS
- ○ DEATHS
- ○ PROPERTY LOSS
- ○ GOVERNMENT FORCES
- ○ CIVILIANS
- ○ LOOTING
- ○ RAPE
- ○ PEACE EFFORTS

GO

Submit An Incident!

Submit Via SMS
Send your SMS to 6006 on
your phone
(Safaricom/Celtel)

	Incident	Location	Date	Description	Images
→	Eldoret Protestors	Eldoret Town	Jan 17, 2008	I just witnessed a group of youth who were rioting being dispersed by general service unit (GSU) policeman near the eldoret's main hospital...	
→	Riots	CBD	Jan 17, 2008	Riot police dispersing people in Nairobi CBD with batons & teargas, one person reported dead (not confirmed)...	

2

2. The first version of Ushahidi, showing reports submitted by Kenyan citizens.
3. Juliana Rotich and David Kobia of the Ushahidi team.
4. (Left to right) Linda Kamau, Juliana Rotich, Erik Hersman, and Brian Herbert of the Ushahidi team at a rare in-person meeting.

media companies such as ABC in Australia use Crowdmap to source information around the Queensland floods of early 2011, and in Chicago, the *Tribune* Crowd mapped the effects of a large snowstorm. The platform is easy to use and extendable, and therefore amenable to various uses. We have seen a Spanish teacher use Crowdmap as an interactive tool for his students to map community happenings, thereby expanding their language skills and learning. The most surprising use of the Crowdmap platform to date has been Blizzard Babies Crowdmap, which links midwives to stranded pregnant moms through community mapping. This is one of the most surprising uses of the technology, one we could never have imagined.

Our hope is that the platform informs communication design by enabling the submission of information from remote areas, to allow those in a rural setting to say, "This is what we see," using the mode of submission that they have at their disposal. We hope the platform can handle data from varying shades of connectivity, and democratize the flow of information to include a broader range of input from a wider group of people, and through whichever mode of information submission the users are comfortable with or have access to. In short, to enable those who use the platform to "listen locally" and encourage bottom-up, grassroots efforts of data sharing, collection, aggregation, and, ultimately, collaboration.

You have stated that the Ushahidi team is "from the Internet." What do you mean?

How is this type of organization a benefit to your work? What implication does this have globally?

JR: Ushahidi would not exist were it not for the connections and collaborations made through the Internet and blogging. The initial idea was posted on a blog and coordinated through email and, in some cases, Twitter to bring it to life. The initial team members were linked to each other primarily through the Internet. The cofounders did not meet in one room for a full year after the organization was created. Crucial support of the idea was from Kenyan and international bloggers, who spread news not only of the situation in Kenya, but also of the ways we were trying to use technology to gather information. Our global community of developers, users, translators, and supporters communicate and work virtually with us. This means we collaborate regardless of distance. The core team is spread over six time zones, with developers and team members in Nairobi, Accra, Atlanta, Florida, Kentucky, and Chicago. It benefits our work because this style of working brings together people who are independent and self-organizing. In addition, we get design input from developers with a keen sense of local needs. We strive to make products that can work anywhere. This relatively new way of working has global implications, as there is true transfer of knowledge—not just one way, from West to South, but in both directions.

What constraints did you encounter while building Ushahidi for Africa? Do you think those limitations have helped the platform's usefulness?

JR: When we first developed Ushahidi, Internet penetration in Kenya was 2.8%; blogging and Internet use were available only to a small population, often the

official map. **Using the Ushahidi platform, the Map Kibera organization worked with local youth to create the first public digital map of their community. What is the future for this kind of democratic information sharing?**

JR: The technical community had started coalescing before Ushahidi, primarily through informal blogger meetings in the Nairobi area. After Ushahidi, the community came together even more, and linkages with Open Street Maps were forged. These linkages saw the community host mapping parties that joined local Kibera youth and Ushahidi developers. The maps provide context to the largest slum in Nairobi. For the residents, it is their home, and it provides them a different perspective when they see information that matters to them. The subdivisions, schools, and community centers that matter to them are now part of the digital world. Map Kibera has spurred similar projects, including Map Mathare, the first digital map of that community. As governments and other agencies allocate resources, there is less reason to overlook these areas as a mass of homogeneous locales with no specific communities, resources, and needs. There are more mapping parties organized in Nairobi, some by organizations that do not put the maps in the public domain. To ensure that information gathered through these efforts benefits a greater group of people, we must support and encourage open-source tools. Dominance of one company over the maps generated by communities would not augur well, as those maps end up being the property of the company and not of the communities themselves.

As an African futurist, what do you envision for the future of technology on the continent? Africa's urban population is projected to triple between 2010 and

elite and the diaspora. Bandwidth was extremely expensive and slow, but this specific constraint actually informed the design choices we made early on. The key consideration that made the tool not just another map mashup was the inclusion of SMS, which meant that information could be gathered from rural areas. I was in Eldoret, a small town in Kenya, when we brought the tool into existence, so this was particularly important to

me. Inclusion of email was also key; in addition, the coupling of a database structure with mapping technology was fundamental to the growth and usability of the platform.

Your organization has been at the forefront of changing the way information flows. In Nairobi, one of the largest informal settlements in East Africa, Kibera, did not appear on any

5

Aid needed - Portail Leogane, Cite L'Ouverture

english:
Please, I need to help, This is the number we can
to find me:36737869 .Certil Mackensy, I live at
Portail Leogane zone city Louverture. ..
creole:
mwen bezyen *d tanpri silvoupl* men numero nou ka
jyenn mwen 36737869 e potay leogane blok cite
louv*ti mwen se certil mackensy

6

5. Volunteers work together on the 2010 Kenyan
constitutional referendum monitoring project,
Uchaguzi.co.ke.
6. An art installation by Chris Blow features
thousands of printed SMS reports sent by Haitian nationals for the Ushahidi-Haiti crisis map.
7. African innovation: an old bicycle turned into
a furnace bellows.
8. African innovation: a bicycle mobile-phone
charger at Maker Faire Africa, 2010.

**2050[1] as people continue to migrate from
rural villages into informal settlements
and slums. There will be an increasing
demand for good governance, proper
housing, sanitation, clean water, and
education. How can innovation, design,
and technology help provide real
solutions for such dramatic shifts?**
JR: Urban migration already presents

immense challenges for Africa's cities.
Case in point: Nairobi's snarled traffic
jams, water and electricity outages,
and lack of accessible information for
urban planning. Locally appropriate
technology that meets the needs of the
city inhabitants will be key—innovation
that is fully embedded in society and a
part of how that society functions. These

real solutions are often best developed
with, and not so much for, the inhabitants.
Technology helps overcome analog
inefficiencies with digital effectiveness,
which can be done via mobile phones and
the Web. We are starting to see this in the
medical-health field with FrontlineSMS
Malawi and with mobile learning in
South Africa. Another consideration is

that technology can be low-tech but appropriate. An example is a bicycle-powered charger. Other innovations are profiled on the blog AfriGadget.

There is an opportunity for emerging and rapidly growing cities to become smart cities. This is one of the ways in which innovation, design, and technology can provide real solutions. Current, near-real-time data can be gathered, with the help of the crowd, to provide pertinent information to urban planners, academics, and leaders. Our hope is that they can make well-informed decisions that take into account the flowing reality of the cities.

As Assaf Biderman, Associate Director MIT's Senseable City Lab, has stated, "Insight from data can be used to leapfrog." There is also the opportunity for education and academia to use participatory systems such as Ushahidi to link science, data, and student participation. Relating the exploration of the built/urban environment to scientific observation, data collection, and analysis is but one way to tackle the challenges of rapidly growing cities. Solutions that have worked in other areas of the world need to be shared with the key planners of cities. The future of technology in Africa is bright, to say the least. I envision growing metropolises that will come up with ingenious ways of dealing with the immense challenges they face—new solutions within Africa, for Africa, by Africans.

Notes

1. UN Habitat, "State of African Cities 2010" report (http://www.unhabitat.org/documents/SOAC10/SOAC-PR1-en.pdf).

Dirty Work: Landscape and Infrastructure in Nonformal Cities

Christian Werthmann

Associate Professor of Landscape Architecture, Harvard Graduate School of Design

In the dense quarters of nonformal cities, the term landscape does not readily cross people's minds. Nevertheless, the evolution of nonformal cities is intimately tied to the morphology of their underlying landscape. Informal settlements are primarily built on ecologically sensitive landscapes, such as floodplains, wetlands, marshes, swamps, riverbanks, riparian forests, river valleys, ravines, steep slopes, and bluffs. Other informally settled landscapes serve as vital infrastructures for urban regions and have hitherto been protected from development—highly productive farmlands, species-rich forests, groundwater-recharge areas, and the watersheds of reservoirs. At times, occupied landscapes are directly tied to infrastructural systems—the interstitial spaces of highway medians, leftover spaces between railroad tracks, landfills—or postindustrial landscapes, including abandoned factories, quarries, and other mining operations.

Landscape as Threat

Despite the hostility and precariousness of these terrains, there is always a strong rationale for low-income populations to settle on them. In nonformal settlements as in real estate, location is the primary impetus. Job proximity forces poor migrants to settle in places avoided by earlier urbanization. In the 1950s, John Turner noted that closeness to potential jobs, which secure income and food, overrules other considerations such as comfort and safety.[1] Given such logic, the ingenuity and resourcefulness of informal settlers to negotiate unsuitable building terrain have been widely admired and described. However, despite their inventiveness, larger forces often overwhelm human constructions and inflict severe damage and suffering upon informal cities and their populations. Mudslides after heavy rains destroy whole neighborhoods and take lives in seconds—events that will only increase due to the effects of

1. By separating the bays of the favela from the polluted reservoir and treating stormwater runoff, the bays can be cleaned and serve as community swimming ponds. Proposal for the favela Cantinho do Ceu by Katie Powell.

climate change. Garbage slides can kill dwellers living next to or on top of landfills. Houses on steep, erosion-prone slopes get washed away in heavy rains. Flooding of low-lying areas and valleys causes severe damage and creates unsanitary conditions; trapped moisture and poor ventilation result in long-term respiratory illnesses. The list of calamities is long, and reaches down to more mundane inconveniences, such as the climbing of hundreds of steps to reach one's house on a steep hill. One could rightfully claim that the hostile landscape conditions hidden under the crowded houses of informal cities are a major source of suffering. Can this unfriendly landscape resurface as a source of delight and opportunity?

Landscape as Asset

As many of the projects to upgrade informal cities over the last two decades have shown, landscape belongs among the primary agents of improvement. After decades of experience, the premier urban-redevelopment projects in Latin America focus less on the provision of housing than on the restructuring of landscape and infrastructure. Ironically, housing is no longer the primary task of Favela Bairro in Rio de Janeiro and the Low Income Housing Agency in São Paulo (SEHAB), Brazil; and the planning agencies of Bogotá and Medellín, Colombia. After studies showed that informal-city dwellers improve their individual houses when their overall neighborhood is improved and when the threat of eviction is removed, the focus of these and other housing agencies turned to the improvement of landscape and infrastructure. Following the principle in first aid of attending to the most seriously wounded first, these municipal agencies prioritize informal cities that are located in the most volatile areas. They relocate at-risk dwellers as close as possible to their former houses in order to help them maintain valuable professional networks and social relationships. The new voids created by these evacuations are then available for engineering projects to open up new spaces, connect dwellings to sewage systems, send storm waters to underground pipes, seal erosion-prone slopes, and

2 (before)

3 (after)

build access roads with utilities below. Over the last twenty years, hundreds of new plazas, playgrounds, parks, festival grounds, outdoor markets, and other spaces have been built on evacuated land and over utility corridors in Rio de Janeiro, São Paulo, Bogotá, and Medellín. Paradoxically, these projects make it apparent that informal settlements built on volatile landscapes can offer more open-space opportunities than favelas erected in stable areas, where residents do not feel the necessity to move and new public areas can only be built in existing voids.

2, 3. A 500m-long promenade built in 1997 along Guanabara Bay in Parque Royal, Favela Bairro, Rio de Janeiro.

4

Moreover, these cities have the potential to become truly remarkable. Their distinctive forms are already shaped by intensive manual labor in difficult terrain, and simple interventions can often turn precarious situations into favorable ones. For example, in Rio de Janeiro's Parque Royal, built in the sensitive littoral zone of Guanabara Bay, a new, 500-meter-long boulevard along the ocean converted shags on stilts in the mudflats into one of the best locations in town, a much-cited flagship project of the Favela Bairro Program (figs. 2, 3). The Cellula Urbana Program developed a similar project for Morro da Providência, the oldest favela in Rio de Janeiro, where new overlooks offer brilliant views over Rio's old city center (fig. 4). In a similar fashion, cable-car stations erected in Medellín and later in Caracas and Rio de Janeiro paired with social programs turned inaccessible hilltop locations into

well-connected areas (fig. 5). Once one absorbs the loss of littoral zones, coastal bluffs, and Atlantic rainforest, these projects show the potential of landscape to be transformed from a threat to an asset.

Conventional Infrastructure and the Externalization of Problems

These successful and socially sensitive municipal programs in Latin American cities may appear to be effective models for improving informal cities by transforming landscapes and public spaces. However, closer inspection reveals that the new civic landscapes are often disconnected from infrastructural upgrades. They are essentially recreational spaces laid over engineering projects that attempt to control the volatile landscapes below the surface. There is not much evidence

4. Spectacular overlooks were sensitively inserted in Morro da Providênçia, Rio's oldest favela.

5

5. Medellín invested heavily in a cable-car system to connect the poorest areas in the hills to the city and create new public spaces below.

to support the notion that they are landscape *as* infrastructure; rather, they superimpose themselves over a conventional model of infrastructure characterized by inefficiencies. In many of these cities, waste is shipped to distant and overflowing landfills. New power plants in faraway locations satisfy increased electrical demands. Sewage, if treated at all, is pumped over long distances to large plants in remote watersheds. New drinking-water reservoirs are built in far-flung areas, while once-remote reservoirs have been engulfed (and polluted) by rapid urbanization. Food is shipped over long distances. As in most cities on the planet, these centralized infrastructural systems rely on the externalization of problems. They aggressively secure and negatively impact distant landscapes to serve their growing needs. Although there is a strong desire for greater effectiveness, the development of closed-loop systems, and more decentralized infrastructure, the maximization of local resources is still in its infancy in the cities of the Global South (and not that much further ahead in the Western world either, where the per-capita consumption and environmental footprint

are abysmally higher). Tragically, in many cases, upgrading today means that informal cities, once characterized by resourcefulness and inventiveness, are hooked up to the wasteful infrastructure systems of the formal city (fig. 6).

A Global Challenge

Obviously, we can no longer afford this model. In forty years, another two and a half billion people will be added to the planet; seven of the world's nine billion inhabitants will live in cities.[2] Three billion, or almost half of them, will live in nonformal cities. Experts are deeply troubled about these new populations. The provision of food and water is among the chief concerns, along with energy questions, disaster management, and increased political instability. Many wonder how the world population will be fed, since the majority of arable land on this planet is already being used. It is expected that food prices will rise in wealthy countries and food shortages and famine will become more common in poorer countries. Since more than three quarters of our fresh-water consumption is used for agriculture, it is expected

6

that the ongoing fight about water will intensify, exacerbated by the effects of climate change that will bring alternately droughts and floods (fig. 7).

Amidst the dark prognostications, there is also good news: Many people are supposed to escape poverty. The number of people described as "middle class"—depending on how it is defined—is projected to grow from a scant one-and-a-half billion to three or perhaps four billion in 2050.[3] On the flipside, experts are worried that this burgeoning group will bring substantial increases in consumption, resulting in greater greenhouse-gas emissions and resource depletion. However, from an ethical point of view, we have to further advance living conditions for all people on the planet.

Without going more into the details of the various scenarios, it is clear that we need nothing short of a revolution. Much of the thrust of this revolution has to play out in the city and its region, where the majority of humankind will live. This revolution will need all sectors of society to initiate change on all levels. As designers, we have to contribute to the holistic development of more efficient urban and regional infrastructures. At the same time, we have to continue to find ways to improve the living conditions of potentially three billion informal city dwellers in unison with the other four billion urban residents. Our task is unambiguous; in the intersection between a more efficient urban metabolism and an increased urban life quality rests the biggest design challenge and opportunity of the twenty-first century.

6. Flood basins take up valuable space next to overcrowded favelas, São Paulo.

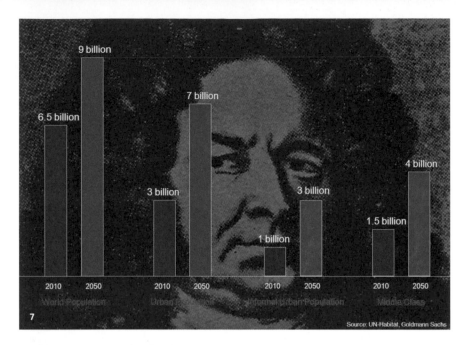

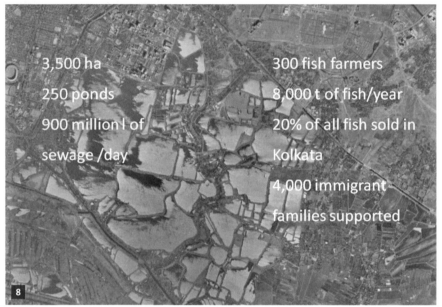

3,500 ha
250 ponds
900 million l of
sewage /day

300 fish farmers
8,000 t of fish/year
20% of all fish sold in
Kolkata
4,000 immigrant
families supported

7. When the current generation of young designers retires and sends their grandchildren to school, the world will look radically different. What will their roles be?
8. Sewage fish ponds, Kolkata, India.

began experimenting with other ways to cultivate fish. In this system, the sewage goes through three stages: The untreated sewage receives a first cleaning in the Kolkata wetlands. Second, it is diverted into 250 ponds stocked with fish, which consume the algae formed by the nutrient-rich sewage. Third, the effluent from the fish ponds is used for irrigating rice paddies. In total, the system cleans about one third of Kolkata's sewage (the city has no sewage plant) on an area of 3,500 hectares (about 8,650 acres), providing income and food for 4,000 families, which produce over 8,000 tons per year, one fifth of all fish sold in Kolkata.[4] (fig. 8)

Composting in Dhaka, Bangladesh: The standout nongovernmental agency Waste Concern runs a large composting operation in Dhaka, employing over 400 workers to collect organic waste from individual households by rickshaw. The material is brought to five composting plants that process up to fifteen tons of organic material a day. The compost is sold as fertilizer to farmers. In addition to creating jobs, the program uses the city's waste to foster organic agriculture in rural areas and positively impacts the appearance of public spaces in the city, which are now less prone to informal garbage dumping. The program has been so successful that Waste Concern just completed the construction of a 700-ton-per-day facility in the periphery of Dhaka, which will employ a total of 16,000 workers coming mostly from lower socioeconomic backgrounds. In its final iteration, it will treat 80% of the organic waste of Dhaka's nine million inhabitants. The increase in scale was partially made possible through the Clean Development Mechanism established by the Kyoto Protocol. Since this composting process reduces overall methane emissions, up to one third of Waste Concern's cost is financed by carbon credits—a model being copied in several other countries.

Urban Agriculture in São Paulo: Cidade desse Fomem (Cities Without Hunger) is a small NGO fostering urban agriculture in the favelas of São Paulo. With the help of community cooperatives,

Landscape as Infrastructure

From the viewpoint of landscape design, there are rich opportunities to integrate new, less wasteful models of basic infrastructure (waste, water, energy, food, and transport) that create new public spaces and provide new sources of income—the best way to improve life quality. Many improved models already exist in the cities of the Global South.

The Sewage Fish Ponds of Kolkata, India: The

sewage fish ponds of Kolkata are a historic example of improving urban nutrient flows. The practice began in 1928 in Kolkata, when the overuse of irrigation dried up the Bidyadhari River and farmers

9

it occupies and converts leftover parcels in the dense fabric of the favelas into productive farmland. Thus far it has established more than twenty urban farms that provide healthy food and income for over 2,600 favela residents, called *favelanos*. In addition, once derelict open spaces are transformed into productive urban landscapes, informal dumping grounds vanish. Although small, Cidade desse Fomem has just received the Dubai International Award for Best Practices to Improve the Living Environment and is expected to replicate further (fig. 9).

The Role of Design and Design Schools
From a design standpoint, it is notable that most of these enterprises are initiated by non-designers. The strength of their implementation is based on the particular engineering and social expertise of their founders; the spatial and experiential effects on landscape and public space are the byproduct. This is a common reality of NGO activities initiated by engineers, doctors, and social activists whose focus on one type of objective, be it sanitation, agriculture, or health, can lead to excellent results in each respective area. However, the disconnected activities of these increasingly powerful NGOs have drawn criticism in recent years, including calls for larger coordinated efforts that achieve long-lasting, systemic change across sectors. (The current situation in Haiti is emblematic of this debate). Design is in a unique position to fill this gap by providing a model of improved urban metabolism on many levels: socially driven, culturally relevant, economically viable, ecologically literate, resource-

9. Cidade desse Fomem, São Paulo.

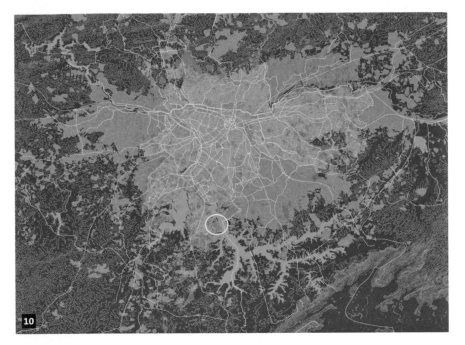

efficient, and spatially delightful. This holistic effort will require an integrated design methodology that comprises many fields and stakeholders—a challenge that can be found in its nascent stages in the municipal upgrading programs of Rio de Janeiro, São Paulo, Bogotá, and Medellín.

In the development of these integrated models, design schools must play a catalytic role. They can develop prototypical projects in which new approaches can be initiated, adapted, and carried on by local carriers. Fortunately, more and more design schools are engaging the topic of informality in research and curricula on a very practical level.

For example, I recently conducted a Harvard Graduate School of Design studio that engaged with a favela-upgrading project initiated by the São Paulo Housing Agency. Cantinho do Céu, a city of 30,000, is a clandestine development built thirty years ago by developers who illegally cleared protected rainforest along the banks of São Paulo's largest water reservoir, parceled the land, and sold the plots to low-income residents. Such developments are a common practice in the Global South. Cantinho do Céu is part of a much larger informal agglomeration near the once-forested watershed of the Billings Reservoir, rendering large parts of the reservoir unusable. Although the lake is heavily impacted by untreated sewage from informal settlements, it is even more damaged by agricultural runoff and by contaminated floodwaters pumped into it from São Paulo proper during the rainy season (figs. 10–16).

Thirteen graduate students and I worked with Fernando de Mello Franco of MMBB, a prominent architect from São Paulo; the São Paulo Housing Agency, led by Elisabete França; and a group of

10. Roughly 20% of São Paulo's population, or close to 4 million people, live in nonformal or clandestine settlements (in orange).
11, 12. Cantinho do Céu, near the Billings Reservoir, São Paulo.

twenty local and international consultants, most notably environmental engineer Byron Stigge of Buro Happold. Since rigid zoning plans have failed, we steered our students away from developing finite master plans toward pursuing discrete tactical operations unfolding over periods of time. Their objective was to initiate a first move and predict its eventual spatial, ecological, and social effects. The ultimate goal was to create a healthy coexistence of the favela and its vulnerable landscape, the 580 km² reservoir.

After detailed analysis, a site visit, community meetings, numerous reviews, and fourteen weeks of intensive work, the students formulated thirteen tactics, including storm-water and sewage-treatment wetlands, community centers and spaces, tree nurseries and street-planting programs, water promenades, and large-scale

13. The poorest houses are typically found right at the edge of the reservoir.
14. Negotiations between the residents of Cantinho do Céu with the electrical company, which runs the reservoir, left some of the steep banks open from informal urbanization.

"O único trabalho que temos no Cantinho estão com pequenas lojas com qualquer carreira. Precisamos de mais postos de trabalho locais. Os jovens precisam de ser envolvidos."

"The only jobs we have in Cantinho are with small shops with no career path. We need more local jobs. Young people need to be involved."

"Nossa educação é fraca. Existem três escolas primárias e uma escola de ensino médio Cantinho estudantes mas não vai continuar a sua educação passado que."

"Our education is poor. There are three elementary schools and one high school in Cantinho. Students will not continue their education past that."

"de mais casas para viver por."

"We need better houses to live in."

"Não há mais patrocinadores locais. ONG's deixaram de vir para o nosso lugar."

"There are no local sponsors anymore. NGO's have stopped coming to that place."

"Eu would gostaria de ter mais linhas de autocarros para para a cidade, demora cerca de três horas de Cantinho."

"I would like to have more bus line to go into the city. It's about three hours from Cantinho."

"gostaríamos de ter uma confiança hospital. Médicos em Cantinho são demasiado jovens e menos qualificados."

"We would like to have a trustful hospital. Doctors in Cantinho are too young and unskilled."

light-rail systems. The best approaches provided environmental services, new sources of income, and, to be sure, improvement of public space. In the end, the project showed that a systemic design approach initiated through landscape operations had the potential to reconcile the coexistence of the informal city and the reservoir. After a presentation to the community, the São Paulo Housing Agency chose five of the thirteen projects as guides for their actual upgrading project (figs. 1, 17–23).

Ten Considerations for the Future
The lessons of this engagement were manifold, but the most important one was that longer engagements are needed between academia and disadvantaged communities to build trust and to assess and correct processes. When I compare the lessons of my academic work with the experience of large-scale upgrading practices in Latin America, and with alternative models of

urban infrastructures, the following considerations emerge for the future development of landscape and infrastructure in nonformal cities:

1. Transdisciplinarity: A holistic approach demands the integration of many sectors and government bodies, where no single discipline is dominant. Designers, who traditionally stand between art and science, are inherently capable of orchestrating such collaborations. In this process, urban engineering must be taken into greater consideration, and landscape architects and utility engineers must work more closely together.

2. Multifunctionality: The high population density of informal cities requires that improvements made to them must serve many connected functions. Hybridized systems have to combine programs not typically juxtaposed—sports fields that serve as sewage-treatment plants, for example, or community centers that serve as recycling nodes.

15. The steep topography of Cantinho do Ceu accelerates stormwater runoff into the reservoir.
16. Results of a community meeting.

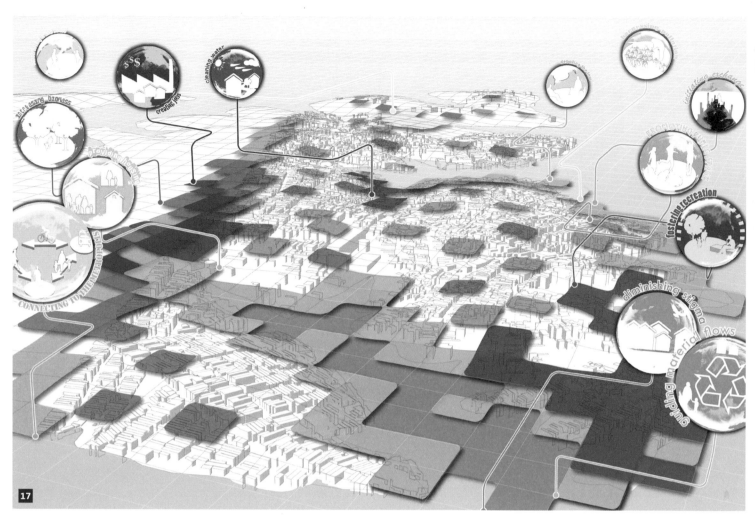

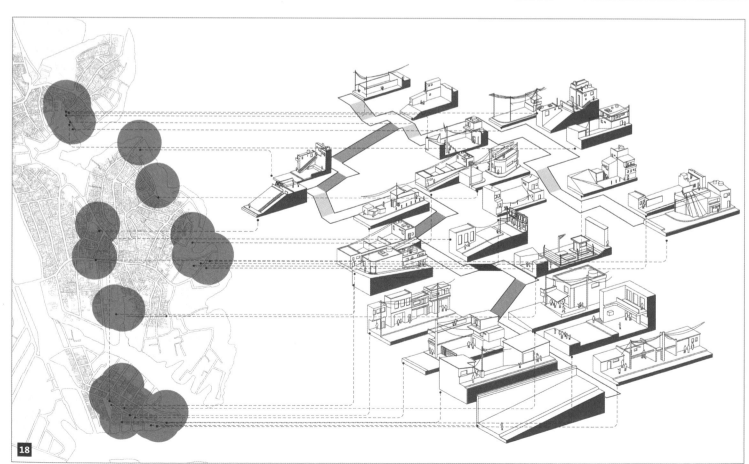

90

19

3. Water as Key Infrastructure: The most common natural threats to nonformal cities are related to water—flooding, erosion, and water pollution—and the provision and management of water in cities will become more and more pivotal. Large-scale, centralized engineering projects have historically done more harm than good. Alternative, decentralized urban water management has to be tested, and if it is successful, it will have a profound impact on the composition of informal cities.

4. Telescopic Approach: Infrastructural and ecological systems operate independently of municipal, site, and property boundaries, and involve large amounts of terrain. The development of socio-ecological infrastructures in nonformal cities means one has to simultaneously monitor the process at all levels—local, regional, and global.

5. Ecology as Economy: The economy of formal and nonformal cities is inextricably linked to the ecology of their terrain and region. There is a historical opportunity to leapfrog informal cities into ecologically beneficial infrastructures that generate new jobs and provide services for the city as a whole.

6. Informal and Formal: Urban metabolism occurs on many scales, independent of the genesis of its neighborhoods. When improving how cities work, the designer has to disregard the dichotomy between formal and informal. The designer has to study and redesign flows—of people, water, material, energy, waste, etc.—for the whole terrain of a metropolis and its supportive regions.

7. Participation: The success or failure of upgrades of nonformal cities is directly tied to community participation. A growing body of knowledge shows that different types of community participation should occur at various times in the project, depending on the size and composition of the populations involved. For projects involving thousands of people, the participation of social workers and specialists is indispensable.

8. Process: The processing and phasing of operations in the nonformal city have to be carefully orchestrated. When urbanism is studied from a landscape perspective, the factor time becomes dominant. In order to develop strategies for the myriad events occurring in nonformal cities, a process-based design methodology has to be

17. The thirteen students pursued thirteen different tactical goals.
18, 19. Despite high population density, Cantinho do Céu has many unused micro-parcels that could be categorized by size, form, steepness, and adjacencies and serve as a small-scale public-space system. Proposal by Andrew ten Brink.

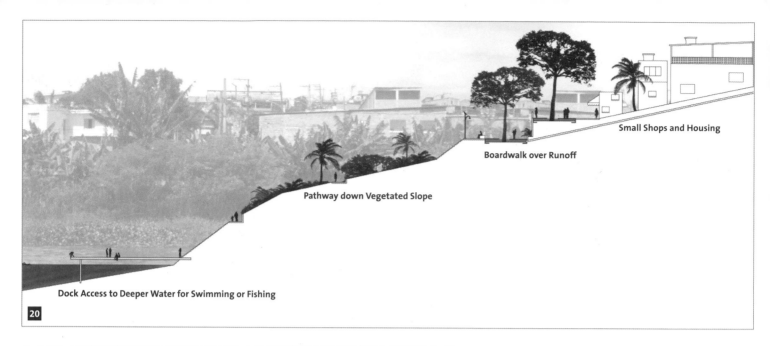

Small Shops and Housing

Boardwalk over Runoff

Pathway down Vegetated Slope

Dock Access to Deeper Water for Swimming or Fishing

20

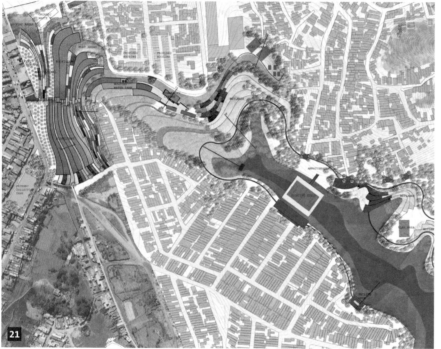

21

20. The edges of the reservoir could be made accessible and the city turned around to face it. Proposal by Katie Powell. 21. A small sewage-treatment plant could be buried on top of a hill. In a tertiary treatment phase, water would be cleaned through terraced wetlands and would eventually irrigate terraced agriculture. Proposal by Rina Salvi.

developed to negotiate between bottom-up and top-down approaches, unfold over time, and adapt to changing demands. That means designers have to accompany neighborhoods over longer periods of time.

9. Representation: Our tools of historic representation are still connected to the exploration of the static object (e.g., "the building"), whereas the representation of dynamic systems such as material flows, energy flows, water and transport flows, and ecological systems is still in its infancy (the mapping movement of the mid-1990s was an

important start in that direction). Today an array of exciting new digital tools for representation of dynamic systems has to be explored and developed to reveal and manipulate urban flows while breaking down the boundaries between the inaccessible technical communication systems of engineering and the overly experiential communication methods of design. For example, one can now develop terrain-sensitive algorithms that can predict future informal urbanization based on topography, land ownership, and utilities. Based on these models, one could develop anticipatory strategies to prepare the land or guide these new settlements.

10. Beauty: Every informal city has its own aesthetic. Designers especially must understand this and situate their work in context. Informal city dwellers are generally stigmatized, and the aesthetic posture of an intervention is an indispensable tool for self-esteem.

There are, of course, many more lessons to be learned on a diverse range of subjects, including governance, creative financing, land-use planning, property laws, the position of the designer, activist practice, and security. Redesigning cities

22

characterized by inequality is an infinitely complex undertaking, and no list can ever be comprehensive. As with any open project, initial considerations such as these need improvement, exploration, and expansion. Given the dimension of our future challenges and the responsibilities that we hold as designers and human beings, there is no time to waste.

Notes

1. Turner, John F. C., and Robert Fichter. *Freedom to Build: Dweller Control of the Housing Process*. New York: Macmillan, 1972.

2. UN-Habitat, "Urbanization: Facts and Figures."

3. Goldmann Sachs, "The Expanding Middle: The Exploding World Middle Class and Falling Global Inequality."

4. http://www.keip.in/bl3/wetlands.php.

22. Floating "cut flower islands" and a new promenade that stores rainwater could give Cantinho do Céu's waterfront a new face. Proposal by Joseph Claghorn.
23. The "cut flower islands" would suck out nutrients from the polluted reservoir, mimicking the functions of existing water hyacinths, and provide income to residents. Proposal by Joseph Claghorn.

CONDIÇÕES ATUAIS: LIMPEZA DE WETLANDS
EXISTING CONDITION: WETLAND CLEANING

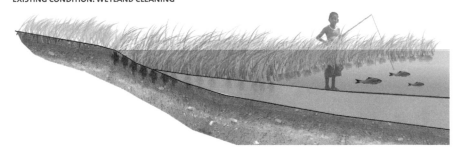

CONDIÇÕES ATUAIS: LIMPEZA DE WETLANDS
EXISTING CONDITION: WETLAND CLEANING

CONDIÇÕES PROPOSTAS: LIMPEZA DE WETLANDS
PROPOSED CONDITION: WETLAND CLEANING

23

Abalimi Bezekhaya

Interview with
Christina Kaba, Field Operations Director
Robert Small, Resource Mobilization Leader, Abalimi Bezekhaya

By Cynthia E. Smith

What is Abalimi Bezekhaya? What is your role at the organization?
Christina Kaba: It means "Grow at home." At Abalimi, we train and support people to grow their own vegetables and fruit and start community gardens. We sell them plants and provide instructions and advice on how to handle seedlings, make their own compost, and otherwise work their land. They can then grow their own food and sell vegetables to make money for themselves and their community.

The organization was founded in 1982; I've been with them since 1989. As Field Operations Director, I coordinate projects and oversee the field workers working in the communities. Although other people might see me as a leader, I think I'm more of a trainer or a pilot. I listen to what the communities around us say they need, and I provide those needs if they match our aims and goals.

What events led up to the formation of Abalimi Bezekhaya in South Africa? When and how did this urban-farming movement begin? How can this help

people living in poor informal settlements in South Africa?
Robert Small: Since the Industrial Revolution, we have been setting up industrial systems, and that includes agriculture. And industrial agriculture has overrun or eliminated small family farming in large parts of the world. In South Africa, this has emphatically been the case. Under apartheid, men from the black tribes were brought to the cities and the mines to work, leaving the women and the elderly in the rural, so-called "homelands."

Fifty years ago, the homelands were full of crops and cattle; the men used to come back and plow during the holidays. Now more than half of those rural areas are empty and unfarmed. That generation has aged, and most of them are not strong enough to carry on farming activities; and the young people have given up. During apartheid, we forced agriculture on black youth, whereas white youth were not forced to study agriculture. There was an attempt to turn blacks into farm laborers and keep them in the rural areas, but it

1. Local farmers grow organic vegetables with the help of Abalimi Bezekhaya on plots adjacent to their settlement, Cape Town, South Africa.

was resisted by the young people. That killed agriculture as a real possibility for a career through two generations.

Commercial farming has grown at a rapid pace. The only successful farming model seems to be the industrial model, and nothing else is taken seriously, at least in South Africa. So what we have in South Africa is a dead small-farm culture. There is no real support being given to these farmers, and that's a worldwide phenomenon.

What we at Abalimi have done since 1982 is reestablish micro- and family farmers in the poor informal settlements of Cape Town. Participants can make money and even create a job with as little as 500 square meters (0.12 acre). Imagine pieces of land like this all over the country, an abundant food source for a whole family plus enough money for a modest living.

2

Why do people in the townships need these community gardens and backyard gardens?

CK: I think that most people come to the big city looking for jobs. When they can't find one, they end up poor and hungry. We help those people put food on their table and learn to make money. Many of the people we train come from rural areas such as Ciskei and Eastern Cape, and they take their knowledge back to their villages. They bring us photos of what they are doing there, and others come to us from those areas to get more training and ideas to bring back home. There are still many unemployed people in the township. They need the land, the open space, to start their gardens, but it's very difficult to get the government authorities' permission.

Can you describe the different stages of development for the urban farmer?

Why do you think Abalimi Bezekhaya's approach, combining traditional and commercial farming methods, is a critical step in providing a sustainable solution?

RS: First is the survival stage, where you just eat what you farm. Second is the subsistence stage, where you eat and produce seasonal surplus once, twice, or three times a year, which you can sell or give away. Third is the livelihood level, a new synthesis of the old, easygoing subsistence way of farming and of a highly disciplined, commercial, straight-line planning approach to agriculture.

The big mistake made by development agencies worldwide—and why agriculture fails over and over again in Africa—is that they try to leapfrog farmers directly to full industrial farming, with no intermediate stage. Moving directly from subsistence or survival into commercial level, they have little chance of success. With the

livelihood level, we say to the small farmers, "Grow five rows of something, say, carrots, and we guarantee that we will buy what you grow if the carrots are of a satisfactory quality and if you follow the procedures." And if the farmers follow the agreement and the quality of their produce is reasonable, they can gain a regular, guaranteed supply of income. Anything left over can be cooked in soups, given away, or composted. If this kind of system can be followed countrywide, poverty—of food as well as cash—can be significantly reduced.

What is Harvest of Hope (HOH)? How does this initiative work?

RS: HOH is a community-supported agriculture (CSA) scheme in an urban context, supplied by poor micro-farmers. People buy organically grown vegetables from the community farmer rather than go to the supermarket. I think this can happen in any city, the connection between local farmers and consumers who do not have the time or desire to farm for themselves. The produce is same-day fresh, straight out of the ground, organically grown. You are creating jobs while reducing your carbon footprint because you are not buying frozen food imported from outside the city. You are supporting agriculture and helping to sustain abundant bird and insect life in the gardens. We even have rare bird species that come live in the urban gardens. They have become an environmental oasis.

What makes Abalimi Bezekhaya's urban farming model successful? Do you think this can be a useful model for other cities?
RS: There are a number of key points that make the Abalimi Bezekhaya model unique. The first point is to provide quality, reliable support to small farmers during the survival, subsistence, and livelihood stages of farming. If you do not support these three stages permanently, you cannot get the commercial element working, and you will drive the peasant family farmers out of business to live in ghettos around cities—which is the current model. All three stages have to be supported permanently, and that support should not have to cost more than 100 rand (about $14.35) per farmer per month, including all the manure, seeds, seedlings, ongoing training, support on the ground, marketing infrastructure, administration, and management.

The second point is to find a guaranteed local market for these small urban farmers. Match the money with the produce, at a fair price. At first, we scratched our heads at the prospect of finding people open to eating vegetables grown locally and organically, while

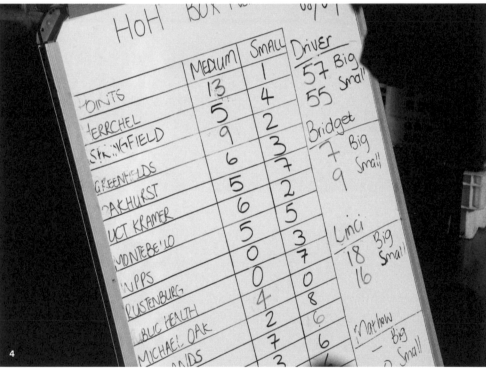

reducing the carbon footprint and creating jobs. We approached local schools, principals, and parents, and the program made sense to them. We have twenty different drop-off points at the moment, and consumers sign up and pay in advance each month. They do not have a choice of what they get, but they know there will be good variety—and the satisfaction of helping to build a good, strong local market.

2. Farmers review the Harvest of Hope vegetable-growing plan, Sinethenba school plot, Phillipi Township, Cape Town, South Africa.
3. People's Garden Centers' logo.
4. A chart keeps track of Harvest of Hope's weekly deliveries, Phillipi Township.

5

6

5. Abalimi micro-farmers prepare Harvest of Hope's "seed-to-table" vegetable boxes, Cape Town.

6. A farmer cultivates common table vegetables on public land next to a settlement, Cape Town.

7. Mabel Bokolo dispenses seedlings to a settlement gardener, Nyanga People's Garden Center, Cape Town.

And the third point is that all profits go back to the farmer through the provision of services. There are no private shareholders. The farmers do not feel exploited, and they receive a fair price for their produce. This model can be replicated in every single city in South Africa and throughout Africa, wherever there are people who want to buy vegetables. It is as simple as convincing people to eat local and seasonal produce, to buy from their local farmers and to have local farmers to buy from.

Why do you maintain garden centers for the urban farmers in the settlements? How many are there? Where are they located?

RS: Under apartheid, black people were not allowed to congregate, except in church and in other very limited social contexts, to discourage political gatherings. We had to be very careful, so we set up two garden centers, first in Nyanga in 1984–85 and then in Khayelitsha, the largest township in Cape Town, in 1989. People could come to us and get seeds and seedlings along with advice and support to plant gardens back home. One of the secrets to supporting urban farmers is to make sure the farmers have access to abundant manure, seeds, seedlings, and water, cheaply or for free. Abalimi runs nurseries and garden centers supporting home gardens in the townships. Even with very little support, these survival-level home gardens can thrive.

You have initiated numerous ground-breaking urban agriculture and environmental renewal projects, including the first grassroots community allotment garden in Macassar, Khayelitsha, in the Cape Flats area of Cape Town. How have these projects improved the lives of the

7

residents and the urban environment?

CK: Khayelitsha is a new township, with around two million residents. We train people to go into communities whose residents know nothing about gardens and instruct them on how to grow their own food. And people spread that knowledge. When people visit friends who live in our township and see their vegetable gardens, they ask how they did it, they come to us for more information, and they bring it back to their communities.

I think the residents of Khayelitsha understand that they can do something for themselves, which makes them want to try different things. And at Abalimi, we want to help them accomplish whatever goal they set. But to me, the vegetable garden was the first project to open people's eyes because it meant food on the table, money that went to the school, even money for lighting their houses. This was especially encouraging to women, many of whom lack education and employment. But now they've got

something to do and feel happy about. I've also been involved in efforts to create parks in Khayelitsha. We now have quite a few parks and a large swimming pool in the township. I love being here, and I love being part of the community.

Why do you think Abalimi Bezekhaya has been successful in cultivating a new food-growing and greening culture in the Cape Flats townships?

CK: I think we have essentially changed attitudes in the township. Through these projects, people, especially women, start to think, I'm not so poor and helpless. I've got things I can do with my hands to get food and money and make my place look nice. And they start home and community gardens around all the townships in Cape Town. We find that more women are becoming involved every day. They come to us with a lot of problems. When they meet each other, they see that others have the same problems they do, and together they try to solve their problems. They share ideas and knowledge.

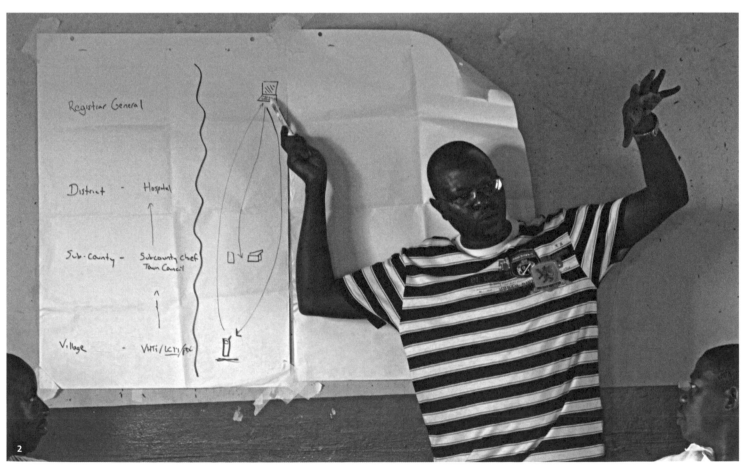

Digital Drum

Interview with
Sharad Sapra, Uganda Representative
and former Director of Division of Communication, UNICEF

By Cynthia E. Smith

As UNICEF's Director of Communication, you created in 2007 an Innovation Team within the agency to use new technologies to benefit its mission to help children around the world. What inspired you to explore this new approach to human development?
Sharad Sapra: Albert Einstein said, "We can't solve problems by using the same kind of thinking we used when we created them." This basic idea has inspired me to approach development challenges from different perspectives.

Who makes up the Innovation Team? How did you engage what is traditionally seen as a large bureaucratic organization? How has involvement spread throughout UNICEF? Can you explain why collaborating with "experts from around the world and from diverse fields such as academia, private sector and civil society"[1] can provide real and lasting solutions?
SS: The Innovation Team is made up of people who are not too firmly entrenched in traditional development work; they are usually young, and they want to challenge

the status quo. While from the outside, UNICEF appears to be a big bureaucratic organization, it provides enough space for those who want to work on "what is" and take it to "what can be." I am a physician by background, and UNICEF, over the past twenty-five years, has allowed me to work in different areas and roles, and experiment and test new ideas and new ways of being. For example, one project, which promoted the use of basic mobile phones and SMS messages (and the RapidSMS platform) to report on and improve program implementation, started as a simple idea but has now spread to more than eighteen countries.

Solutions to the many development challenges we face today no longer rest in the same field of work. For instance, making vaccines available at the right place and the right time is not necessarily a health issue, but a logistical one. Most problems relate to scaling up and reaching the "last mile"—the poorest of the poor, people in the remotest parts of the world, and those who face severe inequities in their ability to access national services.

1. Youths use the first Digital Drum prototype, Maker Faire Africa, Nairobi, Kenya, August 2010.
2. UNICEF Uganda Child-Protection Specialist Augustine Wasago explains mobile phone–based birth registration to community workers.

These inequities might be cultural, economic, geographic, or ethnic. In today's interconnected and interdependent world, no one sector is an island unto itself. An intersection that allows academia, civil society, the private sector, and the affected people themselves to come together and exchange ideas, experiences, and tools offers the best possibility of finding relevant and lasting solutions.

The initiative has resulted in a number of groundbreaking health innovations, such as RapidSMS and ChildCount. What is RapidSMS and how will it improve healthcare for those in most need?
SS: RapidSMS is a framework—essentially a set of building blocks—which allows software programmers to quickly create SMS-based applications for mobile phones. Instead of developing a new tool from scratch every time there is a new

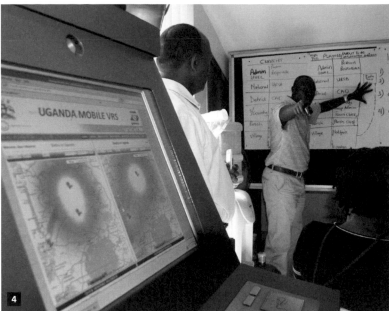

project, RapidSMS allows its users to save time and money by reusing parts from systems that already exist. RapidSMS is also open-source, which for UNICEF means we are supporting a solution that can be fully owned and maintained by the governments and people for whom we work.

RapidSMS was initially developed by UNICEF and deployed to track the distribution of ready-to-use therapeutic food to fight malnutrition in Ethiopia. We are very excited to see it being used by a wide range of organizations and companies worldwide, such as ChildCount and Millennium Villages. A project of the Earth Institute at Columbia University, Millennium Villages is a community case-management application utilized in Kenya, Ghana, and Uganda that allows community health workers to record births, track vaccinations, and monitor diseases. What has made many RapidSMS projects successful is that, in an effort to bridge the last mile, they have been designed with the end users, who rely on basic, locally enabled phones. These successes are being built upon by others, including a disease- and drug-monitoring system deployed by FIND Diagnostics in

Uganda and a UNICEF Rwanda initiative to strengthen prenatal care.

What other projects is the Innovation Team currently working on? How has your move to Uganda to head up UNICEF's efforts helped to generate solutions?
SS: Uganda has offered me a field where the best new ideas and systems can be quickly implemented and developed on a national scale. We will be rolling out a number of projects that were first tested on a smaller scale here and in other countries: the first phase of a mobile phone–based birth and family registration system; a drug-stock reporting system for health centers; a community-based malnutrition monitoring system; and a system to get real-time reports on malaria, diarrhea, and pneumonia, the three main causes of mortality of children under five years of age in the country. We are also setting up a national children's help line and an SMS-based information and reminder system for pregnant women and young mothers. Over 600 young people are already enrolled in uReport, an SMS-based crowd-sourcing system with which village youths can report on the presence of schoolteachers in the classroom, the functioning of the

3. Engineer Andrew Kasola shows community workers how to register births via their mobile phones.
4. Augustine Wasago explains mobile phone–based birth registration to UNICEF staff. Digital Doorway in foreground.

community water point, etc. Through this system we are able to not only inform communities of their entitlements but also engage them to monitor and advocate for them. The data provide feedback to the responders and are also aggregated and used to alert government leaders and functionaries regarding the quality of social services in their area. We are entering into agreements with newspapers and TV and radio stations to start a regular public discourse on the outcomes of these data, thus bringing the voice and the observations of the common people into regional and national policy dialogue. We hope to cover the whole country with uReport in phases over the next eighteen months.

As I mentioned before, one of the roles of the Innovation Team is to bring people, rather than problems, together. This includes those facing the challenges in their own countries, and especially

5. A community healthcare worker in Rwanda receives training in using RapidSMS to report danger signs during pregnancy.
6. Boys at the C&D Youth Center in Moroto, in northeastern Uganda, get their first look at the Digital Doorway kiosk.

maverick freelancers and local innovators full of ingenuity and entrepreneurial spirit. That's why another part of my work here is looking for the best Ugandan and regional examples of innovation and supporting them to reach a bigger audience. East Africa is especially full of novel ideas for mobile phones, alternative energy, and sanitation. We believe that through the exchange of information, experiences, and tools, lasting solutions can be developed quickly, for relatively low cost, and the communities themselves will benefit from new production opportunities.

In the Global South, large numbers of people are migrating from villages to large cities and settling in informal settlements or slums to search for work and a better life. They often lack access to clean water and proper sanitation and health services. The most vulnerable residents in these densely populated **informal cities are women and children. In what ways are the tools you develop impacting and protecting this fast-growing group?**

SS: An informed community is an involved community. The biggest challenge for economic migrants is that they leave behind the social safety networks that

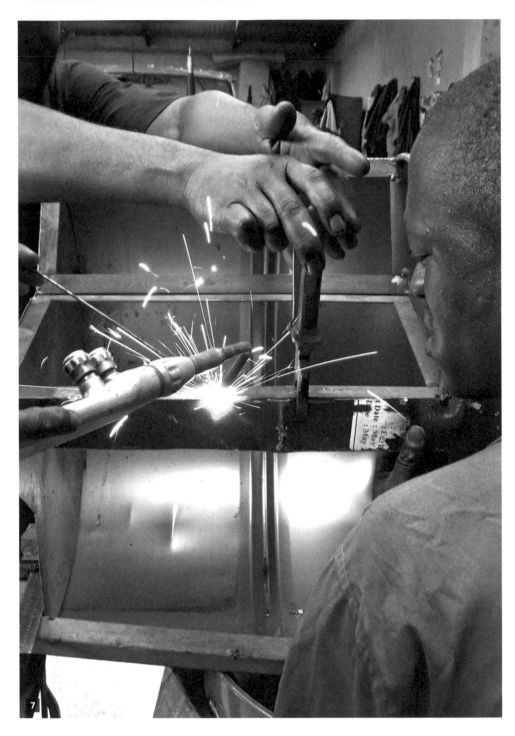

You initially posed a set of questions to provoke innovation at UNICEF, asking how growing mobile-phone use could improve development work, how to connect youth to each other, and how to use social media better educate and inform youth.[2] As technology evolves, are there additional questions that you could ask UNICEF and other UN agencies?

SS: Today, in Uganda and all over Africa, almost half of all children do not complete a primary education due to high absentee rates among teachers and the lack of basic learning and teaching tools in schools. Those who do complete primary school will acquire less than a third of the competencies they are expected to have. Inequities—economic, geographic, ethnic, and cultural—also significantly hinder the quality of learning and future employability of most of these children. The challenge is to make the learning independent of these negative variables, as they are not going to change quickly enough. Therefore, the next question for UNICEF is, How do we provide access to quality education regardless of the existing inequities? Doing more of the same will not solve the problem. We have to reexamine some basic assumptions about learning.

We're doing things in Uganda like building rugged solar-powered computer kiosks to serve as information access points for communities, youth centers, and schools. We're producing a whole series of "top teacher" videos to make classroom lessons by the best teachers in Uganda available to children whose schools lack teachers or who are out of the school system altogether. I believe that the challenges are big but not impossible. We just have to work at them from a different perspective.

they enjoyed in their native areas. The mHealth and uReport systems allow them to have a virtual support community where their day-to-day concerns will be collated, amplified, and brought to the policy table. These systems will also help them become more aware of their rights and give them places to go when they need support. The aggregated data will also allow development planners to identify challenges and allocate appropriate resources to address them.

For me, it's about a government being accountable to its citizens. In so many cities, the worst violations of rights happen right under the leaders' noses. With these tools, I think we can encourage more citizen action and more accountability and responsibility from leaders. They will have the data to act on and the motivation to address the needs of newly vocal and visible groups of people.

7. Auto mechanics build a Digital Drum, Kampala, Uganda.

8. A student in Uganda, which has one of the highest teacher-absenteeism rates in the world.

9. Kids and community members line up to experience the Digital Drum at the Treasure Life Youth Centre in Kamwokya, Kampala, Uganda.

10. UNICEF Uganda software programmer Moses Mugisha explains to UNICEF staff how his software uses maps to display data submitted by village teams using RapidSMS and mobile phones.

Notes

1. "UNICEF wins award for helping malnourished children," in the *Hindustan Times* (January 10, 2009), http://www.hindustantimes.com/UNICEF-wins-award-for-helping-malnourished-children/Article1-365084.aspx (accessed 1/20/2011).

2. UNICEF Innovation, "History," http://unicefinnovation.org/about.php (accessed 1/20/2010).

PROFILES

EXCHANGE
REVEAL
ADAPT
INCLUDE
PROSPER
ACCESS

A

Shack/Slum Dwellers International

Founders: Sheela Patel, Celine d'Cruz, Jockin Arputham, Joel Bolnick, Patrick Magebhula, Rose Molokoane. India and South Africa, 1992.

Affiliates: Angola, Argentina, Bolivia, Brazil, Cambodia, Colombia, DRC, East Timor, Egypt, Ghana, Haiti, Honduras, India, Indonesia, Kenya, Liberia, Malawi, Mozambique, Namibia, Nepal, Nigeria, Pakistan, Philippines, Sierra Leone, South Africa, Sri Lanka, Swaziland, Tanzania, Thailand, Uganda, Venezuela, Vietnam, Zambia, Zimbabwe

A transnational organization with global affiliates in thirty-four different countries in Asia, Africa, and Latin America, Shack/Slum Dwellers International was founded in 1992 out of a series of exchanges and peer-learning experiences among Indian and South African slum and shack dwellers. SDI affiliates are comprised of urban poor, the majority of them women, and range in size from a few hundred members in Zambia to more than 1.5 million in India. They all share a common realization: government alone cannot solve poverty and underdevelopment. SDI is pioneering an alternative route by creating a set of tools to build more inclusive cities through redevelopment and upgrades and by engaging global agencies directly about equitable urbanization.

Horizontal exchange is SDI's primary learning strategy. Groups from different countries visit each other to compare experiences and achievements, such as utilizing savings networks and SDI tools like community enumeration,

mapping, settlement planning, housing design, and infrastructure upgrades. These exchanges have enabled the rapid dissemination of locally developed solutions. Promoting women's participation and building local capacity and leadership are critical components of SDI's strategy to help the poor build cohesion and confidence and create pivotal change in their own settlements.

An example of SDI's reach is in the designing and building of community toilet blocks with improved lighting and ventilation; over 400 toilet blocks have been constructed in India. They are a part of training and envisioning exercises for all housing projects. The process of planning, constructing, and maintaining the blocks strengthens trust among residents, builds local skills, increases livelihood options, promotes women's involvement, and expands the residents' hopes to improve their surroundings and help the entire city. **CS**

A. Informal settlement dwellers, SDI affiliate Mahila Milan, and architects discuss existing and new community layouts, Yerwada Slum Upgrade project, Pune, India.
B. Enumeration in Villa Vista informal settlement, Oruro, Bolivia.
C. House model in Kenya. Colorful pieces of cloth represent walls.
D. Chikhalwadi toilet block, India, 2000.
E. Zimbabwe-Thailand peer-to-peer exchange.

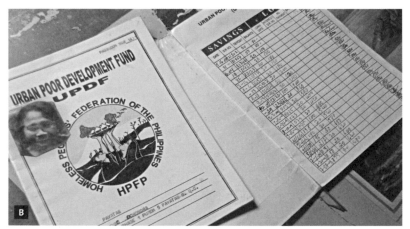

Miraculous Hills Community Resettlement

Payatas settlement community and SDI alliance: Homeless People's Federation, Payatas Scavenger's Homeowner Association, Philippine Action for Community-Led Shelter Initiatives, with Municipality of Rodriguez. Sitio Bangkal, Barangay San Isidro, Rodriguez, Rizal Province, Philippines, 1997–present

Over one million of the 2.68 million people who reside in the northeast district of Quezon City, in the Philippines, live in slums, many in high-risk areas on riverbanks, under bridges, and in alleys on private or public land. Payatas, one of the poorest and largest informal settlements, lies at the foot of a 39.6-meter-high (130-foot-high) mountain of trash—a home and source of livelihood to about 4,000 scavenger families that pick through the garbage to supply recyclable material to waste-recovery and recycling businesses. In 2000, a landslide of garbage killed and displaced scores of residents in the slum.

SDI's Philippine federation has chapters in eighteen cities that use savings to mobilize victims of disasters, ecological crises, and evictions. A founding member of the Homeless Peoples Federation of the Philippines, the Payatas Scavengers Association formed to save money collectively, with the goal of purchasing land for those living under threat of eviction from private land owners around the dumpsite. In 1998, 280 families from the savings group purchased 30,000 square meters (325,000 sq. ft.) of land in Rodriquez, Rizal province, and began designing and constructing the Miraculous Hills resettlement site, comprising sixty-two housing structures for survivors of the landslide. Fifty families live on the site, which is still in development, with drainage, roads, off-grid electricity, well water for drinking, bathing, and washing, a daycare center, and bio-intensive gardening and hog-raising ventures for income. Further design and planning are underway for a comprehensive eco-settlement to improve living conditions through efficient resource use and reduced pollution. Initial ideas include solar-generated electricity, alternative building materials for additional housing, improved drainage, rainwater harvesting, a biogas digester, community kitchen, playground, and bio-diesel production for fuel. **CS**

A. Community row houses, Miraculous Hills, Rodriguez, Rizal province, Philippines. B. Savings books, Payatas Scavengers Association, a founding member of Homeless Peoples' Federation of the Philippines. C. Payatas informal settlement with dumpsite in the background, Quezon City, Philippines.

Sheffield Road Upgrade: Community Mapping

Sheffield Road settlement community and SDI alliance: Community Organization Resource Centre, Informal Settlement Network, Federation of the Urban and Rural Poor, Ikhayalami. Philippi, Cape Town, South Africa, 2009–present.

Sheffield Road is an informal settlement situated on a road reserve set aside for future extension, near the busy N2 freeway in the Philippi township of Cape Town. Residents suffer from problems such as overcrowding, severe winter floods, and lack of tenure and services. The Sheffield Road Upgrade, a joint project between the city of Cape Town and a South African SDI alliance of the Community Organization Resource Centre (CORC), the grassroots organization Informal Settlement Network, and the Federation of the Urban and Rural Poor (FEDUP), a women's savings group that came about after the successful upgrade of the Joe Slovo informal settlement after a fire that left 1,500 residents homeless.

Using SDI's community-mapping tool, Sheffield Road residents drew a physical representation of the settlement, including houses, shops, pathways, water points, and electric poles. Visualizing the physical situation enabled them to plan and prioritize improvements. Maps provide detailed, accurate, firsthand knowledge, effective for planning, mobilizing, and negotiating with local authorities. The survey and map identified 167 shacks, five shops, 542 people, seven functional toilets (78 people per toilet), and no showers (people bathe at home or in public). Another SDI tool, community enumeration, calls for slum residents to count themselves, creating a detailed socioeconomic profile that mobilizes the community and is key to sustaining upgrading projects.

The most urgent need residents identified was sanitation. The city consulted with the community on where to place new taps, drains, and toilets. The alliance, with community residents, re-blocked a portion of the settlement, demolishing and rebuilding shacks in different positions. The first cluster of twelve 15-20-square-meter (161.5-215-sq.-ft.) houses was completed in 2010. Brick thresholds protect the structures from flooding and new safe courtyards provide open space for play and washing. **CS**

A. The community identifies areas of need on their self-produced map.
B. A safe upgraded courtyard.
C. Informal dwellings along Sheffield Road.

Yerwada Slum Upgrade

Yerwada slum settlement community, SPARC
Samudaya Nirman Sahayak, and Pune Municipal
Corporation; with Prasanna Desai Architects and
SDI affiliates: SPARC, National Slum Dwellers
Federation, Mahila Milan. Mother Theresa Nagar,
Sheela Salve Nagar, Wadar Wasti, Bhat Nagar,
Netaji Nagar, and Yashwant Nagar, Yerwada, Pune,
India, 2008–present

Approximately 17% of the world's slum population lives
in India. Rather than evicting the urban poor to demolish
the slums, India's national, state, and city authorities have
partnered with an alliance comprised of SDI affiliates
Mahila Milan, the National Slum Dwellers Federation,
and the Society for Promotion of Area Resource Centres
(SPARC) to plan, design, and rebuild houses in situ.
The Yerwada Slum Upgrade project includes six dense
Yerwada-area slums in Pune, India. In 2009, the alliance
began going house to house with architectural models
to gather ideas for what the community wanted. Maps
visualized the information gathered from enumeration and
socioeconomic surveys, helping the residents and planners
identify fixed and more flexible spaces. Community
workshops with Pune's Prasanna Desai Architects used
three-dimensional models of the existing settlement
to give residents perspective on their communities'
space and relationships, street hierarchy, and density,
an important step in redefining their relationship with
design professionals. Full-size house models, a popular
SDI tool, were constructed from colorful cloth walls and
bamboo framing, allowing slum dwellers to visualize size
and layout, while also inviting the government and public
to review these new secure housing strategies. Residents

helped determine the final layouts, maintaining existing
street patterns and housing footprints.

Part of India's Jawaharlal Nehru National Urban
Renewal Mission, the Yerwada slums are undergoing
redevelopment. A 25-square-meter (270-sq.-ft.), single-
family structure includes an in-house toilet and kitchen.
Microloans help residents secure the 10% required
contribution (30,000 rupees, or about US$675). For those
who cannot pay the 10,000-rupee (US $225) down
payment, Mahila Milan offers construction jobs. As of July
2011, 460 houses were under construction. Once they are
built, each family receives a ninety-nine-year lease and the
community becomes a legal "colony." **CS**

A. Planning with Yerwada
slum dwellers to ensure
each household is allo-
cated 25 sq. m. Each tile
represents a 12.5-sq.-m.
footprint.
B. Full-size house model
with cloth walls and
bamboo frame.
C. Housing construction,
Mother Theresa Nagar
informal settlement,
Yerwada area, Pune, India.

Zabaleen Waste Recycling

CID Consulting, Association for the Protection of the Environment, and Spirit of Youth. Manchiyet Nasser, Ezbet el Nakhl, Tora, Motamedeyya, and Helwan informal settlements, Cairo, Egypt, 1983–present.

In Cairo, one of the larger cities in the world, its population of fifteen million continues to grow, straining basic services such as the collection and disposal of waste. Traditional waste collectors (*Zabaleen* in Arabic) go door to door collecting three tons of household waste a day. They transport the garbage to Mokattam, at the center of one of five recycling neighborhoods ringing Cairo; sort solid waste into piles of plastic, textiles, and glass; and recycle roughly 80–85% of the collected waste. As the city grows and privatizes garbage disposal, the Zabaleen face possible forced resettlement to the city periphery and limited access to their livelihood.

To educate a more competitive generation of waste recyclers, CID Consulting developed innovative partnerships with the Zabaleen and with community-based organizations to meet the demand for recycled materials. The Association for the Protection of the Environment (APE) runs "Learn and Earn" recycling in Mokattam, teaching women and girls—traditionally required to stay out of the public and sort at home—skills for recovery and recycling, such as turning office paper into handmade craft paper and cards and rags into hand-loomed rugs, bags, and quilts, to generate income and support community health clinics and literacy and training programs. The Spirit of Youth group runs a buy-back center and school for boys, established to recover empty Proctor & Gamble shampoo bottles that are fraudulently refilled and resold; enrolled Zabaleen students are paid for each recovered container and are schooled in reading, writing, math, art, drama, and computing skills. The SDI network engaged in a series of exchanges to learn more about this Zabaleen community-based recycling system that generates income for the urban poor—a valuable model for cities throughout the Global South. **CS**

A. Preparing empty plastic bottles for the recycling machine, Cairo, Egypt.
B. Plastic is melted down.
C. Zabaleen waste collector.

Bang Bua Canal Community Upgrading

Bang Bua Canal Network community, Community Organizations Development Institute, and Asian Coalition for Housing Rights, with Prayong Posriprasert, Nattawut Usavagovitwong, and Sakkarin Sapu, Sripatum University. Bang Bua, Bangkok, Thailand, 2004–present

Thailand's Baan Mankong ("Secure Housing" in Thai) Community Upgrading program began in 2003 to improve housing, land-tenure security, and infrastructure for all 5,500 poor urban settlements throughout Thailand. A groundbreaking, large-scale approach that places slum communities at the center of the process, it has improved conditions in 1,546 settlements in 277 cities; in Bangkok, 422 of 1,200 slums are in some stage of improvement. The successful program subsidizes infrastructure and environment upgrades as well as low-interest loans for settlement re-blocking and new housing. Squatter communities and community networks develop their upgrading plans in close collaboration with the independent public organization, Community Organizations Development Institute (CODI), and local governments, professionals, universities, and NGOs.

Three thousand four hundred families live in twelve informal communities along a thirteen-kilometer (8-mile) stretch of the Bang Bua Canal. Many live in stilt houses built directly above the polluted canal, which floods during heavy rains, and use rickety, half-meter-wide (1.6 foot-wide) bamboo and wood plank walkways that only allow one person to pass. The Bang Bua Canal community upgrading project, part of Baan Mankong, was the first canal-wide community-improvement project in Bangkok. After living with insecurity and risk of fire and eviction for close to a century, the canal-side residents, many of them vendors, laborers, and daily-wage workers, joined together in 2004 to plan its redevelopment. Self-selected groups

of five households met to plan, budget, and carry out improvements. They negotiated a thirty-year renewable lease on the publicly owned land. Working with architects from nearby Sripatum University, who designed three basic house types—detached (single), semi-detached (double), and row houses—they built ninety-square-meter (970 sq. ft.) houses, often from recycled doors, timbers, and window frames. Re-blocking for similar-sized houses created a more democratic neighborhood layout, and family adjacencies kept social units connected. The stilt houses that limited access to the canal were demolished and rebuilt on the interior of the community to make way for the public access walkway along the canal, now three meters (9 ft.) wide, for playing, walking, biking, vending and emergency vehicles. The community plans to revive traditional floating markets along the canal.

The upgrade resulted in not just physical, but also many social changes in the community. Planning surveys identified elderly and disabled people who had no one to look after them, so a *baan klang* ("welfare house") was built and financed by residents—a model for other communities. Residents also established a welfare fund to pay the school fees for the poorest children and classes, libraries, and play groups for all children; and even established a children's saving group where each member saves fifteen cents a day. **CS**

A. A Bang Bua resident examines models representing three housing types available for upgrade.
B. Stilt houses built above Bang Bua Canal before upgrade.
C. Public access walkway along canal, upgraded Bang Bua neighborhood, Bangkok, Thailand.
D. (Top) Map of Bang Bua Canal communities after upgrading. (Bottom) Map of Bang Bua Canal before upgrade.

C (after)

D

EXCHANGE

A

Design With Africa: Bicycle Modules

Designers: Roelf Mulder, Byron Qually, Richard Perez, and Ryan Fowler, Dot Dot Dot Ex Why Zed Design. Organizer: Design Institute, South African Bureau of Standards. Rustenburg, South Africa, 2005–present. Bicycle components, found objects and materials, sheet metal

Reflecting the African *Ubuntu* concept of interconnectedness, Cape Town–based industrial design firm ...XYZ launched the Design With Africa initiative in 2009 to encourage dialogue between designers throughout the continent. A shared database of case studies and an open forum for debate on design as a strategic tool for development, it offers a platform for Africa's problems to be solved in a uniquely African manner.

Based on the principle of incremental design, ...XYZ developed Bicycle Modules that can be assembled in a variety of ways. Users are provided with bicycle parts that are difficult to manufacture—wheels, spokes, and frame—and complete the bicycle or cart on their own, engaging their ingenuity and skills to suit their needs. The parts can be assembled easily without special equipment and repaired using scrap metal, wood, fence wire, or other readily available materials. They lack gears and other complicated components, which eases maintenance. The

modular metal pieces can be held together with roofing bolts or wire, easily accommodating reused materials. The Bicycle Modules can be converted into a tricycle or cart to transport patients to clinics or goods to market.

Early concepts resulted from a 2005 Interdesign workshop, at which sixty designers from around the world came together with experts and community members in South Africa to explore non-motorized modes of transport. The South African Bureau of Standards Design Institute then commissioned ...XYZ to develop their modular bike concept. Early prototypes were field-tested in 2008 and received positive feedback from local communities. Initially developed for rural transport, the flexible design is transferable to resource-poor urban and peri-urban locations throughout Africa and beyond. **CS**

A. Concept exploration, Ledig Township, near Rustenburg, South Africa.
B. Concept sketches.
C. Metal bicycle module components. Numerous hole sizes and locations provide flexibility in attachment points.
D. Cart adaptation sketches.

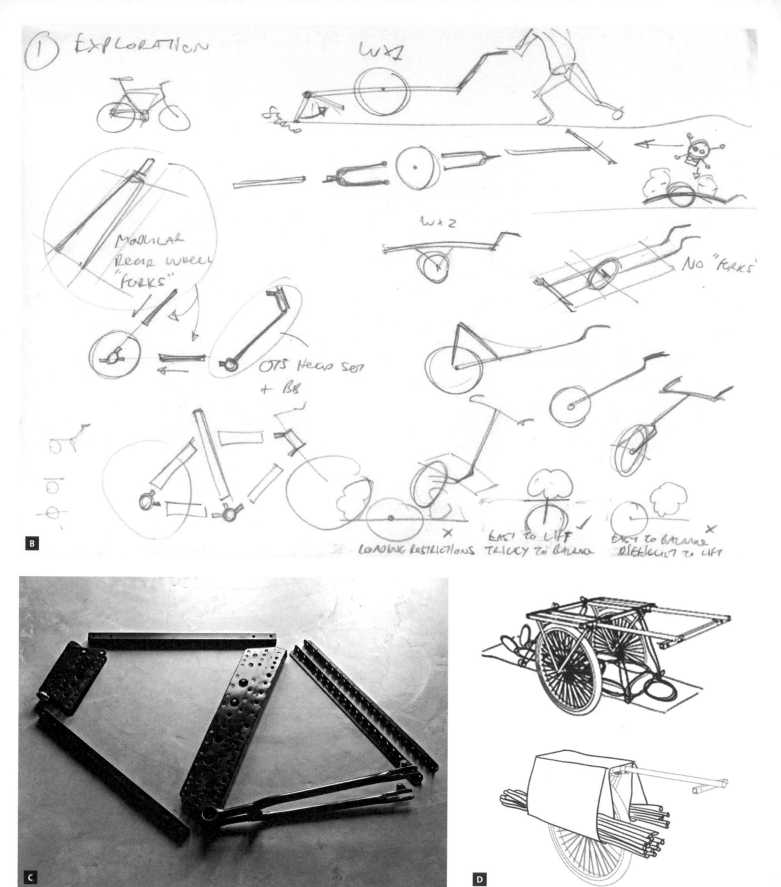

① EXPLORATION

W×1

STAND

MODULAR REAR WHEEL "FORKS"

OTS HEAD SET + BB

W×2

NO "FORKS"

LOADING RESTRICTIONS   EASY TO LIFT   EASY TO BALANCE
                        TRICKY TO BALANCE   DIFFICULT TO LIFT

B

C

D

Incremental Housing

Architects: Alejandro Aravena, Tomás Cortese, Emilio de la Cerda, Andrés Iacobelli, and Alfonso Montero, Elemental. Engineers: José Gajardo, Juan Carlos de la Llera; urbanization specialist: Proingel and Abraham Guerra. Construction: Loga S.A. Client: Chile Barrio. Iquique, Chile, 2003–4. Concrete, brick concrete, wood panels. **Monterrey** Architects: Alejandro Aravena, Fernando García-Huidobro, and Gonzalo Arteaga, Elemental. Collaborator: Ramiro Ramirez. Construction: Constructora AXIS. Client: Instituto de la Vivienda de Nuevo León (IVNL). Santa Catarina, Gob. Nuevo León, Mexico, 2007–8. Concrete, concrete blocks, stucco, plaster, paint

Government-built social housing is generally constructed on low-cost land, often far from opportunities for work, education, transportation, and healthcare. Moreover, the value of subsidized social housing tends to depreciate over time. In Chile, where it is projected that $10 billion will be spent over the next twenty years on housing, the government has hired the Chilean architecture firm Elemental to design a new social housing unit that can increase in value over time.

The architects designed half-built houses, called Incremental Housing, for one hundred families in the poor neighborhood of Quinta Monroy, in Iquique, which they have illegally occupied for thirty years. With only a $7,500 subsidy to pay for the land, infrastructure, and each housing unit, the architects designed the half of the house (30 sq. m. or 323 sq. ft.) the families would never be able to afford—the structure, bathroom, kitchen, and roof. To allow for expansion, only the ground and top floors are constructed; residents are responsible for the rest (72 sq. m. or 775 sq. ft.).

The government of Nuevo León, Mexico, commissioned Elemental to design a group of seventy housing units for a middle-class neighborhood in Santa Catarina. Adapted for the expanded scenario and local climate, Elemental Monterrey features half-built units with a kitchen, bathrooms, stairs, dividing walls, and roof spanning the units. A subsidy of $20,000—more than double the cost of the Chilean project due to higher construction costs and stricter local building standards and codes—builds the more difficult half of the dwelling, and an additional investment of $2,000 by each family, doubling the unit's size, increases its market value to $50,000. **CS**

A. Incremental Housing with residents' self-constructed expansions, Quinta Monroy, Iquique, Chile.

B. Elemental Monterrey half-built housing units, Monterrey, Mexico.

C. Original living conditions for the Quinta Monroy informal community.

D. Community workshop, Chile.

E. Paper models created by residents in community workshop.

micro Home Solutions

Marco Ferrario and Rakhi Mehra, with John Backman, Ellen Chen, Henri Fanthome, Aden Van Noppen, and Vyasdev Yenghom; engineers: Studio Jurina, Studio Albertini; graphic design: Alberto Mazza. Collaborators: BSFL, BASIX, DR AV Baliga Trust. Mangolpuri and Sultanpuri slum resettlement colonies, Delhi, India, 2010–present. Baked clay bricks, concrete-reinforced cement, cementation finishes, steel net, steel bars. **Modular Homeless Shelter** Architects: Marco Ferrario, with Henri Fanthome and Vyasdev Yenghom. Yamuna Pushta, New Delhi, India, 2009–present. Bamboo, baked clay bricks, carpet, canvas

Urban-housing strategies in India have addressed home-ownership models, but have often not accounted for the diverse needs of low-income groups. In response, a firm called micro Home Solutions is developing a housing portfolio based on access to design services, affordable microfinance products, and community engagement. One project is Design Home Solutions, piloted in the government's slum-resettlement colony of Mangolpuri, northwest of Delhi, where residents are moved far from the city and allotted 23-square-meter (250-sq.-ft.) plots on which to build.

Design Home Solutions was initiated to improve self-construction practices and accommodate rental models. In Mangolpuri alone, 60% of residents are renters, and housing demand, coupled with increasing density, is leading to vertical expansion. Plot "owners" self-construct up to three floors to earn supplemental income, but the buildings are often unsafe and inefficient, with poor ventilation and light. Design Home Solutions offers financial products that provide households with access to small, affordable home-improvement loans. Architects work with clients to develop effective, culturally acceptable solutions, and help monitor self-construction to ensure safe building practices. Upgraded houses are safer and healthier, and help meet demand in the rental market while providing additional income for households.

Another project in the mHS portfolio, the Modular Homeless Shelter, built in Yamuna Pushta in New Delhi, serves one of the most concentrated populations of homeless migrants in Delhi. The shelter consists of a bamboo structure, brick floor, and waterproof canvas walls and roof, designed to be easily assembled and disassembled using local labor. A gap between the shelter's double-layer walls can be filled to provide additional insulation during winter months. Additional modules can be added to the base design, including a kitchen, medical facilities, and toilets. **AL**

A. Design Home Solutions: upgraded house, Mangolpuri slum resettlement colony, New Delhi, India.
B. House before upgrading.

A (after)

B (before)

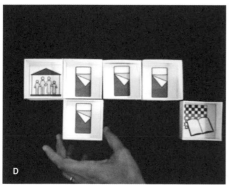

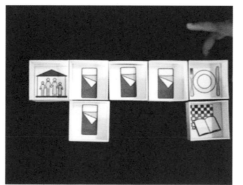

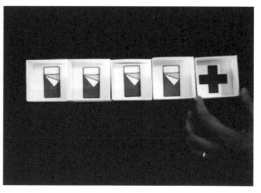

C. Construction of Modular Homeless Shelter.

D. Modular Homeless Shelter modules allow for flexible arrangement of sleeping area, communal space, dining, and medical facilities.

E. Homeless migrants, New Delhi, India.

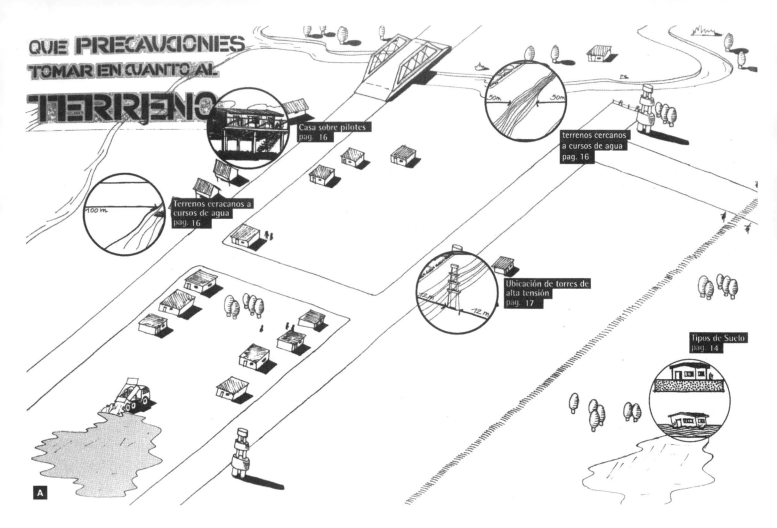

QUE PRECAUCIONES TOMAR EN CUANTO AL TERRENO

Casa sobre pilotes
pag. 16

terrenos cercanos
a cursos de agua
pag. 16

Terrenos ceracanos a
cursos de agua
pag. 16

Ubicación de torres de
alta tensión
pag. 17

Tipos de Suelo
pag. 14

A

Urbanism Manual for Precarious Settlements (Manual de Urbanismo para Asentamientos Precarios)

Viviana Asrilant and Gabriela Sorda, with Leandro Cairuga, Nicolás Cambón, Sabrina Cifre, Giovanni Da Prat, Germán García, Juliana Giménez, Melina Espósito, Eliana Maffulo, Verónica Navas, Guadalupe Tello, and Constanza Tommei, Secretariat of Community Action, Faculty of Architecture, Design and Urbanism, University of Buenos Aires. Collaborators: Buenos Aires settlement communities, Asociación Civil por la Igualdad y la Justicia, Centro de Derecho a la Vivienda y contra los desalojos, Asociación Civil Madre tierra. Villa 31 Bis, Barrio Los Eucaliptos, Barrio San Roque, Barrio Los Pinos, Barrio Indaburu, Buenos Aires, Argentina, 2006–9

While working with local slum dwellers, a group of architects from the University of Buenos Aires found there was a dearth of material on how best to develop a self-built community, as well as of sources outlining local codes, agencies, and basic rights for inhabitants. The university's Secretariat of Community Action, formed to strengthen ties with the community through projects, training, advisement, and field work, designed a fully illustrated and annotated Urbanism Manual for Precarious Settlements.

Distributed for free, the manual is a compilation of urban, legal, and other invaluable tools to create a healthy, adequate urban environment, such as location relative to geography, infrastructure, and waterways; planning for walkways, roads, housing plots, open space, transportation, and gardens; how to work with government agencies; and

listing local and national resources. Sketches made in the field interpret conditions and solutions for new informal settlers and others who may not understand architectural drawings, and real-life testimonies pass on valuable knowledge in organizing improvements to settlements. The workbook is designed to accommodate photocopying to encourage wide distribution. And although it was produced specifically for Buenos Aires, it is also meant to be adapted for other cities. The group works to determine where settlements are emerging and provides the manual to squatters in those locales. Of the one thousand copies printed thus far, 600 have been distributed to mayors, universities, technicians, and organizations working in slums; it is also available free online, filling the gap between a settlement`s rapid construction time and the typically slow government response. **CS**

DEL BARRIO AL BARRIO

A. *Urbanism Manual* illustrations indicate what precautions to take planning a new settlement. B. Using the *Urbanism Manual* as a guide, residents construct a bridge in Los Eucaliptus, José León Suarez, Buenos Aires, 2007. B1) Before construction; B2) laying the foundation; B3) completed bridge; B4) manual illustration of bridge connection.

A

10x10 Sandbag House

Architects: Luyanda Mpahlwa, Uli Mpahlwa, Kirsty Ronne, Westley van Wyk, and Chinedum Emeruem, DesignSpace Africa; structural engineer: Aurecon; surveyor: BTKM. Construction: Tech Homes. Clients: Interactive Africa, Design Indaba. Freedom Park, Cape Town, South Africa, 2008–9. Sandbags, timber EcoBeams, cement plaster, timber cladding, metal sheet roof, steel windows, timber door

In Freedom Park, an informal settlement in the Mitchell's Plain township in Cape Town, corrugated-metal and scrap-material dwellings are being replaced by low-cost, two-story homes built with timber frames and sandbag in-fill construction. The 10x10 Sandbag Houses are architect Luyanda Mpahlwa's response to the 10x10 Housing project initiated by Design Indaba, South Africa's renowned design-advocacy organization, which called for innovative housing solutions costing 50,000 rand (US$7,000)—the national government's housing subsidy—to build. Concurrently, the Freedom Park upgrading project mobilized community members, local organizations, and the provincial government to participate in creating dignified housing.

The design of the 10x10 Sandbag House borrows from indigenous mud-and-wattle building methods. A structural timber frame using EcoBeam technology (timber beams with metal inlays that provide tensile strength) is combined with sandbags reinforced with chicken wire and finished with plaster and timber cladding. The sandbags provide thermal insulation and, thanks to the EcoBeam technology, contributes to a system that is both

wind-resistant (it is heavier than brick construction) and moisture-resistant. Moreover, the building method is cost-effective and energy-efficient, and requires little to no electricity and only minimal transport, since the EcoBeams are manufactured onsite. Little skilled labor is needed for construction, and local community members were involved in building the houses, demonstrating the possibility for replication in other communities. Given the small plot sizes allotted by the government for Freedom Park, the ability to build up rather than out ensures a solution that can accommodate density. Ten houses were completed in Freedom Park in 2009, and the building method can be scaled to help meet the urgent need for housing. **AL**

A. Completed 10x10 Sand-bag Houses, Freedom Park, Cape Town, South Africa.
B. 10x10 Sandbag House under construction.
C. Freedom Park residents fill sandbags.
D. Informal dwellings, Freedom Park.

A

Make a House Intelligent

Architects: Arturo Ortiz Struck, with Pamela Basañes, Salomón Rojas, and Daniela Kleinman, Taller Territorial de México. Collaborators: Carolyn Aguilar, Architecture department, and Elisa Gutierrez, Social Service department, Universidad Iberoamericana AC. Collaborator: Saúl Torres Bautista. Clients: Chimalhuacan area settlers. Chimalhuacan, Mexico City, Mexico, 2008–present (prototype). Gabion, sandbag, hollow concrete block, wire fence, corrugated steel sheet, steel beam

Over half of the Mexico City metropolitan area's twenty million inhabitants live in informal settlements, or *colonias populares*. One settlement, Chimalhuacán, exploded from 20,000 residents in 1970 to over 600,000 in 2010. In 2008, Arturo Ortiz Struck and the urban architecture research firm Taller Territorial de México organized workshops with seventeen families new to Chimalhuacan, with the goal of sharing basic design principles for the residents' self-built houses, planning the layout and construction to "make a house intelligent."

Since the new residents are required to occupy a lot within thirty days, the architects designed a new type of housing that could be built quickly and inexpensively in stages depending on available resources. It also allows for natural ventilation and illumination, is easily adaptable, and uses locally available materials which can be reused.

They devised a flexible system whose principal structure consists of sand, concrete blocks, gabions (metal mesh retaining structures), and steel beams. The gabions are laid out in the desired location and filled with rock or sandbags, and a small concrete slab is anchored with rebar at the top. Secured steel beams provide structure for the inclined sheet-metal roof. Concrete blocks and a layer of sand over compacted soil provide the interior flooring. With all the material at hand, the construction process takes a team of five people between five and seven days to complete the full layout. **CS**

A. Architectural model of gabion house, Arturo Ortiz Struck's studio.
B. The step-by-step building process illustrates ease of construction.
C. Architect Arturo Ortiz Struck discusses the self-built house with a Chimalhuacán community member.
D. Prototype house being built by community members, Pirules section of Chimalhuacán, Mexico.

PROCESO DE ARMADO   BUILDING PROCESS

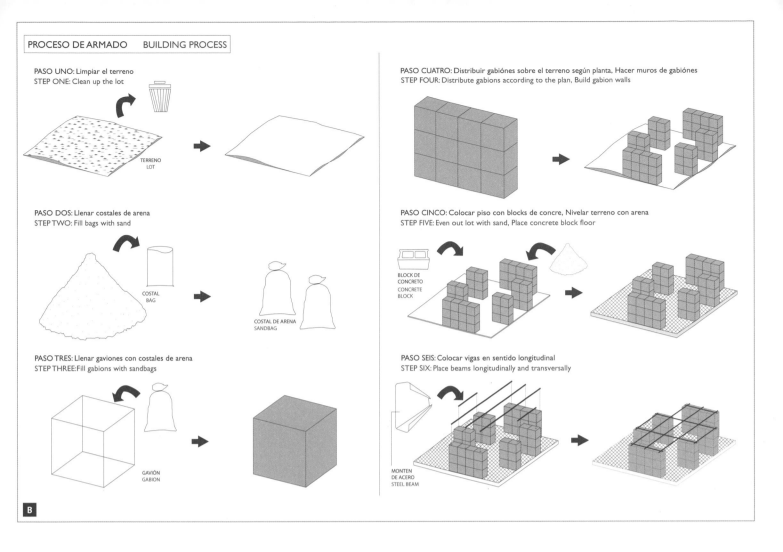

PASO UNO: Limpiar el terreno
STEP ONE: Clean up the lot

TERRENO
LOT

PASO DOS: Llenar costales de arena
STEP TWO: Fill bags with sand

COSTAL
BAG

COSTAL DE ARENA
SANDBAG

PASO TRES: Llenar gaviones con costales de arena
STEP THREE: Fill gabions with sandbags

GAVIÓN
GABION

PASO CUATRO: Distribuir gabiónes sobre el terreno según planta, Hacer muros de gabiónes
STEP FOUR: Distribute gabions according to the plan, Build gabion walls

PASO CINCO: Colocar piso con blocks de concre, Nivelar terreno con arena
STEP FIVE: Even out lot with sand, Place concrete block floor

BLOCK DE
CONCRETO
CONCRETE
BLOCK

PASO SEIS: Colocar vigas en sentido longitudinal
STEP SIX: Place beams longitudinally and transversally

MONTEN
DE ACERO
STEEL BEAM

B

C

D

A

Plastic Formwork System

Designer and manufacturer: moladi. Diepsloot, Tsakane, Blikkiesdorp, Pacaltsdorp, Shayamoya, Hammanskraal, Kwanokuthula, Mitchells Plein, Pomeroy, Despatch and Dukathole informal settlements, South Africa, 1986–present. Formwork: plastic polymer blend, reinforcing steel bars; mortar: granite or river sand, ordinary Portland cement, moladiCHEM

Every year, nearly seventy million people, or 200,000 a day, move from rural areas to urban cities. In South Africa alone, more than 2.2 million homes are currently needed, and an additional 180,000 homes will be needed every year to keep pace with rapid urbanization. The Plastic Formwork System is a method of building cast-in-place reinforced concrete structures, in which the walls of a house can be built in as little as a day by unskilled laborers with locally sourced materials and little waste. The system is comprised of square plastic components that join together to form wall panels from which the house is assembled. The house's infrastructure—steel-reinforcement bars, conduits, window and door frames, pipes and other fittings—is positioned on the wall; once in place, these elements are sandwiched between a second layer of panels, forming a cavity into which a lightweight concrete mortar is poured. After the mortar dries overnight, the Plastic Formwork panels are removed and reassembled for use at the next housing site, minimizing waste and transportation needs.

The plastic formwork kits can each be reused to cast fifty homes, after which the plastic is recycled into household consumer products such as toilet seats. The result is a house that can both withstand natural disasters and provide thermal insulation and moisture resistance. Moreover, it leads to local job creation without compromising quality or integrity. The Plastic Formwork System has been used in housing projects throughout South Africa, and the company has established branches in thirteen countries, including Namibia, Mozambique, and Mexico. **AL**

B

C

A. Plastic Formwork walls form the overall house structure, South Africa.
B. A Plastic Formwork house nears completion.
C. Concrete mortar is poured into a cavity between Formwork layers.

A

Pocket Reconstruction

Designers: Renu Khosla, Nandita Gupta, and Sukant Shukla, Centre for Urban and Regional Excellence, with Deepak Bhatia, Bashobi Dasgupta, Tarun Garg, Sakshi Jain, Tanay Jaithalia, Ishan Puri, and Varun Singh, University School of Planning and Architecture. Door fabricator: Niranjan Aggarwal. Savda Ghevra resettlement colony, New Delhi, India, 2008–present. Models: board, paper, plywood; door: mild steel

Savda Ghevra is a large resettlement colony forty kilometers (twenty-five miles) from the center of New Delhi, India. To create space for New Delhi's new infrastructure, 8,000 slum families were uprooted from their homes, social networks, and livelihoods and relocated to pocket-sized plots of 12.5–18 square meters (135–94 sq. ft.). Starting in 2007 with the first generation of settlers, the Center for Urban and Regional Excellence (CURE), with students from New Delhi's University School of Planning and Architecture and the Aga Khan Trust for Culture, engaged the community in the development of their settlement. The families, armed with knowledge and expertise to take appropriate action, participate in planning meetings and contribute to improved housing plans and basic service designs. With access to microcredit, they help construct their new homes and community spaces, using innovative solutions to get more for less.

CURE's improved housing designs enable independent access for additional rental income. Demonstrating safer self-building methods, modified rat-trap bond brick walls—bricks overlap and break the joint below—bear loads for two floors, as vertical construction is a necessity due to the small plot size. A simple, low-cost redesign of a typical entry door incorporates an open grated top half, yet still provides ventilation, light, and privacy when locked for safety. Since much activity, including household chores, takes place on the street, new streetscape designs increase social engagement; simple colored pavers delineate children's play and learning spaces; a new water-supply network provides clean well water to homes; and proper wastewater removal improves public health. CURE is also developing with the residents, especially women and young people, sustainable livelihoods within the local economy, including waste-collection enterprises and sewing cooperatives. **CS**

A. Architectural models engage residents in the design and construction of three housing options; in background, a redesigned entry door with open wire screens for improved security and ventilation, Savda Ghevra.

B. Modified rat trap bond brick walls provide better thermal quality than normal brick walls and improved stability during earthquakes.

C. Resident builds a house using rat trap bond bricklaying technique, requiring 50% less cement mortar and 30% less brick, resulting in 25% cost savings.

D. Savda Ghevra slum resettlement colony, outside of New Delhi, India.

A

Bamboo (*Tacuara*) Loofah Panels

Designer: Elsa María Zaldívar Rolón, Base ECTA. Villa Clara community, Coronel Oviedo, Paraguay, 2008–present (prototype). Bamboo, crushed loofah, cassava starch waste, sand, water, castor oil, baba de tuna

Scrap metals, wood, and other found materials are often used to make dwellings in informal settlements, resulting in homes that are unsafe and precarious, with little thermal insulation. In Paraguay, Elsa María Zaldívar Rolón develops local, affordable, and replicable building materials made from loofah, a locally grown vegetable known widely for its use as an exfoliating sponge. Zaldívar, who began her enterprise as a means to increase the earning capacity of local women, initially combined the loofah with recycled plastic to form building panels in a specially engineered machine. But when plastic doubled in price and required sealing treatments to reduce humidity stains that appeared over time, the cost became prohibitive.

Her latest loofah panels depend less on technology, as the current process is more closely aligned with traditional wattle-and-daub construction than machine-milling. The raw materials include crushed loofah, cassava starch waste, sand, water, and castor oil, which are mixed together and applied to a bamboo panel. *Baba de tuna*, a gelled material

created from soaking tuna in water for three days, is used to create a waterproof bond on the outside of homes. The building panels, fabricated locally by community members, provide better thermal insulation and acoustic quality than materials typically used in informal dwellings, and the raw materials are incredibly low-cost, ranging from US$0.50 to $1 per square meter (10.75 square feet). The solution is environmentally sustainable and the technology is easily replicable in other areas using local materials. **AL**

A. Residents mix the raw materials of crushed loofah, cassava starch waste, sand, water, and castor oil, Villa Clara community, Paraguay.
B. Preparing a bamboo panel.
C. The loofah mixture is applied to the panel.
D. A waterproof bond is applied to the panels.

EcoFaeBrick

Designers: Syammahfuz Chazali, Irawan Nurcahya, Wusana Bayu Pamungkas, Erma Melina Sarahwati, Fika Nurfitriyani, Indri Yuni Handayani, Marseliana, Teuku Winnetou, and Yusuf Aria Putera dan Fatmawati, Prasetiya Mulya Business School. Indonesia, 2008–present. Cow dung, soil extracts

Cheap, plentiful building materials are needed to meet the massive demand for sound dwellings in informal settlements. In Indonesia, clay bricks could offer an alternative to scrap metal and wood housing, but the quarry mining techniques used to make bricks are expensive and damage the land. EcoFaeBricks, developed by students from Prasetiya Mulya Business School, are made from cow dung with soil extracts and are cured using biogas, reducing the carbon dioxide emitted during the traditional process of using wood-fire heat. The result is a building material that is 20% lighter than clay bricks and has 20% greater compressive strength. Because they make use of a replenishable waste product, EcoFaeBricks are also less expensive than clay bricks. EcoFaeBricks are made in partnership with local communities, providing work opportunities and helping to preserve agricultural land devastated by clay quarrying. Groups in India, Kenya, and Mexico have expressed interest in the technology to meet their own rapid urban development needs. **AL**

A. Mixing the soil extracts with cow dung.
B. Molding the bricks.
C. Molded bricks are prepped for drying.

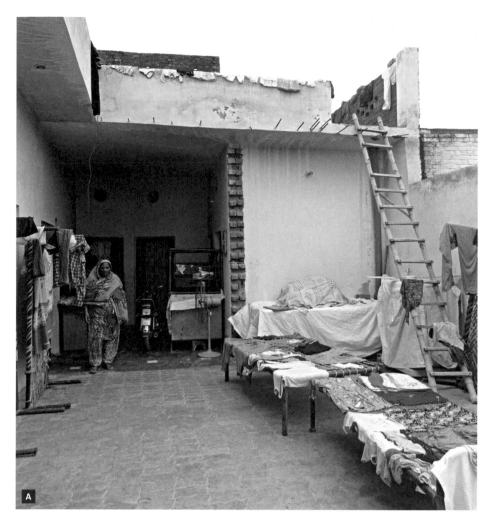

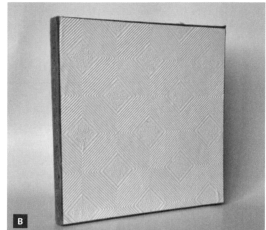

Ghonsla Insulation Panels

Designers: Zehra Ali, Monica Hau Le, Emmanuel Arnaund, Mubarik Imam, and Katelyn Donelly, Ghonsla; manufacturer: Packages. Collaborators: Bheri Village community, World Wide Fund for Nature–Pakistan, UN-Habitat. Lahore, Pakistan, 2008–present. Straw, paper sludge (byproduct of paper and board manufacturing), paper liner, paint, plaster, embossed PVC sheets or jute

Corrugated-metal roofs are ubiquitous—it is estimated that close to a billion people today live under them in urban informal settlements and disaster-affected areas. The poor thermal performance of the corrugated metal, however, makes dwellings unbearably hot in the summer and deafeningly loud during rainstorms. In winter, homes become incredibly difficult and expensive to heat, leading to overconsumption of fuel resources and increased indoor air pollution. Ghonsla's low-cost panels, developed in Lahore, Pakistan, in partnership with Pakistani packaging manufacturer Packages, are designed for installation under existing corrugated-metal roofs to improve insulation performance. *Ghonsla* ("nest" in Urdu) panels feature core insulation made from straw and sludge from the paper industry blended with water, which is pressed in a mold, dried in the sun, and finally smoothed in a heat press before the surface finish is applied. The resulting panels are durable, lightweight, and easy to install. Made from local renewable and waste materials, the panels reduce heating

costs by 30% and decrease indoor air pollution, resulting in healthier indoor environments. In summer, the panels can also lower indoor temperature by more than 10° Celsius (18° Fahrenheit), important in a region that sees temperatures up to 45° Celsius (113° Fahrenheit).

Ghonsla is creating jobs by building capacity for distribution and installation in local communities, and plans to establish decentralized production and support entrepreneurs, with the aim to reach scale in the Pakistani market. Interest in the insulation panels has come from other countries with corrugated-metal dwellings and similar climates, including India, Afghanistan, and Peru. **AL**

A. Due to extreme indoor heat during summer months, residents sleep outdoors, Lahore, Pakistan.
B. Insulation panel with embossed PVC plastic finish to increase room brightness.
C. Panels dry in the sun.

Interlocking Stabilized Soil Blocks

Designer: Moses Kizza Musaazi, Technology for Tomorrow. Manufacturer (block press): Makiga Engineering Services. Kampala City, Uganda, 1993–present. Soil, Portland cement

In Uganda's urban areas, where 53,000 homes are needed annually to maintain population growth, fired clay bricks are among the most common building materials. However, unmonitored clay extraction increases soil erosion and degradation. Trees are cut down to fire bricks, contributing to deforestation and air pollution and reducing fuel sources needed for other activities. Interlocking Stabilized Soil Blocks (ISSB), an affordable and environmentally sustainable alternative to fired bricks, are made from soil stabilized with 5% cement, compressed in manually operated machines, and dried in the sun. In the 1990s, Moses Kizza Musaazi of Technology for Tomorrow developed a double-interlocking system for the blocks, similar to a tongue-and-groove joint—when stacked, ridges on the top of one block fit into slots on the bottom of the next block, and side ridges fit into side slots of corresponding blocks. Musaazi introduced both straight and curved blocks, the latter used in the construction of water tanks, granaries, and biogas digesters. The blocks perform better than clay bricks by increasing the structural stability of built walls while reducing the amount of cement needed as mortar. ISSB are made onsite, reducing transportation, fuel, and construction costs. The building technology is easily transferable and culturally appropriate in urban areas where building with earth bricks is already common. **AL**

A. A wood model of the curved ISSB demonstrates how blocks interlock, Moses Kizza Musaazi's office, Kampala, Uganda.
B. Curved ISSB used in construction of above-ground water tank.
C. Stacks of straight and curved ISSB.

The waste collection and recycling system of the Municipality of São Paulo (red) will be extended through cooperative models that will be incorporated in the local community of Heliopolis in collaboration with the MAS Urban Design and Reserach Studio of the ETH Zürich.

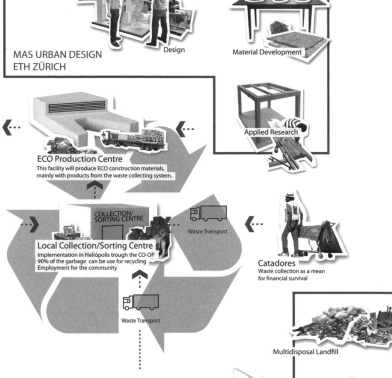

MAS URBAN DESIGN
ETH ZÜRICH

Design

Material Development

Applied Research

Building Materials/
Construction Systems

ECO Production Centre
This facility will produce ECO construction materials, mainly with products from the waste collecting system.

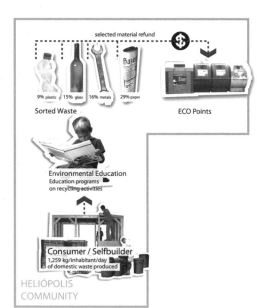

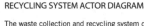

selected material refund

9% plastic   15% glass   16% metals   29% paper

Sorted Waste

ECO Points

Environmental Education
Education programs on recycling activities

Consumer / Selfbuilder
1,259 kg/inhabitant/day of domestic waste produced

HELIÓPOLIS
COMMUNITY

A

COLLECTION/
SORTING CENTRE

Waste Transport

Local Collection/Sorting Centre
Implementation in Heliópolis trough the CO-OP
90% of the garbage can be use for recycling
Employment for the community

Catadores
Waste collection as a mean
for financial survival

Waste Transport

Multidisposal Landfill

Collection Points
Unsorted waste disposal

Waste Sorting Facility
Only 3% of the material is good for recycling

Processing Facility
New products production

MUNICIPALITY OF SÃO PAULO
SEHAB SECRETARIAT FOR HOUSING

Urban Mining

Designers: Marc Angélil and Rainer Hehl, with Tomas Polach, Rafael Schmidt, and Julia Sulzer, Urban Design, Department of Architecture, ETH Zürich. Collaborators: Vanessa Padiá, Elisabete França, Maria Teresa Diniz, and Ligia Miranda de Oliveira, Secretariat for Housing, Municipality of São Paulo (SEHAB), Heliópolis settlement community. Heliópolis, São Paulo, Brazil, 2011–present

Informally settled by rural migrants in 1970s, Heliópolis is the largest favela in São Paulo, with 70,000 residents living on an area of land less than a third that of New York's Central Park. Urban design researchers from the science and technology university ETH Zürich, partnering with the city's Municipal Housing authority (SEHAB), propose to engage local residents to recycle discarded materials, which will be combined with either concrete or polymer to create new materials used to make prefabricated elements for favela upgrading. Part of an effort by the World Bank Institute, the Carbon Finance Capacity Building program promotes sustainable development and reduced CO_2 emissions in the Global South's megacities. São Paulo, one of four pilot cities, is focusing on decentralized waste management for two of its informal housing settlements, Heliópolis and Paraisopolis. The planned first phase for the Urban Mining program will restructure local waste collection and build a recycling and prototyping center for composite materials and building systems.

Concrete, a familiar construction material in the favela, when combined with industrial and urban waste products, such as polystyrene, expanded clay, recycled plastic, or natural fiber, is lighter in weight and improves insulation and tensile properties. Polymer mixed with recycled paper, plastic, or textiles produces a material that is lightweight, flexible, weather-resistant, structurally sound, and durable for easier maintenance, transport, and use. The composite materials allow for a modular building system which can be used to construct affordable self-built housing units, collaboratively designed with residents. In addition, collecting and using waste material for upgrades adds to the local economy and generates income for its inhabitants—a model sustainable upgrading system for other informal settlements. **CS**

A. Recycling system diagram illustrates key collaborators and outcomes, Heliópolis settlement, São Paulo, Brazil.
B. Rendering of self-built vertical housing units proposed for Heliópolis.
C. Rendering of prefabricated composite structural components.
D. Rendering of modular building system.

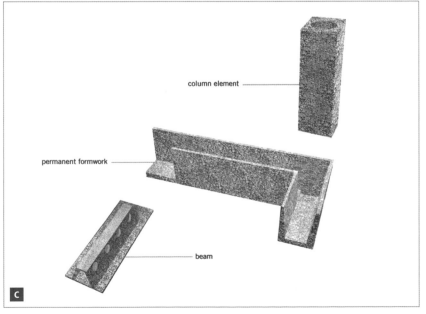

column element

permanent formwork

beam

28 Millimetres: Women Are Heroes

Artist: JR, with Kibera and Morro da Providência settlement communities. Kibera informal settlement, Nairobi, Kenya, and Morro da Providência, Rio de Janeiro, Brazil, 2007–9. Photographic reproductions on vinyl, ink, paper

A. Large-scale portrait pasted on stairway, Morro da Providência favela, Rio de Janeiro, Brazil.
B. Morro da Providência murals at night.
C. Aerial view of women's portraits, Kibera informal settlement, Nairobi, Kenya.

In most informal settlements around the world, women are often central community members, yet they remain the most invisible. Self-described "photograffeur" (part graffiti artist, part photographer) and "urban activist" JR draws attention to the persistent strength of women in these communities with his Women Are Heroes series, part of his broader 28 Millimetres project. Using a wide-angle 28mm lens, JR captures extreme close-ups of women's faces and covers informal settlements with large-scale reproductions of the images. The women actively participate by telling their stories and taking part in the artistic process. In Kibera, an informal settlement in Nairobi, images of ten women's faces and eyes cover 2,000 square meters (21,528 sq. ft.) of corrugated metal rooftops, and are visible from Google Earth satellites and the city's elevated train tracks. The images are printed on water-resistant vinyl that protects the homes underneath. Images of women's eyes also cover the train that passes through Kibera twice a day; the rest of the women's faces are pasted on the slope beneath the train, so in the moment the train passes, the women's portraits are complete.

In the Morro da Providência favela of Rio de Janeiro, ten women's portraits are pasted onto the sides of houses and public stairways along a steep slope, positioned to look toward the city center. A number of them are of relatives of three young men killed in the favela, caught in the turf wars between corrupt military police and drug traffickers. The photographs reveal not grief or despair, but their identity and humanity. Such intimate portraits pasted in these urban landscapes allow passersby to encounter these women as large, central figures in their communities. **AL**

Grassroots Mapping

Designer: Jeff Warren, Center for Future Civic Media, MIT Media Lab. Collaborators: Shuawa Arts Organization, Neokinok, Escuelab, Manzanita "A." Cantagallo, Lima, Peru, 2010–present. Trash bags, balloons, plastic bottle, braided nylon string, reel, tape, digital camera, rubber band, helium

Mapping is an important tool in exploring, documenting, and planning communities. Those in informal settlements cannot always depend on the government to map their territories, and so many are undertaking mapping efforts themselves. Grassroots Mapping is an open-source, participatory approach that enables communities to create their own maps using inexpensive equipment. Residents own the resulting images and maps, which they can use to support land-title claims or to aid in upgrading efforts.

Started by Jeff Warren as part of his master's research at MIT Media Lab's Center for Future Civic Media, Grassroots Mapping consists of a digital camera with continuous mode shooting lofted by a kite, balloon, or inflated trash bag to snap aerial images. Snapshots are geographically

referenced, stitched together, and overlaid on Google Maps, but with a resolution one hundred times higher than existing Google imagery. In Cantagallo, an informal settlement in Lima, Peru, Warren partnered with local residents and Shuawa, a Cantagallo art collective, to generate maps with the community. For the first time, residents saw their settlement from overhead, enabling them to better understand the relationship of their community to the surrounding city. Despite being forced to relocate by the municipality, residents are interested in mapping their new land, which will help in land-title claims offered by the municipality. **AL**

A. Residents prepare their Grassroots Mapping kit, Cantagallo informal settlement, Lima, Peru.
B. Local children use inflated trash bags to loft a camera.
C. Residents' aerial snapshots are stitched together and overlaid on a Google satellite map.
D. Aerial image of local participants.

Informal Settlement World Map

Designers: Christian Werthmann, with Elizabeth Randall and Fiona Luhrmann, Harvard Graduate School of Design. United States, 2011

Creative visual graphics can enhance the understanding of statistics. Based on population size instead of land mass, the Informal Settlement World Map displays global population growth in informal settlements in a way that makes the numbers more meaningful. Current slum populations are represented as orange squares distributed in a checkerboard pattern over black squares, which show overall population. Future population projections are depicted in shaded tones—light orange for slum growth, gray for overall population growth. The resulting image shows what many viewers have likened to a "firebrand raging across the southern hemisphere." The shadows of future growth immediately illustrate the explosion in Africa and Asia. The design team used quantitative data from various sources, including UN-Habitat, which counts informal settlements, or "slum households," as any that fulfill at least one of five criteria: inadequate housing, insufficient living space, insecure land tenure, and lack of access to improved water and improved sanitation. **AL**

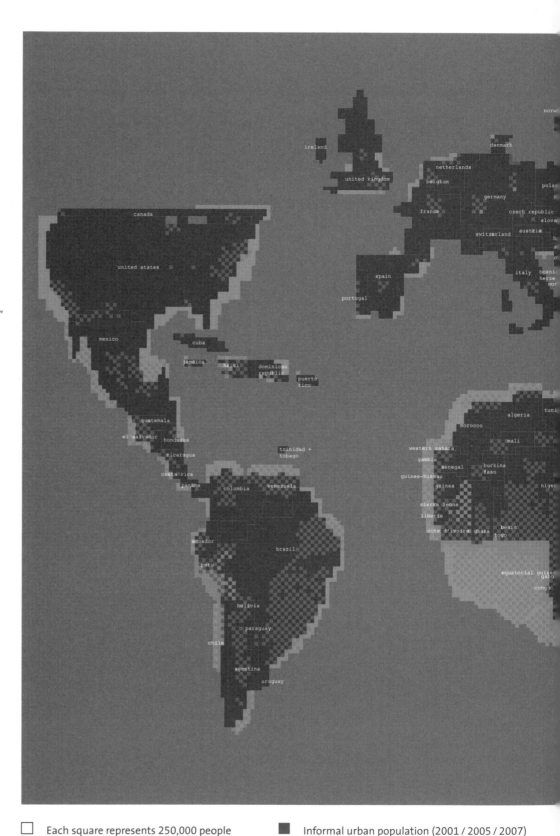

☐ Each square represents 250,000 people

■ Population 2010

■ Informal urban population (2001 / 2005 / 2007)

■ Population growth (20 years at 2001 growth rates)

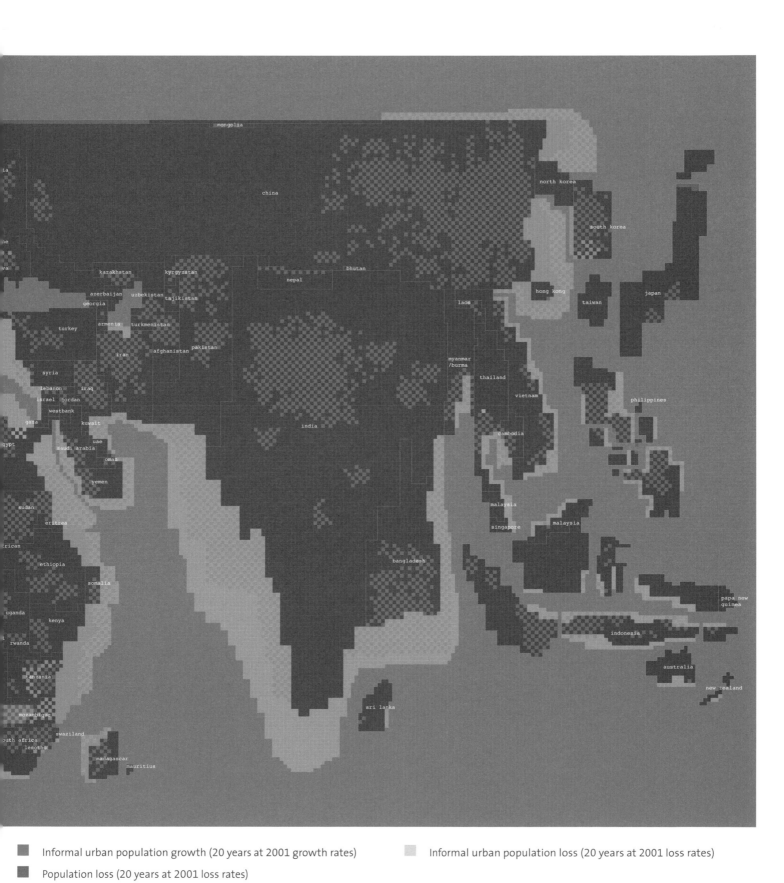

Informal urban population growth (20 years at 2001 growth rates)

Population loss (20 years at 2001 loss rates)

Informal urban population loss (20 years at 2001 loss rates)

mongolia

china

north korea

south korea

kazakhstan

kyrgyzstan

bhutan

nepal

hong kong

japan

azerbaijan

uzbekistan

tajikistan

taiwan

georgia

laos

turkey

armenia

turkmenistan

iran

afghanistan

pakistan

myanmar
/burma

thailand

philippines

syria

vietnam

lebanon

iraq

israel

jordan

westbank

cambodia

gaza

kuwait

india

uae

gypt

saudi arabia

oman

yemen

malaysia

sudan

singapore

malaysia

eritrea

rican

ethiopia

bangladesh

somalia

papa new
guinea

uganda

kenya

indonesia

rwanda

australia

tanzania

new zealand

mozambique

swaziland

uth africa

lesotho

sri lanka

madagascar

mauritius

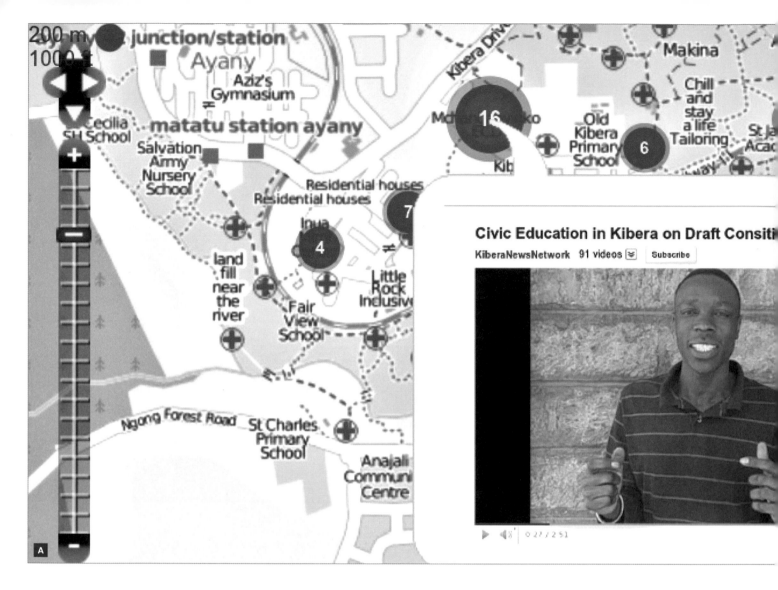

A

Map Kibera

Designers: Erica Hagen and Mikel Maron, GroundTruth Initiative, with Jane Bisanju, Simon Kokoyo, Primoz Kovacic, and Jamie Lundine. Collaborators: Kibera mappers, Kibera News Network, Voice of Kibera, Carolina for Kibera, Community Cleaning Services, Kibera Community Development Agenda, Ushahidi. Kibera informal settlement, Nairobi, Kenya, 2009–present

Kibera is home to an estimated 750,000 to 1.5 million people in an area two-thirds the size of New York City's Central Park, making it one of the largest informal settlements in eastern Africa. Satellite images show a dense, vibrant settlement with many small, informal businesses, even as it appears as a blank spot on official maps. Mapping what exists in the community is a critical first step in understanding what is required to improve living conditions.

Map Kibera is a crowd-sourced community-mapping project. Using tools from the volunteer global mapping project OpenStreetMap, the GroundTruth Initiative partnered with community organizations and local youth to create Health, Education, Water/Sanitation, and Safety/Security layers by pinpointing every water and sanitation

location, security problem, school, church, mosque, and health clinic. The information is uploaded directly onto an online map or gathered in workshops by marking and tracing over aerial imagery for the most current and reliable information. As part of the project, Voice of Kibera allows residents to share community information via news, videos, and SMS messages, which are added to the map using the Ushahidi platform.

Map Kibera was the GroundTruth Initiative's first pilot project. To sustain the impact, it is partnering with other organizations to develop a direct link between the community and government agencies. Building on the success of Map Kibera, the organization plans to expand their citizen mapping and media to other invisible settlements. **CS**

A. Voice of Kibera screenshot detail of the Map Kibera education layer identifying schools and education centers. Geolocated citizen reporting local events via Kibera News Network.
B. Voice of Kibera Web site showing Water/Sanitation filter, community-generated news, videos, and SMS reports.
C. Kibera residents mark security problems on a map overlay before uploading to the online digital version.

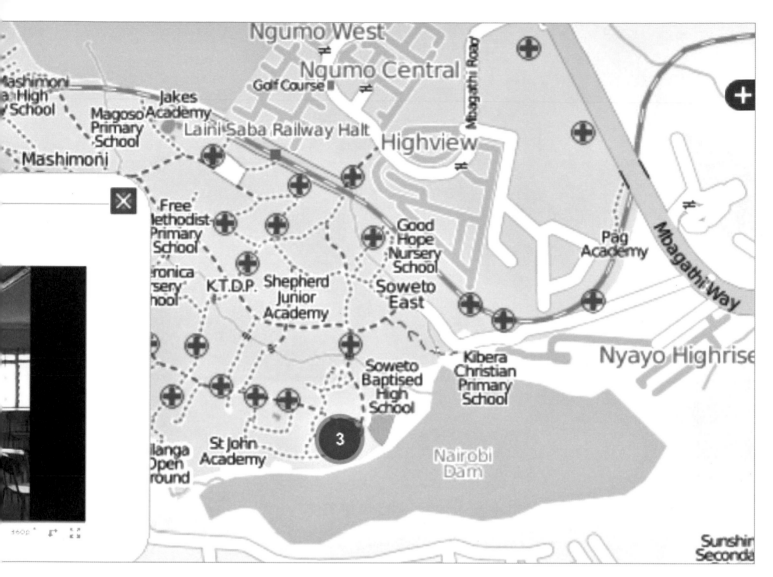

Praça Cantão, Favela Painting Project

Artists: Jeroen Koolhaas and Dre Urhahn, Haas&Hahn, with Santa Marta favela community youth.
Santa Marta, Rio de Janeiro, Brazil, 2009–10

Favelas ring Rio de Janeiro's hillsides, and many of their residents still experience clashes between police and the gangs that control the neighborhoods. In 2007, Jeroen Koolhaas and Dre Urhahn, of the Dutch partnership Haas&Hahn, conceived the Favela Painting Project to bring art and beauty to the built environment and also drive international media attention to the need for improvements. In 2010, they employed local youth to paint murals over 7,000 square meters (75,000 sq. ft.) of the public square, thirty-four surrounding houses, streets, and the interior of a popular samba studio in the Santa Marta settlement. The design for Praça Cantão uses a flexible concept of colorful rays, which can easily be expanded further throughout the favela. Trainers from TintasCoral paint company, as part of their "*Tudo de cor para Santa Marta*" community project, instructed twenty-five local youth on proper safety and painting methods.

The Favela Painting Project was covered by news agencies around the world, including CNN, Fox News, and Al Jazeera. In Brazil, the paintings attracted reporters from every major newspaper and television station. With broad applications, the project's work is spreading to other countries. The team is planning a project in Philadelphia. **CS**

A. Central square at the entrance to the Santa Marta favela, Rio de Janeiro, Brazil.
B. Demarcating a colorful ray.
C. Local community painter.
D. Detail.
E. Local community painter.
F. Interior of popular samba studio.

148

A

Sangli Inclusive Planning

Designers: Shelter Associates, with Baandhani Federation. Collaborators: Indira Nagar settlement community, Sangli-Miraj-Kupwad Municipal Corporation. Indira Nagar, Sangli, Maharashtra, India, 2009–present

Many local governments in India lack data about the poor in their cities, often a significant percentage of the population. If they do exist, much is outdated or scattered among different departments. A team of architects, social workers, GIS (geographic information system) specialists, and community workers from the Pune-based NGO Shelter Associates began, in 1999, to combine socioeconomic data and informal settlement maps to visualize results spatially.

In Sangli, India, a small city of a half million people 400 kilometers (250 miles) south of Mumbai, nearly 15% of the population is estimated to live in slums. Inadequate infrastructure and housing have not kept pace with urban growth. When Shelter Associates developed a citywide plan of the urban poor, for the first time, city officials could see exactly where the slums were. Spatial querying generated critical data, such as caste, house ownership, fuel type,

electricity connection, construction type, and building use, on maps to aid in city planning, design, and development that could engage the entire city.

Shelter Associates worked with Baandhani, an informal federation of poor women and men, to mobilize 3,800 families—almost 50% of the poor across 29 slums—to participate in Sangli's slum-development and housing initiatives. The organization used Google Earth to show slum dwellers their current and new locations in the city, and fought to help them avoid being uprooted from their occupations, markets, and schools. The site design incorporates passive and active open and public spaces, while housing plans remain flexible for the residents to customize their personal space. A model-house exhibition allowed slum residents to experience the new house proposals at full-scale. **CS**

A. Shelter Associates discusses housing designs with Sangli community, India.
B. Full-size layout allows residents to experience a proposed home at a meaningful scale.
C. GIS map spatially locating caste data.
D. GIS map spatially locating building-use data.
E. Google satellite map used to show residents re-location strategy for Sangli.

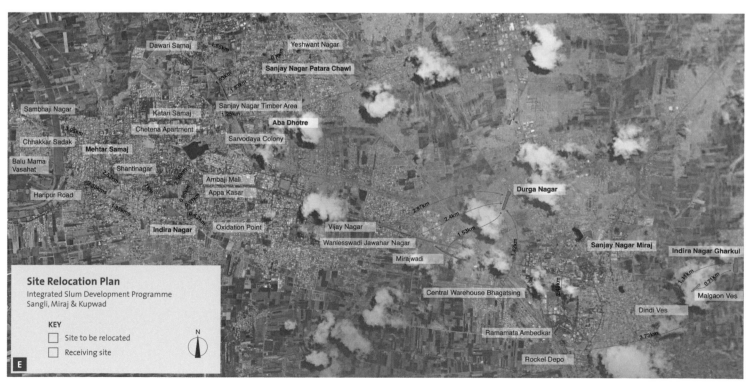

Dawari Samaj · 1.85km · 0.76km · Yeshwant Nagar

Sanjay Nagar Patara Chawl

· 1.93km · 1.83km · Sanjay Nagar Timber Area i.25km

Sambhaji Nagar · Katari Samaj · **Aba Dhotre**

· 1.65km · Chetena Apartment · Sarvodaya Colony

Chhakkar Sadak · **Mehtar Samaj** · Shantinagar · 2.3km · 2.36km

Balu Mama Vasahat · Ambaji Mali · Appa Kasar

Haripur Road · 2.28kms · 1km · 0.95km · **Durga Nagar**

· 1.85km2 · 6.62km · **Indira Nagar** · Oxidation Point · 2.97km · 2.4km

Vijay Nagar · 1.53km · **Sanjay Nagar Miraj** · **Indira Nagar Gharkul**

Wanlesswadi Jawahar Nagar · 1.42km · 1.14km · 0.71km

Mirajwadi · Malgaon Ves

Central Warehouse Bhagatsing · 2.05km

Site Relocation Plan

Integrated Slum Development Programme
Sangli, Miraj & Kupwad

Ramamata Ambedkar · 3.73km

Dindi Ves

KEY

☐ Site to be relocated

☐ Receiving site

N

Rockel Depo

E

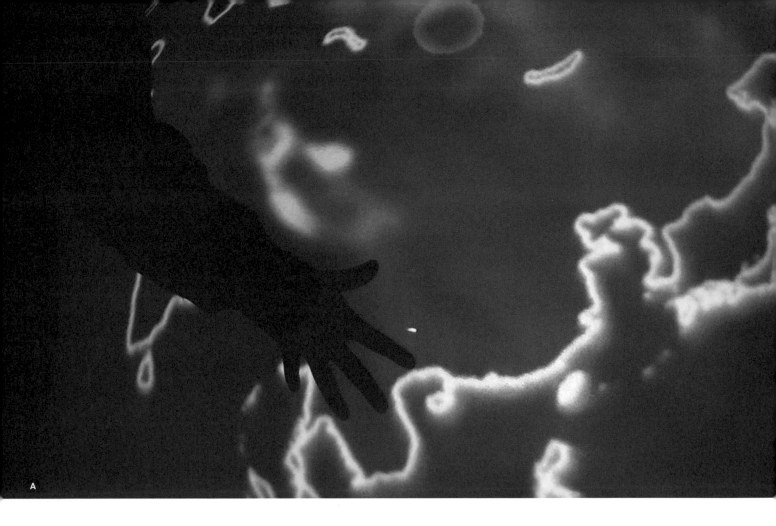

A

Tangible Earth

Designer: Shinichi Takemura, with Ryuichi Iwamasa, Takahiro Shinkai, Kensuke Arakawa, Jun Nishimura, Hideo Shiba, and Shoko Takemura. Japan, 2001–present

Tangible Earth is the first interactive digital globe that dynamically visualizes scientific data. By displaying Earth at a scale of ten million to one, Japanese anthropologist and professor Shinichi Takemura's design aims to give a real sense of our living planet and a better understanding of our environmental and cultural issues. The "public sensory platform" illustrates the unprecedented urbanization and vulnerability of world cities through a series of real-time and simulated climate-hazard visualizations, such as sea-level rise, flooding, hurricanes, and water scarcity. A recreation of Japan's 2011 devastating earthquake and tsunami exposes cities' vulnerability to seismological events. When Tangible Earth is connected to the Internet, one mode provides real-time natural-disaster warnings.

The model, 1.28 meters (50 in.) in diameter, combines digital technology and analog tactility. It can be spun in any direction, and users pushing on the surface activate sensors which translate the pressure into rotation speed and direction. A high-resolution projector with wide-angle lens mounted at the center projects vibrant 3D satellite images that detail every continent.

Inspired by Buckminster Fuller and Marshall McLuhan, Takemura created a museum of senses for the Internet age in 1995. One project, called Netsound, "listened" to Internet traffic; another, called Breathing Earth, visualized fluctuations and conveyed earthquake risks from compiled seismological data. Tangible Earth units have been installed at the 2008 G8 Hokkaido Toyako Summit and at the United Nations Climate Change Conferences in 2009 (COP15) and 2010 (COP10). **CS**

A. Dynamic visualization of scientific data.
B. User interacts with globe by pressing on surface.
C. Shinichi Takemura spins Tangible Earth.

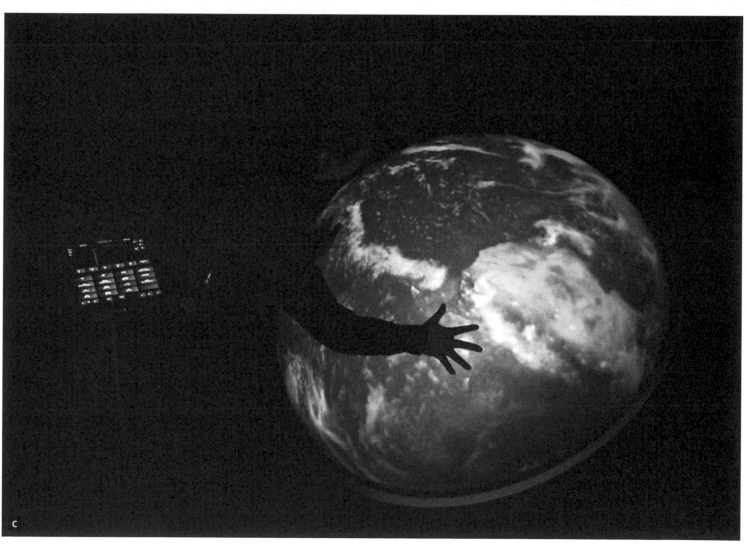

Floating Community Lifeboats

Mohammed Rezwan, Shidhulai Swanirvar Sangstha. Atrai, Barnoi, Gurnoi, Nandhakuja, Gumani, and Boral Rivers, Natore, Pabna, and Sirajganj districts, Bangladesh, 2002–present. Community lifeboats: sal and other woods, bamboo, angle iron, iron sheet, flat bar; SuyraHurricane solar lamps: 4 Ah 6 V sealed lead-acid batteries, 5 W high-efficiency compact fluorescent lamp, switch, recharging socket, charge controller, inverter circuit, lantern casing

One-third of Bangladesh floods annually, with increasing frequency in recent years. In the flat, low-lying Ganges-Brahmaputra Delta, the most densely populated area in the world, six million people could lose their homes if water levels rose just half a meter (19 inches). Architect Mohammed Rezwan witnessed this firsthand growing up in the country's northern Natore region. During monsoon season, many children could not attend classes and often dropped out. Rather than design buildings that would be underwater in his lifetime—Bangladesh is projected to lose 17% of its land by 2050—Rezwan used $500 from a scholarship to found Shidhulai Swanirvar Sangstha in 1998 and designed the first floating school in 2002. Shidhulai currently operates fifty-four floating schools, libraries, health clinics, and a training center for parents, serving close to 90,000 families.

Working with area boat builders, Rezwan modifies traditional flat-bottom riverboats using local materials and building methods. Sitting low in water, they incorporate a metal truss to allow for column-free open spaces, flexible wooden floors, higher ceilings, and waterproof roofs outfitted with solar photovoltaic panels. Eighty percent of Bangladeshis lack regular access to electricity. The boats charge computers, lights, mobile phones, medical equipment, and SuryaHurricane lanterns—low-cost, portable solar-powered lamps made from recycled kerosene lanterns. Rezwan has also designed cluster housing outfitted with cooking facilities and toilets and a three-tier farming structure built on floating platforms. The floating farm's first tier is a planting bed made of water hyacinth and a bamboo truss for growing vegetables, beneath which fish are raised within net enclosures, while poultry can be raised on the top tier. **CS**

A. One-tier community lifeboat with solar panels installed on roof, Bangladesh.

B. Design of column-free open space permits flexible use—health clinic.

C. Multi-tier floating farming structure.

D. SuryaHurricane lanterns powered by solar energy collected from boats' rooftop solar panels provide hours of quality light in homes at night.

E. Lifeboat school's are outfitted with libraries, printers, computers with high speed Internet, and mobile-phone connectivity.

A

Integral Urban Project

Architects: Marines Pocaterra, Isabel Pocaterra, Silvia Soonets, and Victor Gastier, Proyectos Arqui5 C.A., with San Rafael settlement community; hydraulic engineer: Ahmed Irazabal; road designer: Freddy Iriza; geologist: José Francisco Mártinez; structural engineer: José Luis Garcia Conca. Client: Caracas Mejoramiento de Barrios. San Rafael-Barrio Unido sector, La Vega settlement, Caracas, Venezuela, 1999–present

The city of Caracas is situated in a valley, and its informal settlements ring the steep mountain slopes surrounding the central city. La Vega is one of the largest, with a population of 95,000 living within 400 hectares (1.5 sq. miles). Working with the San Rafael-Barrio Unido community in La Vega, a team of architects, engineers, a road designer, and a geologist assessed the settlement's conditions. The architects, Proyectos Arqui5, concluded that the vertical typography (with steep slopes higher than 50% or 2:1 run-to-rise) was the determining condition, limiting accessibility, services, and public spaces.

Based on community-established priorities, the team devised the Integral Urban Project to help solve the main challenges. First, a new road system was designed, with one main road around the top hills and a secondary road connecting smaller streets, which allowed better access to public transportation and circulation. The existing pedestrian walkways were a series of resident-built stairs, narrow in width, with variable step size, no handrails, high slopes, and no stairs higher up the hill. To connect neighborhoods and improve residents' daily commute, the team designed a network of stairs which incorporated basic services such as electricity, drainage, sewer, gas, and water. Every spare space was integrated into walkways, and public landings inserted at intervals acted as new spaces for social interaction. Most important, families were able to remain in their homes, which was critical to maintaining social cohesion. **CS**

A. Before and after—stair upgrade with integrated basic services, San-Rafael-Barrio Unido, La Vega, Caracas, Venezuela.
B. Before and after—public landings inserted at intervals in the new network of improved stairs.
C. Section illustrating integrated infrastructure.
D. Steep and densely populated slopes of Caracas.

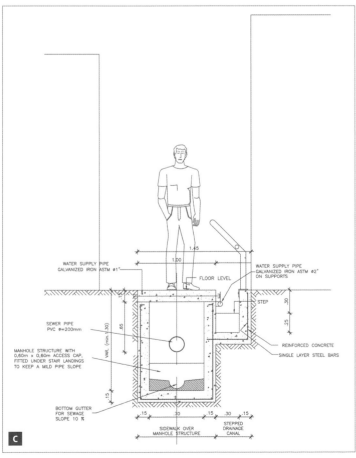

WATER SUPPLY PIPE
GALVANIZED IRON ASTM Ø1"

FLOOR LEVEL

WATER SUPPLY PIPE
GALVANIZED IRON ASTM Ø2"
ON SUPPORTS

STEP

SEWER PIPE
PVC Ø=200mm

REINFORCED CONCRETE

SINGLE LAYER STEEL BARS

MANHOLE STRUCTURE WITH
0,60m x 0,60m ACCESS CAP,
FITTED UNDER STAIR LANDINGS
TO KEEP A MILD PIPE SLOPE

BOTTOM GUTTER
FOR SEWAGE
SLOPE 10 %

SIDEWALK OVER
MANHOLE STRUCTURE

STEPPED
DRAINAGE
CANAL

Millennium School Bamboo Project

Architect: Eleena Jamil; structural engineers: DCCD Engineering Corporation; mechanical and electrical: ACC Engineering Services. Clients: Illac Diaz, My Shelter Foundation, Philippines Department of Education. Nato High School, Camarines-Sur, Philippines, 2008– 10. Bamboo, reinforced concrete, woven reed, metal decking

The Philippine islands are hit with twenty to thirty typhoons every year, causing damage at a cost of up to 20 billion pesos (US$465 million) annually. In order to promote the change of investment priorities from post-disaster assistance to safer, more sustainable infrastructure solutions that could save lives and property, Illac Diaz of My Shelter Foundation organized in 2008 the Millennium Schools Design Competition. Diaz called for the design of a school structure—often the place of refuge for poor residents during a typhoon—which could withstand 150-kph (93-mph) winds. Typical schools in this part of the world are hot, dark, and built with concrete, wood, and metal. The disaster-resistant design needed to be low-cost, use local and sustainable materials, minimize construction waste, incorporate natural light and ventilation, and be replicable in similar regions around the world.

The winning design, by Eleena Jamil of Malaysia, was built in 2010 on the Bicol Peninsula, an area heavily hit by typhoons. Inspired by vernacular houses found in the Philippines and Southeast Asia, the large, sloping roof and shaded veranda on one side provide shade for informal teaching or play. The simple design and arrangement of side-by-side classrooms allows for cross-ventilation, shade,

and natural light. The bamboo and traditional woven-reed ceiling allows airflow and is easy to build and maintain. Lastly, a raised concrete platform keeps floors dry in the rainy season. The Millennium School is the first school in the Philippines to be constructed from bamboo—an inexpensive, strong, flexible, abundant, and sustainable material that can be harvested in three years (versus ten years for timber)—making Bamboo Project ideal for high-wind locations. **CS**

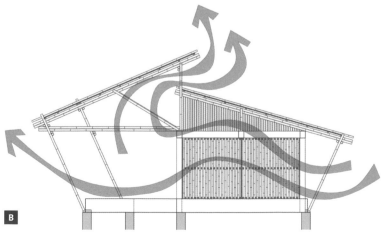

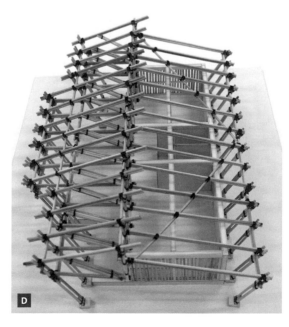

A. Exterior of completed Millennium School Bamboo Project, Philippines.
B. Section illustrating clerestory windows that reduce wind pressure inside building.
C. Local students.
D. Model showing repetitive structural elements to ease construction and reconstruction.
E. Pinned and lashed connections allow movement of joints during strong winds.

A (after)

B

Proyecto Rehabitar

Architects: Eduardo Bekinschtein, Lucía E. Calcagno, Domingo Pablo Risso Patron. Collaborators: Secretary of Housing and Urban Development of Argentina, Argentina Central Society of Architects, Ernesto Pastrana and Verónica Di Francesco, Department of Social Sciences, University of Buenos Aires. Argentina, 2008–present

In response to a housing shortage in the 1970s and 1980s, the Argentine government built scores of housing developments across the country, but due to a lack of resources, poor planning, and little oversight, the developments have since dramatically deteriorated. Tearing the structures down and rebuilding would not only temporarily displace up to a million residents, but would be cost-prohibitive. Estimates suggest the cost of rehabilitation is only 25% that of new construction. Proyecto Rehabitar (the "Rehabilitation Project" in Spanish), led by architect Eduardo Bekinschtein, brings together Argentina's Housing and Urban Development Secretary with the Central Society of Architects to evaluate and propose modifications to existing social housing stock. After quantifying the problem—750 developments consisting of 250,000 households—the team is integrating buildings with the city, generating more effective public spaces, and engaging communities to ensure user participation. Housing that is deteriorated beyond repair is torn down. Rehabilitation work will be implemented in partnership with the housing secretary, municipal agencies, and community groups. Initial interventions have begun in Fuerte Apache, located on the outskirts of Buenos Aires. The grid of city roads ends abruptly at the barrio, creating a rupture within the city with few access points. New routes through the neighborhood will connect it with the city grid. Improved pedestrian connections between buildings, new equipment, and refurbished interior spaces including stairwells and walkways will improve quality of life in the community and ensure better integration with the city. **AL**

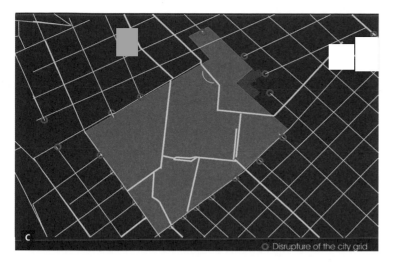

C

Disrupture of the city grid

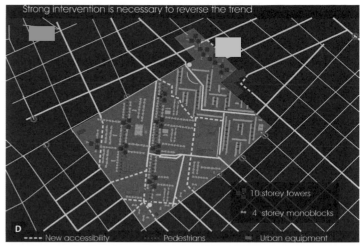

Strong intervention is necessary to reverse the trend

D

10 storey towers

4 storey monoblocks

New accessibility .... Pedestrians ▣ Urban equipment

E (before)

A. Rehabilitated building connector in Fuerte Apache informal settlement, Buenos Aires, Argentina.

B. Rehabilitated building façade in Fuerte Apache.

C. Plan of existing grid disrupture. Yellow lines denote city streets, which end at Fuerte Apache (blue area).

D. Proposal to reconnect neighborhood to city grid.

E. Building connector prior to rehabilitation.

F. Deteriorated building façades and lack of regular waste disposal services in Fuerte Apache.

F

ATLANTIC OCEAN

WASTEWATER PURIFICATION

MBOTIPOM

NDIRENE

Bare gravel filters

Recipients

Collective drains

WAGUE

SICAP

A. Septic

KEY

- ● Recipients
- ---- Tonghor limits
- ------- Neighborhood limits
- ▲▲▲ Ridgelines
- — – Existing network
- — – Network 2
- ▢ Bare gravel filters
- ▢ Flowmeters
- ▢ Collective drains
- ▢ Septic

Yoff Sustainable Wastewater System

Designer: Environment and Development Action–Relay for Participatory Urban Development, with Yoff area community. Yoff, Dakar, Senegal, 2002–11. Manholes, pits, PVC pipes, drains, gravel filters

Yoff, an urban area bordering the Atlantic Ocean in the dense city of Dakar, Senegal, is rapidly urbanizing. Its population has doubled since 1988, putting increased pressure on land in which open space is quickly subsumed by housing. Inadequate urban planning has resulted in insufficient infrastructure and services. Narrow streets prevent access for water and sanitation trucks to properly dispose of wastewater, such as greywater generated from household bathing, laundry, and dishwashing. It was common practice for Yoff's residents to dump used household water on the beach, resulting in not just significant loss of water—a valuable resource in the arid community—but also coastal pollution and unsanitary conditions.

In 2002, a branch of Environment and Development Action (ENDA), a leading international development organization that is headquartered in Dakar and works in twenty-one countries across Africa, South America, and Asia, collaborated with Yoff residents to design and implement a sustainable, gravity-fed wastewater system. Based on an earlier pilot project in the town of Rufisque, Senegal, the system collects household greywater in small settling tanks before sending it "downstream" to larger collection basins, or lagoons, where it is treated and purified with aquatic plants. The recycled greywater is then used for irrigation, urban agriculture, and toilet systems. The community established a committee to manage the system, and signs painted by community members educate others on proper disposal of used water in the system. **AL**

A. Map of Yoff wastewater system, Yoff, Dakar, Senegal.
B. Hand-painted murals next to collection tanks educate users about proper wastewater disposal.

Community Cooker (*Jiko ya jamii*)

Architects: James Howard Archer and Mumo Musuva, Planning Systems Services. Technical support: Arup Cause, Chris Print, Noel Johnson. Laini Saba village, Kibera informal settlement, Nairobi, Kenya, 1993–present. Stone, iron sheets, wire mesh

The majority of Kenya's forty million inhabitants use wood and charcoal fires for cooking. These fires cause respiratory diseases, contribute to greenhouse gases, and denude local forests and scrub lands. One alternative is the Community Cooker (*Jiko ya jamii* in Swahili), a communal oven that uses trash as fuel for the Laini Saba community in Nairobi's Kibera informal settlement.

In the mid-1990s, Nairobi-based architect Jim Archer was increasingly concerned about the amount of discarded refuse piling up in Kenya and many other developing countries. He designed the Community Cooker as a simple, inexpensive machine, easily built and repaired by local communities, with minimal operating expenses. It is described as "cash-free heat": residents collect, transport, or sort the trash in exchange for time cooking or heating or distilling drinking water. Others pay five Kenyan shillings (about six cents)—less than the cost of kerosene or charcoal—to use the cooker.

Under the management of the community-based organization Ushirika wa Usafi ("corporation of cleanliness"), the trash is sorted onto racks, dried, and shoveled down a slide into the burn box. Recyclables are placed in bins to be sold and non-combustibles like rubber and glass are set aside. Biodegradable scraps that fall through become compost manure. A resident *jua-kali* ("informally trained") engineer's innovative oil and water combustion enables the oven's high heat of 875° Celsius (1607° Fahrenheit)—hot enough to burn plastic, paper, garbage, and old rags without toxic fumes, or even melt metal for a possible smelting business. Each oven is large enough to bake ten loaves of bread, roast a goat, or fire clay pots. There are also eight submerged hotplates that people use to boil eggs for sale or cook meals for their families, and five stalls to take hot showers. **CS**

A. Residents gather at the Community Cooker, Kibera informal settlement, Nairobi, Kenya.
B. Concept sketch by architect Jim Archer.
C. Sorting and drying refuse behind the cooker's burn box.
D. Stoking the burn box.
E. Community Cooker with Kibera in background.

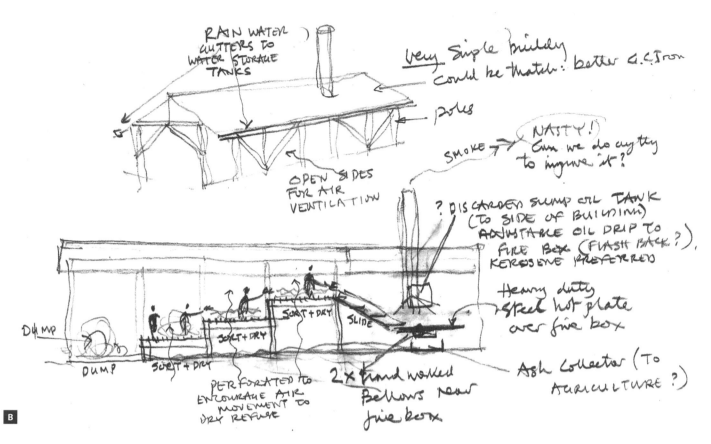

RAIN WATER
GUTTERS TO
WATER STORAGE
TANKS

Very Simple building
Could be thatch: better G.C. Iron

poles

OPEN SIDES
FOR AIR
VENTILATION

SMOKE → NASTY!
Can we do anything
to improve it?

? DISCARDED SUMP OIL TANK
(TO SIDE OF BUILDING)
ADJUSTABLE OIL DRIP TO
FIRE BOX (FLASH BACK?)
KEROSENE PREFERRED

Heavy duty
steel hot plate
over fire box

Ash Collector (TO
AGRICULTURE?)

DUMP

DUMP

SORT + DRY

SORT + DRY

SORT + DRY

SORT + DRY

SLIDE

PERFORATED TO
ENCOURAGE AIR
MOVEMENT TO
DRY REFUSE

2 X hand worked
Bellows near
fire box

B

C

D

E

A

Diadema Reurbanization

Housing Secretaries: Márcio Luiz Vale, Josemundo Dario Queiroz, Jorge Hereda, Mario Wilson Pedreira Reali, Lício Gozanga Lobo Júnior, João Alberto Zocchio, Amir Khair; for mayors Mario Reali, José de Filippi Jr., Gilson Menezes, José Augusto Silva Ramos; with Diadema informal settlement community. Diadema, Brazil, 1983–present

Diadema, near São Paulo, is an industrial city with close to 400,000 residents that has successfully upgraded—or, in the words of former mayor José de Filippi Jr., "reurbanized"—its informal settlements. Filippi points out that favelas have already been urbanized. "The slums are urbanism without urbanists," he observes, paraphrasing Bernard Rudofsky. In the early 1980s, three out of ten Diadema residents lived in favelas, and by the 1990s, homicides had increased 49% from previous years. Efforts to reduce these figures focused on social and physical inclusion through participatory budgeting and planning. The community helped determine priorities for the annual budget, "distributing resources in a democratic way," notes Filippi. The community also had a voice in reurbanization meetings with architects, engineers, and social workers from the Housing Secretariat, suggesting upgrades and approving projects on work, part of which was performed by community members themselves.

As a result, a municipal land-tenure program, the first of its kind in Brazil, was established in 1985 to grant favela residents located on public land a "right to use" the land for 90 years, encouraging improvements in homes and neighborhoods. Households located in unsafe locations were cooperatively relocated into new housing built in partnership with the municipality. Residents widened and paved narrow streets and built clean water and sanitation access to the neighborhoods. State-of-the-art hospitals such as the Quarteirão da Saúde, completed in 2008, provide quality healthcare to the city's poorest residents, and community health agents deliver aid to the most vulnerable residents. Today, only 3% of Diadema's residents live in favelas, and the homicide rate has dramatically dropped from 140 to 14.3 people killed per 100,000. **AL**

A. Community effort to pave Margaridas Street, Diadema, Brazil, 1990.
B. Aerial image of underdeveloped Inamar Eldorado, 1962.
C. Inamar Eldorado, 2006, showing urban growth.
D. Improved streets and housing, Vila Olinda neighborhood, Diadema.

E. Precarious dwellings before reurbanization, Vera Cruz neighborhood, Diadema.
F. Quarteirão da Saúde, a state-of-the-art health facility serving Diadema's low-income residents.

A

Kaputiei New Town

Initiated and designed by Jamii Bora Trust and its members. Architect: Mohammed K. Munyanya. Construction: Kaputiei New Town community. Kisaju, Kajiado district, Kenya, 2002–present

Jamii Bora Trust, meaning "good families" in Swahili, is a microfinance organization founded by Ingrid Munro, a former architect and urban planner and head of the African Housing Fund, and fifty beggar families from Kenya's urban informal settlements, with the mission to pull thousands out of poverty. Today there are more than 170,000 members, who can each borrow up to twice as much as they have saved, no matter how little. In 2002, at the behest of its members and self-management team, Jamii Bora procured 293 acres of land in Kisaju, 65 kilometers (40 miles) south of Nairobi, on which to build Kaputiei New Town.

Designed around eight neighborhoods of 250 houses each, Kaputiei New Town will provide homes for 2,000 families. To be eligible for a home loan, a borrower must have been a Jamii Bora member for three years and managed at least three business loans. A loan for a two-bedroom house costs 3,000 Kenyan shillings (US$32) a month over a ten- to fifteen-year repayment period. Members produce building materials—roof tiles, concrete blocks, laundry basins—at an onsite factory and construct the town's houses and roads. Houses have running water and flush toilets, unheard-of luxuries in informal settlements. Solar panels provide energy for LED (light-emitting diodes) lighting. A wetlands wastewater facility recycles up to 70% of the town's wastewater for irrigation.

To date, two neighborhoods have been built and a third is underway. A primary school has been built and a secondary school is planned. Additional amenities include a market, post office, library, and health center. The town's open spaces and facilities are maintained by associations made up of Kaputiei New Town members. The sense of community and solidarity has enabled members to defy the ethnic divisions that are common in Kenya—as one resident says, "The only ethnic group in Kaputiei New Town is Jamii Bora." **AL**

A. Students walking to school, Kaputiei New Town, Kenya.
B. Local women prepare materials for making tiles.
C. A Kaputiei New Town resident waters his garden.
D. Former living conditions in informal settlements.
E. Community members tile roofs.

A

Kibera Public Space Project

Architects: Chelina Odbert, Jennifer Toy, Arthur Adeya, Luke Clark Tyler, Anthony Opil, Julius Muiru, Ellen Schneider, and Kotch Voraakhom, Kounkuey Design Initiative; environmental engineers: Byron Stigge, Joe Mulligan, Greg Tuzzolo, Buro Happold; volunteer collaborators: Yvonne Hung, Jean Yang. Community partners: Kiki Weavers, New Nairobi Dam Community Group, Riverside Usafi Group, Ushirika Wa Usafi, Youth Development Forum. Soweto East and Silanga villages, Kibera informal settlement, Nairobi, Kenya, 2006–10.
Reclaimed timber and steel, stone, plaster, red soil, cement, gum poles, corrugated metal

Currently, one in seven people worldwide lives in a slum or refugee camp. Kounkuey Design Initiative (KDI) is a nonprofit design firm formed in 2006 to design and build physically, economically, and socially sustainable public spaces in informal settlements. The team of urban planners, architects, landscape architects, and graphic designers developed a community-driven process to build Productive Public Spaces (PPS), which use unoccupied waste spaces to address needs such as sanitation, environmental hazards, and income generation.

First working in Kibera—estimated to be the largest informal settlement in sub-Saharan Africa—KDI converted a former waterlogged dumping site located on a highly polluted Ngong River tributary. The new space features amenities and opportunities for microenterprise— community refuse is turned into compost for sale to urban farmers, and a pavilion doubles as a drying rack for water hyacinth that are woven into baskets and sold at market. Partnering with local contractors and engineers from Buro Happold, the site, open to all residents, also houses a public park, playground, rainwater-fed water tap, and a new bridge that shortens commute time.

Part of a larger vision to "reclaim the river," several community-based sites along the same river form a network that creates a larger watershed and settlement-scale impact. Site two includes a sanitation center that replaces toilets that drained into the river, as well as a set of kiosks, playground, and park. Revenue from the toilet block, a kiosk bakery, and a wholesale brick-making cooperative will offset maintenance costs. The third sits at the bottom of a steep slope, into which sewage and waste drain. In response to residents' needs, the site provides flood control and improved drainage and includes toilets, a water tap, playground, daycare, meeting hall, and a women's health clinic expected to serve 500–800 residents. Two more sites are planned for 2012.

Applying these same design principles to other locations around the world, KDI has transformed a Haitian town's open-air market into a PPS; local community group Tête Ensemble will design, build, and manage Bonneau PPS. KDI's first site in America, St. Anthony PPS in Coachella, CA, starts construction in 2011. The productive space designs include a sheltered meeting space, play structure, community garden, and small-business incubator to help mobilize the area's Pueblo Unido community. **CS**

A. Children at a playground, the first Public Space Project site in Kibera informal settlement, Nairobi, Kenya.
B. Concept drawing of third site in Kibera, where the "river need not be an eyesore."
C. The community pavilion is a popular gathering space.

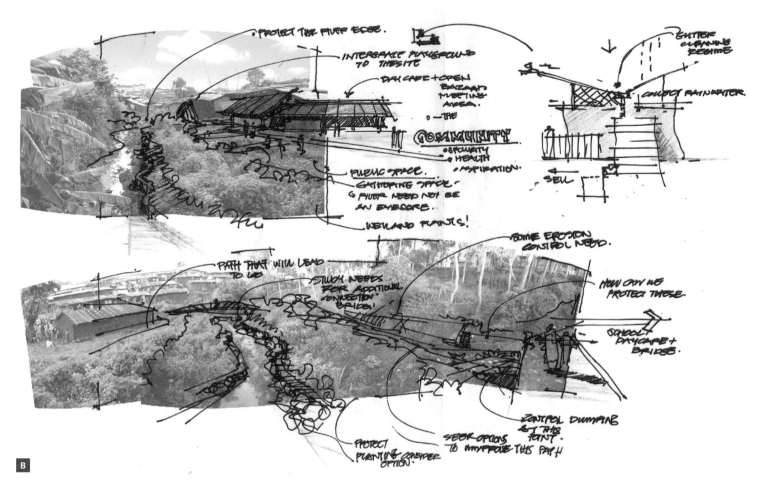

Platform of Hope (*Ashar Macha*)

Designers: Khondaker Hasibul Kabir, with Fourkan Pervez, Nasima Pervez, Faria Farzana Tithi, and Tuhofa Tasmi Tisha. Construction: Odut Ahmed, Saiful Islam. Plant/seed collection: Abdun Nime. Korail, Dhaka, Bangladesh, 2008–11. Bamboo, nuts, bolts, nails

With a population of 120,000, Korail is the largest slum in the fastest growing megacity, Dhaka. UNEP projects that Dhaka will grow to twenty-three million people and become the world's second largest city by 2015. Open public space is rare in Korail, and children make do playing in the narrowest open space. Living with one of Korail's families, Khondaker Hasibul Kabir, an architect, landscape architect and lecturer at BRAC University, collaborated with the local Pervez family to initiate a new public space, the Platform of Hope. Over a three-year period starting in 2008, Kabir and the Pervez family, with help from a local carpenter and bamboo worker, designed and built the 5.5 x 11 meter (18 x 36 ft) platform extending over Gulshan Lake. A bamboo bridge connects it to a lush community garden. Designed for children living in the settlement, it is a clean, new space in which they can play, sing, dance, interact, and read books from a small library. In the evening, families gather for relaxation and enjoy the view over the water.

The Platform of Hope stands in stark contrast to the constant threat of eviction with which the Korail residents live, without security of tenure, on land that is becoming more valuable in the densest city in the world. Yet local residents have the skills and willingness to change their unhealthy surroundings. With knowledge shared on the platform, nearby dwellings are slowly transforming, with better lighting and ventilation. The platform and garden have generated hope for a cleaner and greener place. **CS**

A

B

C

A. Local carpenter and bamboo worker help construct the platform, Korail informal settlement, Dhaka, Bangladesh.
B. Children gardening on the new bamboo platform.

C. View of platform from the water.
D. Platform of Hope, built over Gulshan Lake, with Dhaka in background.

D

A

Vertical Gym (*Gimnasio Vertical*)

Architects: Alfredo Brillembourg and Hubert Klumpner, Urban Think Tank, with Thomas Auer, Ruedi Baur, Felix Caraballo, and Jose Miguel Peres; structural engineer: Andres Steiner; electrical engineer: Freddy Ferro. Caracas, Venezuela, 2004–present. Bolted steel structure assembled on site with prefabricated pieces on reinforced concrete foundation slab; exterior materials: galvanized expanded metal mesh, Carbolux polycarbonate translucent opaque panels

Limited land and high crime rates in the dense informal settlements and slums of Caracas made it unsafe for children to play and participate in sports. Urban Think Tank (UTT) transformed a rundown sports field in Chacao's Barrio La Cruz into Chacao Vertical Gym (*Gimnasio Vertical*), a four-story sports, recreation, and cultural event facility. Taking cues from residents who are unable to expand out, the architects built up on the 1,000-square-meter (10,700 sq. ft.) site without displacing any families. The popular new public space, with 15,000 users a month, has helped to reduce crime in this barrio by over 30% by offering a safe, open space that nurtures fair play, tolerance, and a civic community through sports competition.

UTT's prototype structures are conceived as a kit of parts, which allows flexible design and construction. Stacked volumes are reassembled and programmed for different locations in response to local needs. Caracas's government is constructing four additional *Gimnasios Verticals*—Baruta GV includes an outdoor market; Los Teques GV has an

aquatic sports center; Ceiba GV incorporates a library and metrocable station; and El Dorado GV includes space for informal vendors.

A prefabricated bolted-steel construction system is erected onsite. A ramp provides access at every level, eliminating the expense of an elevator. The latest design incorporates recycled materials, wind towers, solar panels, and rainwater collection to reduce environmental impact and operational costs. UTT is changing the way people think in other parts of the world about sports areas in dense, low-income neighborhoods. Hybrid Vertical Gyms are proposed for several New York City public schools, as well as in Rusaifah, Jordan, and Hoograven, the Netherlands, which is planning a dynamic sport, cultural, and commercial complex. **CS**

A. Interior of Chacao Vertical Gym, Barrio La Cruz, Caracas, Venezuela.
B. Rendering of proposed Vertical Gym with solar panels, wind turbines, and local-artist-made façade.

C. Vertical Gym's kit of parts: 1) triple-height space with volleyball, basketball, gymnastics, martial arts, multipurpose hall, and gym entrance; 2) double-height space with cardio and weight machines, locker rooms; 3) running track, locker rooms; 4) basketball, football, seating.

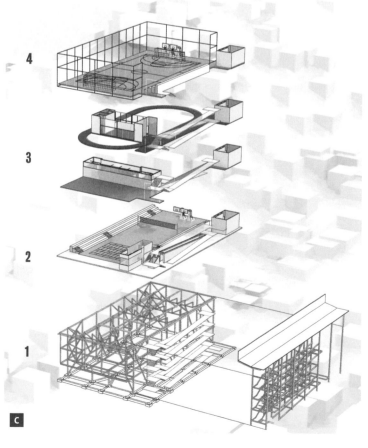

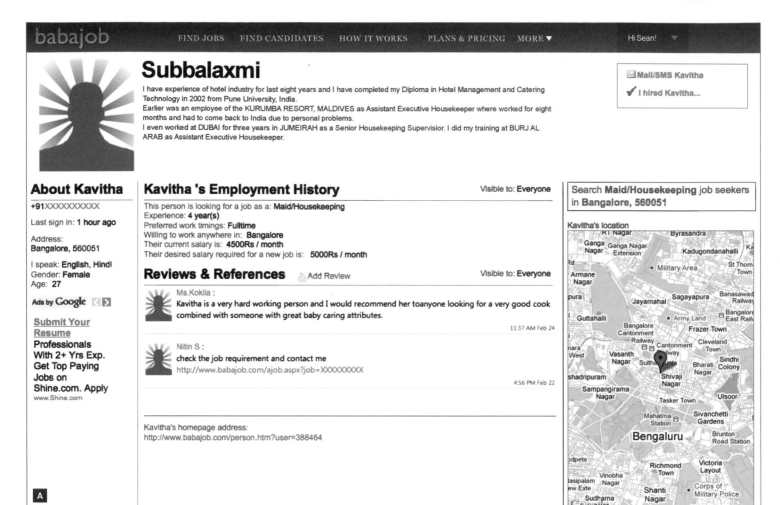

A. Job seeker profile page, Bangalore, India.

Babajob.com

Designers: Sean Olin Blagsvedt and Aditya Dipankar, Babajob.com Services. Bangalore, India, 2007–present

Urban poverty in India is high—80 million people, over 25% of the urban population, live below the poverty line—not because there are no jobs, but because, as economist Anirudh Krishna has observed, informal workers lack connections to better jobs. Without Internet or computer access, informal workers, such as housekeepers, drivers, and clerks, often find jobs through people they know, just as employers look to their social network to find informal workers.

Babajob.com expands the reach of both employers and job seekers, in many ways mimicking the social networks through which Indians customarily find and fill jobs. Job seekers register via mobile phone using SMS texts or USSD (a menu-driven mobile application), providing information such as preferred salary, location, languages, and skills. For the equivalent of two cents a day, they receive daily SMS alerts about jobs in their neighborhood. Their profiles are added to the Babajob Web site, and for a fee, employers can filter and sort candidates as well as post jobs. Information is available in six languages, including Hindi, Tamil, and Telugu. For nonliterate users, a text-free version of Babajob.

com is in development featuring simple icons to guide users through the site as well as speech-to-text services. An automated voice interface available in three languages will also enable nonliterate users to navigate relevant jobs and apply for them by leaving messages with employers. Piloted in Bangalore, Babajob.com has reached almost 150,000 users, posting over half a million jobs and sending two million job alerts every month, with plans to expand the site to the rest of India. **AL**

A. Job seeker profile page, Bangalore, India.
B. Promotional cards, distributed at small shops where job seekers recharge their phones, provide instruction on how to use Babajob.com.
C. Babajob postings in local languages are sent to mobile phones using SMS.
D. Employers sort job candidates.

How Babajob works

1 Register & Create your profile for free.

2 Search for jobs

3 Babajob will send you 2 matching jobs right away!

4 Apply for a job, interview and get hired!

SMS **9972 00 2222**
CALL **080 - 4262 2777**

B

How to search for jobs

JOB MAID
560025

Options | Clear

SMS **JOB** *< MAID, DRIVER, CASHIER, SALES, etc >* *< Your Pin Code >* to **9972 00 2222**

Bangalore Maid Jobs: 1. Maid Rs4000 Ashok Nagar

Options | Back

You will receive 2 jobs that match your criteria!

JOB 1

Options | Clear

SMS **JOB1** *or* **JOB2** *to apply, or* **JOBS** *for more jobs!* *to* **99 7200 2222**

Jobs available for

Maid	Housekeeping	Data Entry	Marketing
Cook	Aayah	BPO	Admin
Helper	Driver	Receptionist	
Guard	Manager	Cashier	& lots more...

Fold this up and use this to store your cards and other important papers

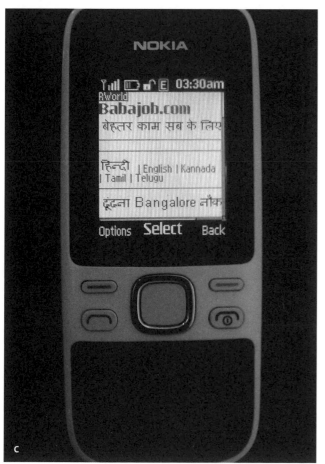

C

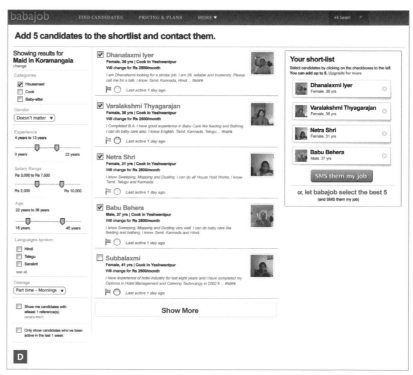

babajob   FIND CANDIDATES   PRICING & PLANS   MORE ▾   Hi Sean!

Add 5 candidates to the shortlist and contact them.

Showing results for **Maid in Koramangala** change

Categories
☑ Housemaid
☐ Cook
☐ Baby-sitter

Gender
Doesn't matter ▾

Experience
4 years to 13 years
0 years   22 years

Salary Range
Rs 3,000 to Rs 7,500
Rs 2,000   Rs 10,000

Age
22 years to 36 years
18 years   46 years

Languages spoken
☐ Hindi
☐ Telugu
☐ Sanskrit
see all

Timings
Part time – Mornings ▾

☐ Show me candidates with atleast 1 reference(s)
(what's this?)

☐ Only show candidates who've been active in the last 1 week

☑ **Dhanalaxmi Iyer**
Female, 36 yrs | Cook in Yeshwantpur
Will change for Rs 2500/month
I am Dhanalaxmi looking for a similar job. I am 26, reliable and trustworty. Please call me for a talk. I know Tamil, Kannada, Hindi ... more
🚩 ○ Last active 1 day ago

☑ **Varalakshmi Thyagarajan**
Female, 36 yrs | Cook in Yeshwantpur
Will change for Rs 2500/month
I Completed B.A. I have good experience in Baby Care like feeding and Bathing I can do baby care also. I know English, Tamil, Kannada, Telugu... more
🚩 ○ Last active 1 day ago

☑ **Netra Shri**
Female, 31 yrs | Cook in Yeshwantpur
Will change for Rs 2500/month
I know Sweeping, Mopping and Dusting. I can do all House Hold Works. I know Tamil, Telugu and Kannada.
🚩 ○ Last active 1 day ago

☑ **Babu Behera**
Male, 37 yrs | Cook in Yeshwantpur
Will change for Rs 2500/month
I know Sweeping, Mopping and Dusting very well. I can do baby care like feeding and bathing. I know Tamil, Kannada and Hindi
🚩 ○ Last active 1 day ago

☐ **Subbalaxmi**
Female, 41 yrs | Cook in Yeshwantpur
Will change for Rs 2500/month
I have experience of hotel industry for last eight years and I have completed my Diploma in Hotel Management and Catering Technology in 2002 fr ... more
🚩 ○ Last active 1 day ago

Show More

Your short-list
Select candidates by clicking on the checkboxes to the left. You can add up to 5. Upgrade for more

Dhanalaxmi Iyer
Female, 36 yrs

Varalakshmi Thyagarajan
Female, 36 yrs

Netra Shri
Female, 31 yrs

Babu Behera
Male, 37 yrs

SMS them my job

or, let babajob select the best 5
(and SMS them my job)

D

Cristal de Luz

Designer: Maria Teresa Tetê Leal. Produced by COOPA-ROCA Collective. Rocinha, Rio de Janeiro, Brazil, 2006–present.

Cotton, plastic, aluminum

Many livelihood models combine craft and design to generate income for poor communities, but perhaps none has been more successful than COOPA-ROCA, an artisanal cooperative founded by Maria Teresa Tetê Leal, known as TT, in Rocinha, a favela in Rio de Janeiro. Rocinha, home to an estimated 180,000 people, was established when job seekers migrated to Rio. Many of Rocinha's female residents found jobs as domestic workers in the wealthy gated communities nearby, but many more remained unemployed. TT founded COOPA-ROCA to improve the lives of these women by increasing their earning ability through traditional craft production. The cooperative has since partnered with global designers including Cacharel, Paul Smith, Tord Boontje, and Ernesto Neto, and has earned an international reputation for its unique, high-quality craftsmanship.

The Cristal de Luz represents a new direction for the cooperative. Designed by TT in collaboration with COOPA-ROCA artisans, the light is sold under the cooperative's own label, established in 2010. By creating and launching its own fashion, accessories, and design products, COOPA-ROCA seeks to build a self-sufficient business model that expands work opportunities to even more female artisans in the favela. For the Cristal de Luz, the artisans make cotton and viscose crocheted covers over industrially produced white globes, reflecting the dexterity and skilled craftsmanship for which the cooperative is known. With more than a hundred members, COOPA-ROCA continues to increase the scale of its production. Through more products like this, it endeavors to improve livelihoods in the favela and demonstrate the possibilities for generating successful businesses in low-income communities. **AL**

A. Detail of Cristal de Luz with lakshimi pattern.
B. COOPA-ROCA artisans crochet Cristal de Luz covers, Rochina favela, Rio de Janeiro, Brazil.

A

iTRUMP: Warwick Junction

Project managers: Richard Dobson (architect), with Sue Wilkinson and Hoosen Moolla, eThekwini municipality; design and implementation: Gavin Adams, Jonathan Edkins, Ken Froise, Nic Combrink, and Nina Saunders, eThekwini municipality; commissioned architects: Architects Collaborative, Emmett & Emmett, Kooblal & Steyn, Langa Makhanya & Associates, Laren Beni, Lee Saunders, Lees & Short, MA Gafoor Architects, Matic van Zyl, Mike Legg Architects, Richard Dobson Architect, OMM Design Workshop. Client: eThekwini municipality. Warwick Junction, Durban, South Africa, 1995–present. Locally sourced masonry units, concrete, steel, timber, corrugated sheeting

Warwick Junction, in Durban, South Africa, is the area's primary transport hub, accommodating 460,000 commuters a day along with 5,000 traders who form several robust markets. During apartheid, the area became neglected, unsafe, and congested. Warwick Junction is one of nine iTRUMP (Inner Thekwini Regeneration & Urban Management Program) districts established in the 1990s by the eThekwini municipality to improve conditions, placing strategic value on the inner city in a quest to become a sustainable city. The pioneering work of incorporating the informal economy into the larger city required stakeholder participation. Heading the efforts, the nonprofit group Asiye eTafuleni ("bring it to the table" in Zulu) used a bottom-up approach, consulting formal and informal businesses, residents, and commuters to overcome gender, cultural, racial, and language biases.

Traders in the Traditional Medicine and Herb Market used to work on the pavement in dangerous conditions, and, lacking storage, many traders protected their goods by sleeping overnight next to them. New designs transformed dormant freeway ramps into sheltered trader stalls with locked storage. Bovine heads, a Zulu delicacy, were boiled over open fires on the pavement, with excess water and grease drained into the city's stormwater system. In the redesigned Bovine Head Market, pre-cast concrete cooking cubicles and steel serving tables reduce pollution and hazards. New designs for trading spaces and kiosks, tailor-made storage facilities, and new widened pedestrian routes have vastly improved trading conditions, and these improved markets have further enabled other "invisible" employment opportunities throughout the city and region.
CS

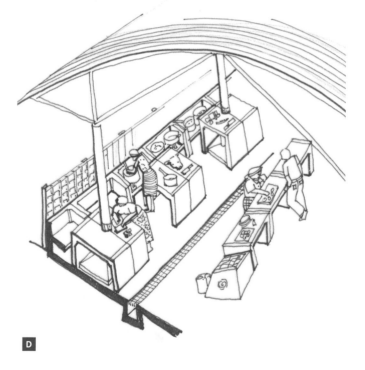

A. Fresh produce stalls in the renovated heritage building that houses the Early Morning Market, Durban, South Africa.

B. Aerial view of Warwick Junction identifying design interventions.

C. Upgraded Bovine Head Market.

D. Design sketch of pre-cast cooking cubicles and steel serving tables for Bovine Head Market.

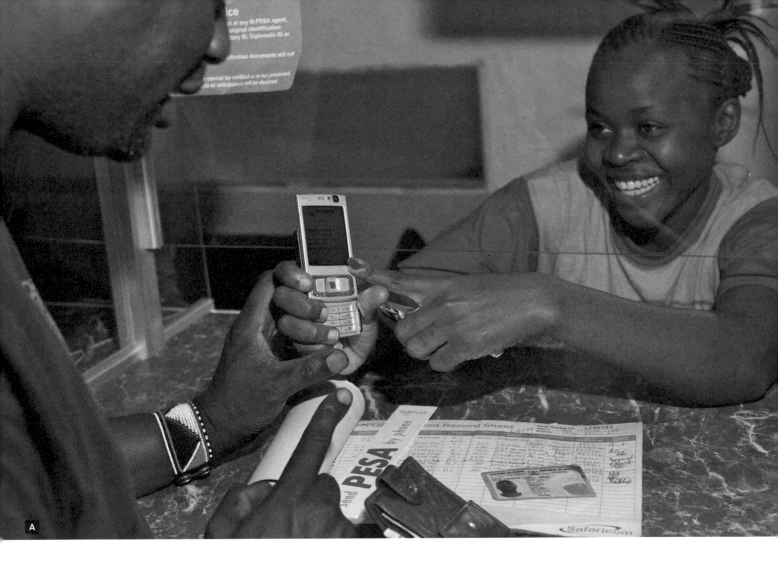

A

M-PESA Money-transfer System

Initiated by Safaricom, Vodafone, and Commercial Bank of Africa. Kenya, 2007–present

Urban workers traditionally send money home to their families in rural villages by post, unreliable couriers, or by delivering it themselves, which can take days of travel and makes them vulnerable to robbery. Since 2007, when Kenya's M-PESA was launched, recipients can receive money with a simple text message on their mobile phone. The ease, speed, and safety of this mobile money transfer have led to its unprecedented success—over two million users in the first year, growing to thirteen million over the following two and a half years.

The M-PESA (the M is for mobile, and *pesa* means "money" in Swahili) system includes a grassroots network of over 22,000 agent outlets throughout Kenya, where users exchange M-PESA money for cash. Kenya's leading mobile-network operator, Safaricom, in partnership with Vodafone, designed M-PESA so that people could use the SMS service installed on their SIM cards. M-PESA is flexible and works across platforms or operating systems. First, a mobile money account is created and linked to the user's

phone number. A simple menu allows the user to securely send money to any mobile phone subscriber in Kenya, who is added to an M-PESA account or by voucher if on another network. Using this code and the recipient's phone number, an M-PESA agent will be able to verify the transaction and pay the correct cash amount.

This simple, person-to-person, mobile-payment method has evolved into a financial tool for both individuals and businesses. Over one million people now pay their monthly bills through the Pay Bill function, larger corporations have started paying their workers' salaries through these accounts, and it has proved a safer option for informed traders dealing with cash. There are plans to expand the program to Tanzania, Afghanistan, India, Egypt, and South Africa. **CS**

A. An M-PESA agent assists a customer, Kenya.
B, C. M-PESA outlet in Kibera informal settlement, Nairobi, Kenya.
D. M-PESA mobile withdrawal.
E. M-PESA outlet.

A

Spaza-de-Move-on

Architect: Doung Anwar Jahangeer, Dala, with Moses Gwiba. Fabricator: Rebcon Engineering. Durban, South Africa, 2001–present (prototype). Galvanized steel, mild steel

In South Africa, hundreds of thousands of workers commute daily from the outlying townships or informal settlements into the cities. This has given rise to the rebirth of the trade in refreshments, loose cigarettes, sweets, and snacks along sidewalks and public spaces. A redesign of the "café-de-move-ons," or coffee carts, popular in the 1960s, the Spaza-de-Move-on, first prototyped in 2008, is an efficient, durable metal cart designed to give street vendors dignity, convenience, and relief in the streets of Durban. The design incorporates a seat, trolley handle, wheels, storage area, and foldout display table. Its evolution involved bottom-up collaboration between architect Doung Anwar Jahangeer and street vendor Moses Gwiba, who formed a relationship while Jahangeer conducted CityWalks, an initiative of the city's sustainable city planning program.

Dala, a South African creative collective, produces art and architecture for social change. It engages creative practitioners—artists and performers, architects and designers, researchers and urban planners—the municipality, and the people and organizations that live and work in the Durban metropolitan area. Spaza-de-Move-on is one of Dala's livelihood initiatives that explore informal livelihoods and entrepreneurial networks. Jahangeer's work embodies a philosophy of "architecture without walls." Rather than focusing on physical walls that divide, his work explores urban spaces that unite. Part of an ongoing process, the Spaza-de-Move-on is a product that embodies the possibility of a new attitude, methodology, and philosophy of urban design for African cities. **CS**

A. Street vendor Moses Gwiba on the Spaza-de-Move-on, Durban, South Africa.
B. Concept sketch.
C. Cardboard mock-up.
D. Moses setting up the Spaza-de-Move-on.

184

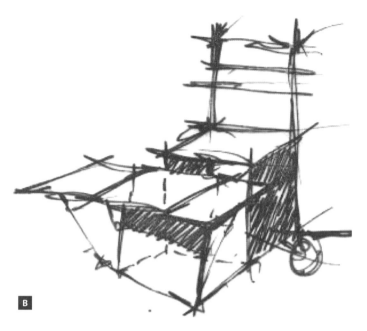

B

C

D

A

Abalimi Bezekhaya

Co-directors: Rob Small, Christina Kaba, and Roland Welte, with Dave Golding, Moraig Peden, and Peter Templeton. Collaborators: Business Place Phillipi, South African Institute of Entrepreneurship, Catholic Welfare & Development Network. Khayelitsha, Delft, Nyanga, Phillipi, and Gugulethu informal settlements, Cape Town, South Africa, 1982–present

The Cape Flats townships northeast of Cape Town are populated by economic refugees from Ciskei and Transkei, formerly Xhosa-speaking, self-governing territories under apartheid. Officials estimate the townships' unemployment rate at 30–40%, with 1,200 new refugees arriving every month. Formed in 1982, Abalimi Bezekhaya ("farmers or planters of the home" in Xhosa) is an organization that combats poverty in the informal settlements of Khayelitsha, Delft, Nyanga, Phillipi, and Gugulethu through a network of organic "micro-farms." Abalimi teaches local communities to grow organic vegetables first for survival, then to sell surplus produce to markets outside of the townships, with the goal of generating a livelihood. Farmers cultivate common vegetables such as onions, tomatoes, carrots, and potatoes, and Abalimi provides ongoing training, technical advice, cheap bulk inputs, irrigation, and other services.

Abalimi Bezekhaya serves 3,000 micro-farmers a year, the majority of them women. Two People's Garden Centers dispense seedlings to sustainable farmers, inculcating a new organic-gardening culture that is becoming a permanent feature among the poor in Cape Town. Their community gardens are adjacent to informal settlements on public land, on unused plots within public-school grounds, and on municipal commonage. Abalimi further builds community cohesion with peer-to-peer learning events and savings groups. In 2008, the group launched Harvest of Hope, which contracts Abalimi's micro-farmers to harvest and deliver vegetables to local Cape Town schools, guaranteeing a steady income for the farmers. **CS**

A. The Nyanga People's Garden Center dispenses seedlings to settlement gardeners, Cape Flats, Cape Town, South Africa.
B. A community garden located on public land adjacent to an informal settlement.
C. Harvest of Hope organic vegetable boxes ready for delivery.
D. Abalimi micro-farmers prepare Harvest of Hope "seed-to-table" vegetable boxes.

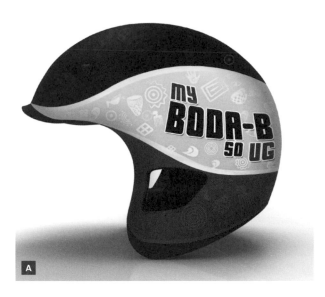

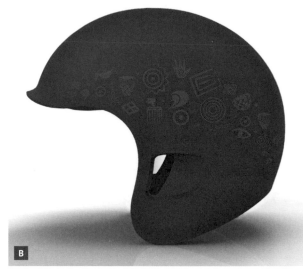

A B C

bePRO motor-taxi helmet

Concept: Vanja Steinbru, Design Without Borders; development: Gonzaga Ntege, Kristoffer Leivestad Olsen, and Marianne Godding Boye, Design Without Borders, and Marcus Martinuzzi; graphic design: Ivan Bargiye, Design Without Borders. Partners: Richiencoy Services Ltd., Injury Control Center–Uganda, Technology Development and Transfer Centre, Makerere University, Norsk Form Foundation for Design and Architecture. Kampala, Uganda, 2009–present (prototype). Polyamide (nylon)

In Uganda, *boda boda* is the term for the uncomfortable and accident-prone motorcycle taxis available throughout the country. Motorcycle-helmet use is mandatory by law; approximately 70% of boda boda drivers own helmets, but only half wear them. Seventy-five percent of hospital-reported injuries in the capital city of Kampala are from boda boda–related accidents; the World Health Organization estimates that helmets can reduce head-injury severity by nearly 75%.

Industrial designer Vanja Steinbru's research in Kampala with boda boda drivers and passengers elicited numerous reasons as to why the majority of them choose not to wear helmets, including prohibitive cost, limited availability, and little understanding of the risks. Certified helmets are expensive and not designed for hot climates; they cover the ears, impeding drivers from hearing potential customers; and passengers are wary of sharing helmets for hygienic reasons.

Steinbru, with other Norway-based Design Without Borders designers, partnered with Makarere University in Kampala, Richenkoy Production Company, the Injury Control Center-Uganda (ICCU), and the Norwegian sports-helmet brand Sweet Protection to develop a new helmet aimed to reduce injuries for boda boda riders. The bePRO helmet will be locally produced using a readily available fiberglass composite, will meet safety standards, and be affordable. The design includes integrated ventilation, holes for hearing, durable closures, a hairnet worn under-helmet, and exterior graphics by urban artists. The first batch of helmets will have extra padding that conforms to a variety of head sizes. **CS**

F

D

E

A–E. Renderings of bePRO helmets with Ugandan artists' graphics: "My Boda-B, So UG" ("Boda B" is slang for boda bodas, "UG" for Uganda).

"*Kampala si kibuga kya bafala!*" ("Kampala is no place for fools!").
F. Testing the durability and impact resistance of resin composite material for

helmets, Kampala, Uganda.
G. Boda boda taxi riders without helmets, Kampala.

G

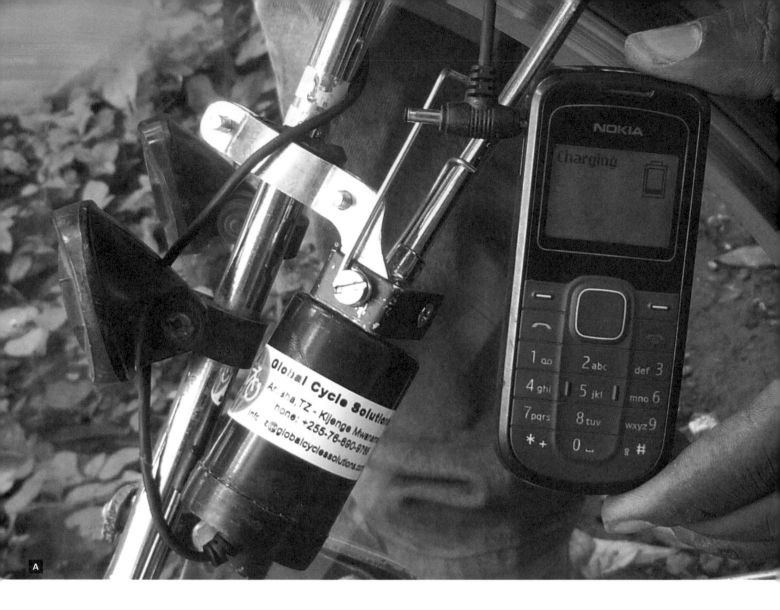

A

Bicycle Phone Charger

Designer: Bernard Kiwia, with Global Cycle Solutions. Collaborators: Suprio Das, International Design Development Summit 2009, Massachusetts Institute of Technology. Arusha, Tanzania, 2007–present. 470 microfarad capacitor, 7806 transistor (voltage regulator), cell phone cord, 12V DC motor, metal u-bracket, rubber roller, brake pipe, brake clamp, spoke, spring wire, 8mm nylon rod

In Tanzania, the majority of people live without electricity, yet a third of the country uses mobile phones. Bernard Kiwia, a trained electrician and vocational-school instructor, collaborated with the for-profit social enterprise Global Cycle Solutions (GCS) to design a phone charger from scrap bike and radio parts. Made from spokes, brake tubes, clamps, motors, and capacitors, the device generates power when its roller comes in contact with the bike's spinning wheel as one rides it.

At MIT D-Lab's inaugural International Design Development Summit (IDDS) in 2007, Kiwia was introduced to design solutions developed with locally resourced materials. Seeing a real need in Tanzania, he made a prototype of the charger from old bicycle spokes and brake cables. Further refinements came after he partnered with another

innovator at the second IDDS, India's Suprio Das, who contributed his small-scale manufacturing experience when certain parts were difficult to source.

In Tanzania, the devices are sold in urban retail stores and via sales ambassadors in rural villages, and are now also distributed in Uganda and Zambia. GCS, comprised of MIT-educated engineers and social entrepreneurs, sells a range of bicycle-powered products. It plans to distribute the phone charger globally. Kiwia has also designed a phone charger that regulates the voltage coming from a motorbike's battery to recharge the mobile phone. An open-source design GCS helped bring to market, the bicycle charger costs approximately US$10 and the motorcycle charger approximately US$5. **CS**

A. Bicycle Phone Charger charging a mobile phone, Tanzania.
B. Bernard Kiwia working on the charger.
C. Kiwia installing the charger to a bike frame.

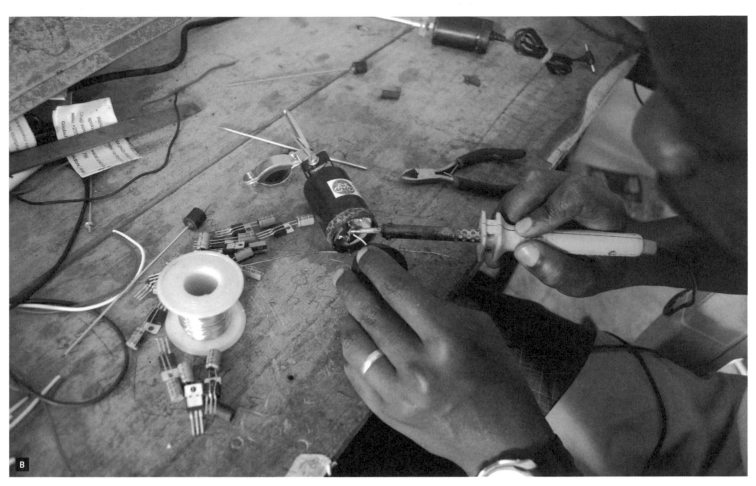

BioCentre

Designers: Michael Francis, Josiah Omotto, Peter Murigi, and Malcolm Ormiston, Umande Trust. Collaborators: Halcrow Foundation UK, Athi Water Services Board, Oxfam, Goal Ireland, UN-Habitat. Kibera, Korogocho, Mukuru, and Mathare informal settlements, Nairobi; Manyatta, Obunga, and Nyalenda informal settlements, Kisumu, Kenya, 2006–present. Bricks, sand, cement, ballast, reinforcement bars, timber, roofing materials

In the slums and informal settlements of Nairobi, there is only one latrine for every 150 people. As a result, many resort to "flying toilets" or use open spaces after dark, which is a security risk for women and girls. Most latrine blocks are inaccessible to children, the elderly, and physically challenged. Waste overflow pollutes nearby streams, leading to diseases such as diarrhea, typhoid, and tuberculosis. Water costs four to five times higher at kiosks inside the slum so that many residents cannot afford to meet their daily needs, while dilapidated pipes leak and expose water to contamination.

Kenya-based Umande Trust worked with residents and artisans in the slums of Nairobi and Kisumu to plan, design, cost, procure, and construct the BioCentres. Built from conventional, locally available technology and materials and unskilled labor, the multi-story BioCentres convert human waste in situ without requiring infrastructure. The bio-latrine uses anaerobic, or airless, digestion, in which bacteria transforms human waste into fertilizer and methane-based gas for cooking and heating water, reducing carbon emissions. A shallow pit latrine feeds into a domed underground bio-digester and expansion chambers, which need little maintenance since there are no moving parts. Generated bio-gas and liquid fertilizer can be sold for income. BioCentres provide toilets free to children, washrooms and showers at a minimal fee, kiosks selling affordable clean water on the ground floor, and community and livelihood spaces on upper floors. **CS**

A. Multi-level BioCentre in Kibera informal settlement, Nairobi.
B. Section elevation of BioCentre.
C. Bio-digester under construction by local artisans.
D. Unsanitary conditions in Kibera informal settlement.

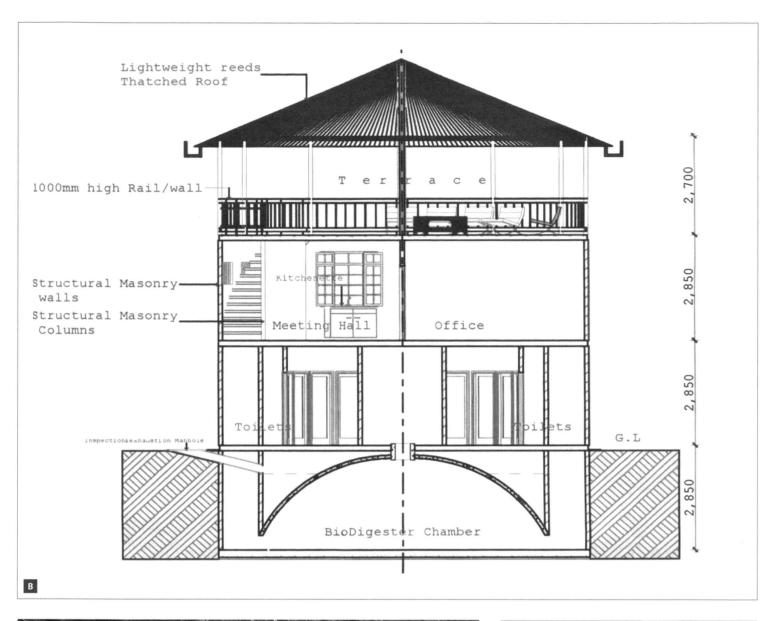

Lightweight reeds Thatched Roof

1000mm high Rail/wall

Structural Masonry walls

Structural Masonry Columns

Terrace

2,700

Kitchenette

Meeting Hall

Office

2,850

Toilets

Toilets

2,850

Inspection&exhaustion Manhole

G.L

BioDigester Chamber

2,850

B

C

D

Chennai Sustainable Transportation Network

Initiated by Chennai City Connect, with Institute for Transportation and Development Policy and Sustainable Mobility & Accessibility Research & Transformation, University of Michigan. Architects: Madras Office of Architects and Designers. Chennai, India, 2009–present

In emerging economies, increased traffic congestion results in lost productivity and negative health impacts, and Chennai, India's fourth largest city, is no exception. Chennai City Connect, with the Institute for Transportation and Development Policy (ITDP) and SMART-University of Michigan, is envisioning a regional transportation plan to ease congestion, designing pilot projects with the Madras Office of Architects and Designers (MOAD). They propose to link surrounding towns and villages to Chennai via a 5,000-square-km (1,900-square-mile) network of transportation corridors. The network connects districts and towns with a growing IT corridor and industrial and economic clusters. The plan incorporates readily available technology and services, optimizes local transport, and does not require governmental policy changes or "mega-sized plans" to streamline implementation.

The pilot projects focus on integrating various modes of transport—pedestrian, bicycle, auto-rickshaw, rail, bus, motorbike, etc. Aiming to reduce private vehicle use in Chennai's central business district, the T Nagar Redevelopment Project, the first of its kind in India, will create new pedestrian zones, reorganize bus routes, and establish mobility hubs for easy transfer from different modes of transportation. Currently, 70% of Chennai's citizens walk, cycle, and commute by bus. The Vadapalani Metro Rail pilot project focuses on improving pedestrian access, bicycle parking, and pick-up/drop-off, for roll out at all thirty-four stations. **CS**

A

A. Map of existing transportation lines and proposed expansion of regional transportation corridors, Chennai, India.
B. Rendering of proposed pedestrian zone for T Nagar Redevelopment Project, Chennai.

C. Multi-modal plan for Vadapalani Metro Rail station, Chennai, India.
D. Motorbikes, motorized rickshaws, cars, bicycles, and pedestrians share congested traffic lanes in Chennai's T Nagar district.

B

METRO STATION

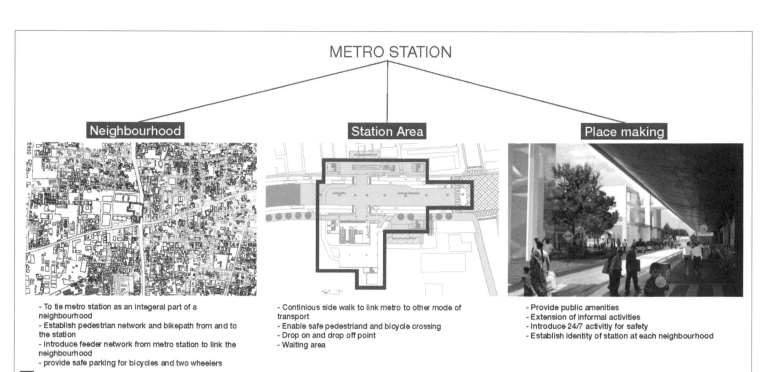

Neighbourhood

- To tie metro station as an integeral part of a neighbourhood
- Establish pedestrian network and bikepath from and to the station
- Introduce feeder network from metro station to link the neighbourhood
- provide safe parking for bicycles and two wheelers

Station Area

- Continious side walk to link metro to other mode of transport
- Enable safe pedestriand and bicycle crossing
- Drop on and drop off point
- Waiting area

Place making

- Provide public amenities
- Extension of informal activities
- Introduce 24/7 activitiy for safety
- Establish identity of station at each neighbourhood

C

D

Digital Drum

Concept: Khalid Arbab, UNICEF; prototype 1: Jean-Marc Lefébure, UNICEF, and Grant Cambridge, Council for Scientific and Industrial Research Meraka; prototype 2: Jean-Marc Lefébure, UNICEF; prototype 3: Seth Herr and Jean-Marc Lefébure, UNICEF. Fabrication: Jean-Marc Lefébure, Grant Cambridge, Emmanuel Ezabo, Seth Herr, Islam Khairul, Cissy Majoli, Malik Abdul, Abdul Ahmed, Francis Ssemukte, Hamid Bbossa, Jacob Odere, Amos Okello, Fred Kiyemba, Charles Mubiru, Fred Ssenyimba, Henry Samula. Partners: UNICEF, Motor Care Clinic Ltd. Kampala, Uganda, 2010–present. Steel oil drum, steel bar stock, steel sheet, threaded bars, Plexiglas, sealant, nuts/bolts, bicycle inner-tube (seal), car inner-tube (laptop fastening), weatherproof keyboard, laptops, solar panel (3x55W), charge controller, battery

Access to information is an important tool in empowering individuals, combating corruption, and promoting good governance in cities experiencing rapid urban migration. The Internet is available in Uganda via mobile phones, yet less than 3% of Ugandans over the age of sixteen use it, compared with 15% in neighboring Kenya. In 2010, UNICEF Uganda representative Sharad Sapra and his team devised a simple, cost-effective way to bridge this digital divide. Inspired by the successful "Digital Doorway" deployed by the Council for Scientific and Industrial Research in South Africa, the creative team developed a rugged solar-powered computer kiosk called the Digital Drum. Built affordably with readily available materials, the first prototype was created in three days in a car-repair shop in Kampala using oil drums, basic angle grinders, and a metal arc welder. Mechanics switched from fixing UNICEF vehicles to working with its engineers to fabricate and weatherproof the keyboards and laptops with inner tubes and sealant.

UNICEF plans more Drums, which will include critical information such as the national education curriculum; school-safety guidelines; and videos on topics such as school lessons, public health, campaigns encouraging girls to stay in school, and efforts to combat widespread teacher absenteeism. UNICEF plans to have local vocational schools manufacture more Drums, and will install them in up to a hundred outdoor locations throughout the country over the next two years, with the eventual goal of making the Drum cheap and easy enough to manufacture for every city and village in Uganda. Once finalized, the Drum's design will be made open-source. Madagascar, Fiji, and the United States have shown early interest. **CS**

A. Wall-mounted Digital Drum at the Treasure Life Youth Centre in Kamwokya, a neighborhood in Kampala, Uganda.
B. Installing a keyboard.
C. Freestanding Digital Drum.
D. Local auto mechanic welding two oil drums together for a Digital Drum, Kampala.

Garden-in-a-Sack

Solidarités International, with community members from Nairobi area settlements. Kibera, Mathare, Kiambiu, and Mukuru Lunga-Lunga informal settlements, Nairobi, Kenya, 2008–present. Empty sugar sack, loamy soil, manure, stones, oil tin, seedlings

When post-election violence erupted in Kenya in 2008, food markets were destroyed and prices soared. In response, Solidarités International, a French NGO, designed Garden-in-a-Sack, a low-cost urban gardening system targeting 20,000 households living in the crowded Nairobi slums of Kibera, Mathare, Kiambiu, and Mukuru Lunga-Lunga. Garden-in-a-Sack is a simple three-step process. The sack gardener fills the base of an empty sugar sack with a mixture of loamy soil and manure. Small stones are placed down the center for proper drainage using a small, empty *kasuku* oil tin. Holes are then cut in the sack for planting kale, spinach, onion, or coriander seedlings. On average, households harvest enough vegetables for four meals per week, improving food security and diet diversification in informal settlements, where food is often more expensive than outside the settlements due to restricted supply.

Having migrated from rural villages, many urban poor possess the skills necessary for urban agriculture. Over 55,000 individuals have become active sack gardeners; and sixty community groups have adopted sack gardening, forty of which are generating modest incomes by selling excess vegetables. Despite challenges posed by limited space, crop and sack damage by animals, pests, and disease, and limited availability to clean soil, manure, seedlings, and water, the sack gardens provide many collateral benefits, such as developing social cohesion and empowering women and marginalized groups. **CS**

A. Settlement micro-farmer with sack gardens overlooking Kibera informal settlement, Nairobi, Kenya.
B. Hand-drawn posters in Kibera instruct users on how to create a sack garden.
C. Garden-in-a-Sack.

A (after)

Guangzhou Bus Rapid Transit System

Design team: Zhang Guangning, former Mayor of Guangzhou, and Su Zequn, Executive Vice Mayor of Guangzhou, The People's Government of Guangzhou Municipality; Guangzhou Municipal Engineering Design & Research Institute, Institute for Transportation and Development Policy, Guangzhou Municipality Construction Commission, Guangzhou Municipality Communications Commission, Guangzhou Traffic Improvement Leading Group Office, Guangzhou Metro Design Institute, and Guangzhou Public Transport Management Office. BRT design consultants: Pedro Szasz, Derek Trusler, Edgar Sandoval, Remi Jeanneret. Guangzhou, China, 2004–10

Guangzhou, one of the fastest growing cities in the world, has gained almost three million inhabitants in the past decade. The resulting increase in traffic congestion led the city and its agencies, including the Guangzhou Metro Design Institute, to design a new high-capacity public-transit system, the Guangzhou Bus Rapid Transit (GBRT), to help cut carbon emissions, reduce gridlock, and reclaim streets and public spaces for residents. Curitiba, Brazil, developed the first Bus Rapid Transit system, and it has spread to Bogotá, Mexico City, Hanoi, Seoul, Istanbul, and more recently to Ahmedabad and Johannesburg.

The GBRT system's ridership of 800,000 a day, second only to Bogotá's Transmilenio, surpasses that of each of the five subway lines. The sustainable system features dedicated bus lanes and infrastructure improvements to move buses 30% faster; intermodal integration with subway lines and a bike-sharing system; and a pre-ticketing smart card, multiple large doors, and flush platforms to reduce boarding time.

GBRT is the first in China to include bike parking in its stations and to connect BRT stations to the subway via tunnels, reducing transfer time. Its twenty-six stations and forty-two bus routes are laid out along Zhongshan Avenue, whose innermost lanes form a 23-kilometer (4.3-mile) dedicated bus corridor linking the city center to the fast-growing eastern section of the city, twenty poorer urban villages, and business and residential areas, meeting the transportation needs for a cross-section of the population. This model high-capacity transportation system, built with minimal infrastructure investment in a short period of time, can be transferred to other locations in China, Asia, and cities around the world as demand for sustainable transportation increases. **CS**

Guangzhou Bus Rapid Transit (BRT) system
and connecting metro lines and bike sharing

B

Legend

🚌 BRT station   BRT corridor

🚲 Bike-sharing station   BRT routes

.5   1   1.5   Metro line

Kilometers

C

D (before)

E

A. Gangding station and
BRT corridor, Guangzhou,
China.
B. Map showing BRT
corridor and stations
with connections to
bike-sharing stations and
subway lines.
C. Station platforms align
with bus floors to enable
rapid boarding.
D. Congestion in
Guangzhou prior to the
BRT system.
E. Bike-share at the
Huajing Xincheng BRT
station.

Health Volunteer (*Shasthya Shebika*) Kit

BRAC. Bangladesh, 1977–present. Medicine, sanitary napkins, delivery kit, soap, salt, registrar, pictorial dosage instructions

BRAC, the world's largest nongovernmental development organization, headquartered in Dhaka, engages a legion of community health volunteers, or *Shasthya Shebikas* in Bangla, to go door to door in slums and villages to disseminate information on prenatal and child care, family planning, immunization, water and sanitation, and personal hygiene and nutrition. Trained to diagnose and treat common ailments such as dysentery and pneumonia, they are at the core of BRAC's Essential Health Care program, which reaches one hundred million people in all fifty-four districts of Bangladesh by expanding basic health services for the poorest and most vulnerable, especially women and children.

The Shasthya Shebika mobile medical kit acts as a portable pharmacy, providing essential medicines, vitamins and minerals, delivery kits, pregnancy tests, sanitary napkins, iodized salt, and soap to families in Dhaka's informal settlements and rural villages. Visiting fifteen households a day, each volunteer generates a modest income from selling medicine and health commodities. Selected by their communities, the more than 85,000 Shasthya Shebikas are the first point of contact between community members and a network of public and private healthcare providers. The successful program has spread from Bangladesh to Afghanistan, Sri Lanka, Pakistan, Uganda, Tanzania, Southern Sudan, Liberia, and Sierra Leone. **CS**

A. A health volunteer with kit, Bangladesh.
B. Health volunteers visit local resident.
C. Over 3,200 Shasthya Shebikas live and work in the informal settlements of Dhaka, Bangladesh.

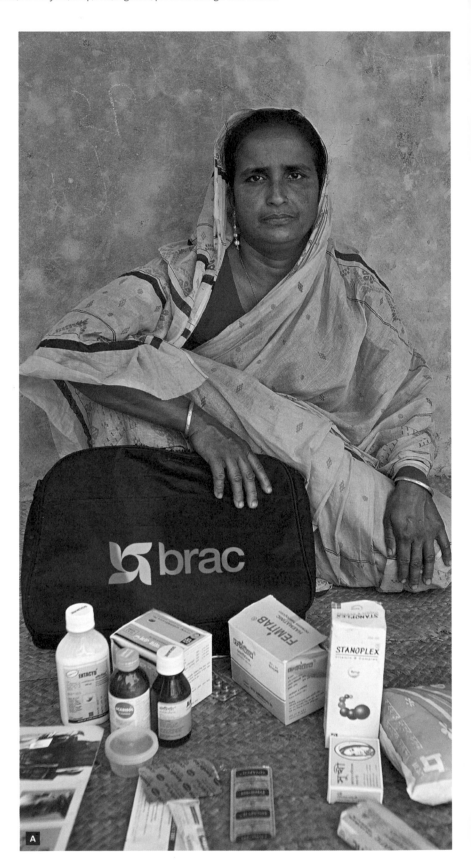

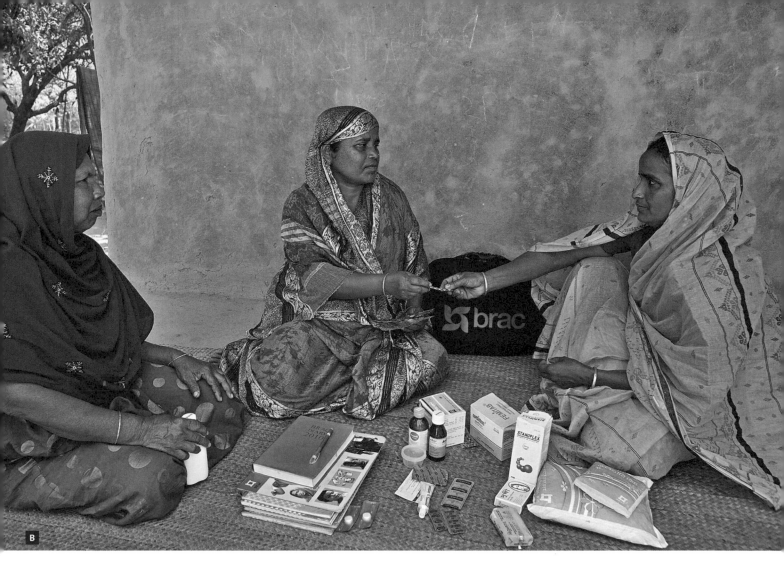

A

Medellín Metrocable and Northeast Integral Urban Project

Metrocable Architects: Edison Escobar and María Patricia Bustamante; technical designers: Bocarejo Engineers, Alpe Etudes, ERIC; equipment design and manufacturer: Pomagalsky; civil work: Conconcreto; installation: Termotécnica. **Integral Urban Project** Architects: Alejandro Echeverri Restrepo, Carlos Mario Rodríguez Osorio, and Carlos Alberto Montoya Correa, with Luis Fernando Arango Arboleda, Eliana Idárraga Castaño, Carmen Elisa Hurtado Figueroa, Esteban Henao, Andrés Benítez Giraldo, Héctor Javier Cruz Londoño, Francesco Maria Orsini, John Octavio Ortiz Lopera, Mauricio Iván Mendoza Martínez, Ana Milena Vergara Monsalve, Oscar Montoya, Diego Armando Pino Pino, Claudia Juliana Portillo Rubio, Carlos David Montoya Valencia, Oscar Mauricio Santana Vélez, and Isabel Arcos Zuluaga; engineer: Cèsar Hernández. Partners: Enterprise for Urban Development, Aburrá Enterprise Limited for Mass Transit, Medellín mayor's office. Medellín, Colombia, 2003–9

Medellín, Colombia, is a tale of two cities: a formal, consolidated city built along a river valley; and a densely populated informal city that grew among the surrounding hillsides. In 1991, Colombia's second largest city was the most violent in the world. By connecting marginalized parts of the city to its safer, more established areas, Medellín's government has transformed it into an inclusive metropolis. Public transportation entwined with social and physical interventions has brought the homicide rate down from a high of 381 to 26 homicides per 100,000 residents in 2007.

Running twenty hours a day, elevated cable cars link remote informal settlements to the central metro system. What could take up to two hours on a crowded minibus now only takes seven minutes. Integral Urban Projects (Proyectos Urbanos Integrales, or PUI) focused the city's resources on specific locations characterized by poverty

and social unrest with a grand vision of providing the best public buildings and transportation system for the poorest parts of the city. The first of four PUI, the project consolidated efforts for eleven Northeast neighborhoods and the construction of a 2-kilometer (1.2-mile) long Metrocable Line K reaching 170,000 residents. Barrio centers were redefined with the location of the cable pylons, adjacent public libraries and parks, and improved streetscapes. The first, Santa Domingo Library and Park, supports library services and created space for recreation and community events. Ten new public schools were built and another 130 were renovated. New pedestrian walkways and bridges unite neighborhoods previously ruled by rival gangs. There is now a greater sense of participation, and residents from the rest of the city visit Santa Domingo and other reclaimed neighborhoods for social outings. **CS**

A. Santa Domingo station, Metrocable Line K, Medellín, Colombia.
B. Parque de los Niños, a newly integrated space between the Metrocable Line K station and Parque Biblioteca España.
C. Granizal sports facility near the Metrocable station and Parque Biblioteca España.
D. The El Mirador footbridge connects the La Francia neighborhood to the Andalucía Metrocable station.
E. Area before upgrading.

B (after)

C

D

E (before)

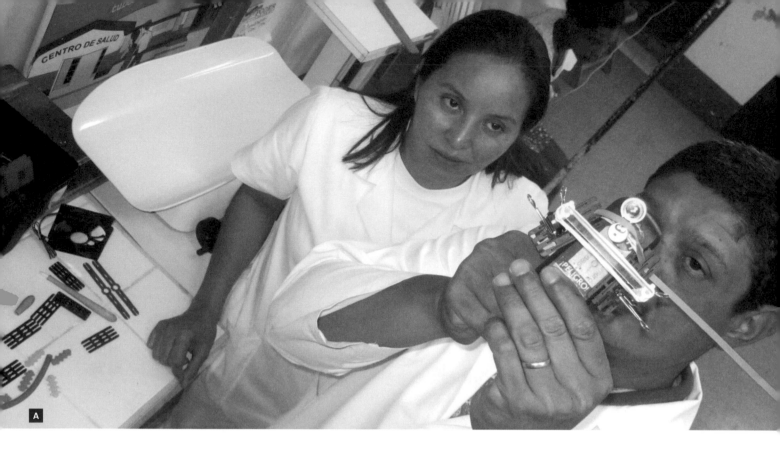

A

MEDIKits

José F. Gómez-Márquez, Anna K. Young, Ryan Scott Bardsley, and Amy B. Smith, Innovations in International Health, Massachusetts Institute of Technology, with Miguel Orozco, Bety Soto, and Ezequiel Provedor, Centro de Estudio de Investigacion de la Salud. Designed United States, Nicaragua, and Ecuador, for use in Managua, Ocotal, and Carazo, Nicaragua, and Quito, Ecuador, 2009–present. Drug Delivery kit: nebulizer, surgical tubing, bike pump, syringes, needles, small surgical tubing; Diagnostics kit: lateral flow strip "puzzle pieces" embedded with reagents, chromatography paper, chemical reagents; Microfluidics kit: glass slides, double-sided tape, transparency sheets (acetate), polydimethylsiloxane (PDMS), scalpels, surgical tubing, syringes, needles, PDMS hole punch, reaction reagents, food dye, test tubes, waste container, microfluidic channel "puzzle pieces", jig. Vital Signs kit: Arduino and MSP430 microcontrollers, optical sensors, buzzers, LCD displays; Agricultural Prosthetic kit: adjustable arm braces, attachable basket, blade, grabber, extender, string, scissors

Ninety-five percent of the medical equipment found in public hospitals in developing countries is imported from the developed world, most of which is quickly rendered useless due to a lack of replacement parts and personnel trained to repair the devices. MEDIKits are medical toolkits that enable healthcare workers in resource-poor communities to develop their own low-cost medical devices from locally available, inexpensive parts. There are currently five versions of the kit available—Drug Delivery, Diagnostics, Microfluidic Blocks, Agricultural Prosthetic, and Vital Signs. The MEDIKit demonstrates to users that even complex devices and tests can be made from affordable component parts and customized to meet their medical needs.

Developed by a team led by José Gómez-Márquez, the MEDIKit empowers users to tinker, hack, modify, and build innovative devices as co-designers. A handheld field microscope attached to a mobile phone enables healthcare workers to take pictures of pathogens and relay images via MMS messages. An alarm for IV bags made from a spring and circuit signals before the bag empties—useful in understaffed health centers, where nurses cannot regularly check bag levels. A nebulizer powered by a bicycle foot pump converts liquid medicine into vapor for easier delivery, particularly for children. Plastic toy helicopters become asthma inhalers, using the propeller as an agitating mechanism. The MEDIKit is leading user-driven, disruptive innovation in some of the world's poorest locations, including Nicaragua and Ecuador. **AL**

A. Medical workers join a field microscope and camera phone with Diagnostics MEDIKit assembly blocks to send images of pathogens for analysis via MMS messages, Ocotal, Nicaragua.
B. Drug Delivery MEDIKit prototype.
C. From the Drug Delivery MEDIKit, a disposable paper spacer to use with inhalers provides an easy and disposable way to get more medication into the lungs.
D. A plastic toy helicopter becomes an inhaler, in which the propeller is used as an agitating mechanism, to help deliver asthma medicine to children.
E. A nurse in Quito, Ecuador, mapping out prototype ideas on a global health innovation compass chart.
F. An abandoned microscope, Trinidad, Nicaragua.

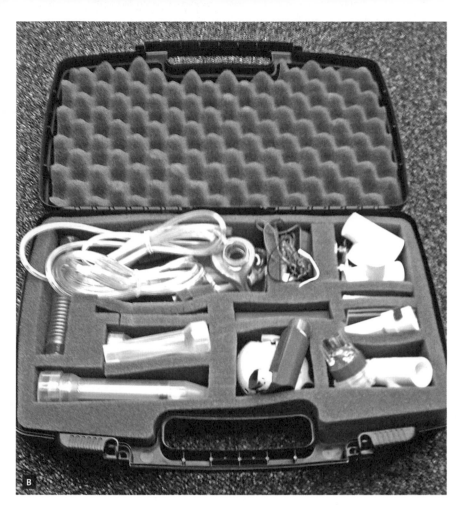

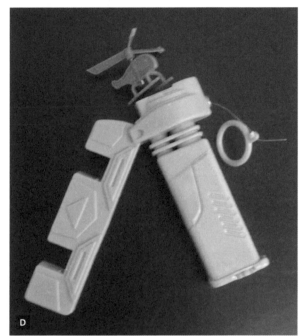

A

Project Masiluleke

Designers: Tony Meredith, Nick De LaMare, Robert Fabricant, Rachel Regina, Yoo-Jung Kim, Sean Lee, Michele Tepper, Jennifer Bettendorff, Ben Fineman, and Allison Conner, frog. Collaborators: iTeach, Praekelt Foundation, Poptech, MTN, Ghetto Ruff. KwaZulu Natal settlement, South Africa, 2007–present. Folded card stock, digital or screen-print graphics, SD Bioline HIV 1/2 3.0 test pouch containing: test device, absorbent packet, Sensa HIV-1/2/0 Tri-lin test pouch containing: test device, absorbent packet, assay dilutant, pipette, lancet, alcohol swab

South Africa has more HIV-positive citizens than any country in the world. The province of KwaZulu Natal is among the most affected, with infection rates of more than 40%. Project Masiluleke (meaning "hope" and "warm counsel" in Zulu) is a collaboration in KwaZulu Natal by the U.S.-based design firm frog, the HIV/TB service organization iTEACH, mobile-based solution incubator Praekelt Foundation, social innovation network PopTech, and telecommunications company MTN South Africa. Since close to 90% of South Africans own a mobile phone, Project Masiluleke uses mobile technology to raise awareness, encourage testing, and guide people into care.

The project's first phase delivered one million "Please Call Me" (PCM) messages a day in local languages, driving users to HIV call centers for information, counseling, and referrals for testing and treatment. The PCM messages—a type of free SMS messaging unique to Africa and primarily used by low-income communities—have resulted in over 1.5 million calls to the country's national AIDS helpline. The project's second phase focuses on delivering testing and counseling services in people's homes, encouraging earlier diagnosis and treatment. The free HIV self-testing kit features simple instructions that rely on minimal literacy and provides a message of health and wellness. Its components can be easily assembled, enabling a scalable solution. The kit includes a number to free counseling that supports the testing process and diagnosis. **AL**

**A. A blood-based HIV self-testing kit prototype.
B. Step-by-step kit instructions (also available in Zulu).
C. A resident tests the prototype's instructions, KwaZulu Natal, South Africa.**

SET UP

① Look for these items inside your test kit.
You should also have a cellphone available.

HIV Test · HIV Test · Test Strips (2) · Alcohol Swab · Lancet · Solution · Pipette · Cellphone

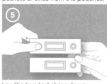

② Tear open the test strip pouches.

③ Remove the test strips and small packets of silica from the pouches.

④ Throw away the small silica packets.

⑤ Lay the two test strips down on a flat, clean surface.

TEST

⑥ Open the alcohol swab packet. Use the swab to clean your finger.

⑦ Twist off the cap of the lancet and prick your cleaned fingertip.

⑧ Draw blood from your fingertip with the pipette.

⑨ Squeeze a drop of blood into the sample well of each test strip.

⑩ Squeeze four drops of solution onto both blood samples.

⑪ Wait 10 minutes, then read the results. Do not wait longer than 15 minutes.

RESULTS

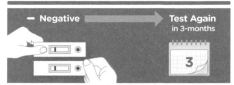

– Negative → Test Again in 3-months

If both test strips have 1 line, you tested HIV-negative.
Questions? Please call **079 876 7782**

+ Positive → Go to Clinic get a CD4 count

If both test strips have 2 (or 3) lines, you tested HIV-positive.
Please call **079 876 7782**

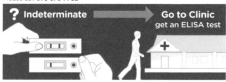

? Indeterminate → Go to Clinic get an ELISA test

If the number of lines on the test strips do not match, or you are confused:
Please call **079 876 7782**

B

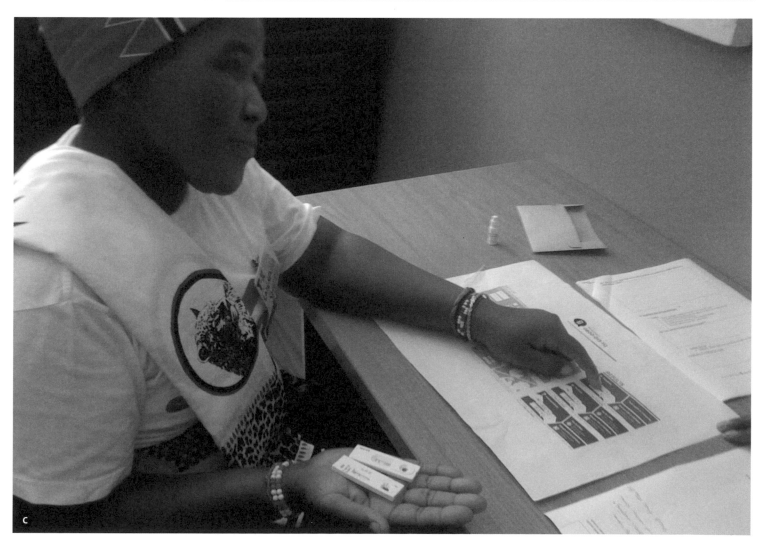

C

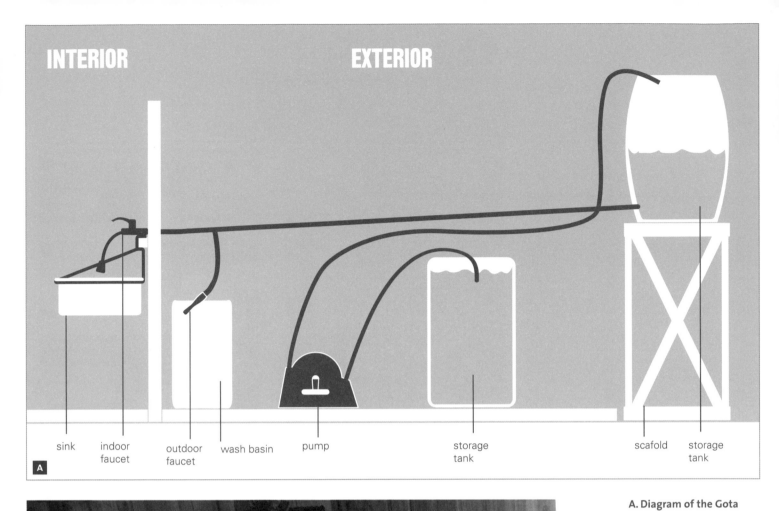

INTERIOR

EXTERIOR

sink | indoor faucet | outdoor faucet | wash basin | pump | storage tank | scaffold | storage tank

A

B

A. Diagram of the Gota a Gota gravity-fed water system.
B. Art Center College of Design students Stella Hernandez and Jaqueline Black conduct field research with resident, Mireya, Campamento Fundo, San José, Chile.
C. Typical water storage barrels outside a dwelling in Campamento San José.
D. Indoor faucet with flexible nozzle.

Safe Agua Water System

Penny Herscovitch, Dan Gottlieb, and Liliana Becerra, Designmatters, Art Center College of Design; Gota a Gota designers: Stella Hernandez, Nubia Mercado, and Diane Jie Wei. Relava designers: K. C. Cho, Jacqueline Black. Collaborators: Un Techo para Mi País Social Innovation Center, Campamento San José community. Santiago, Chile (prototype Pasadena, CA), 2008–present. Gota a Gota: plastic barrel, wood frame, hose, injection-molded plastic faucets, ABS plastic faucets, bicycle parts; Relava: powder-coated wire frame, plastic tubs, drain connector

For residents of Chile's *campamentos* (informal communities), running water is a luxury few can afford. Instead, families, and particularly women, expend tremendous energy, effort, and time carrying large containers of water to complete daily tasks—washing dishes and laundry, cooking, and cleaning. To resolve this, a team of faculty and students from the Designmatters program at Art Center College of Design collaborated with the Chilean NGO Un Techo para Mi País and local community members to develop a gravity-fed water system called *Gota a Gota* ("drop by drop"). Water collected in an elevated storage tank flows down a hose to indoor and outdoor faucets that have flexible nozzles and on/off handles. But to get water up to the elevated storage tank, the team included a foot pump, easy enough for women, children, and the elderly to operate, that moves water from a ground-level tank.

To conserve water and provide a dedicated kitchen workstation, another team developed the Relava sink for use at the indoor faucet, allowing women to wash dishes with more efficiency and dignity. It repurposes two affordable 16-liter plastic tubs as wash and rinse basins, held by a collapsible wire frame that hangs from the wall. For those in the campamentos, these solutions help relieve the burden of living without running water and improve their quality of life. **AL**

C

D

A

School on Wheels

Designer: Door Step School. Pune, India, 2000–present

India's rapidly expanding urban areas rely on migrant workers to build new developments. As each new construction project begins, informal temporary settlements are erected for the workers and their families, who move to and from sites based on the job's requirements. For the underprivileged children of these workers, even a basic education is difficult to come by. Many are not enrolled in school, and for those who are, high drop-out rates and low attendance are common. The children move when their parents move, and few have access to books or a place to study. The Door Step School brings quality education to these children with innovative programs that accommodate their transient lives. The School on Wheels is a bus equipped as a classroom that picks children up daily from settlements. It provides a stable setting in which students learn basic literacy and arithmetic skills, and ensures regular attendance. Buses can accommodate up to twenty-five children; there are two buses currently in operation in Pune and four in Mumbai.

When children move, it is difficult to track them and ensure they continue to receive an education. MyBook eases these efforts with another simple solution—providing students with a handbook to take with them when they are next uprooted. All children in the Door Step School's various projects are given a MyBook, in which teachers maintain a record of the student's academic progress. Importantly, it contains a list of phone numbers to free education centers in the city. The books are intended to help children learn with as much continuity as possible. **AL**

A. A School on Wheels classroom, Bavdhan, Pune, India.
B. School on Wheels.
C. MyBook card with contact information in Marathi and English.

212

SONO Water Filter

Abul Hussam, Center for Clean Water and Sustainable Technologies, Department of Chemistry and Biochemistry, George Mason University, and Abul K. M. Munir, Manob Sakti Unnayan Kendro. Bangladesh, Nepal, and India, 1999–present. Sand, composite iron matrix, wood charcoal, brick chips, plastic buckets, tubing, metal

Arsenic, a deadly poison abundant in Bangladesh's soil and rock, has leached up through the water table into wells across the country, exposing an estimated seventy-five to ninety-five million people, including thirty-five million children. Major portions of northern India, where five hundred million people live, may also be affected by arsenic and other groundwater contaminants. The World Health Organization has called it "the largest mass poisoning of a population in history," bigger than the accidents at Bhopal and Chernobyl.

Abul Hussam, a chemistry professor from George Mason University, designed SONO water filter, an inexpensive method to filter drinking water, developing the active material, a composite iron matrix (CIM) absorbant. The low-cost, two-bucket system strains contaminated groundwater through sand, the CIM, charcoal, and brick chips to remove toxins, producing potable water. More than

225,000 SONO water filters, at a cost of US$35, have been distributed in Bangladesh, Nepal, and India. Production started in 1999 in Bangladesh by the nonprofit Manob Sakti Unnayan Kendro (MSUK), which manufactures and distributes SONO in Bangladesh and India; the NGO Filter for Families produces them in Nepal. Quality control and technical details are handled by SONO Technology and Research in Bangladesh. SONO and MSUK buy back and recycle spent composite iron matrix.

Test results indicate SONO can remove arsenic, manganese (a neurotoxin), iron, and all transition metal ions. Filters can last at least fourteen years at the present usage rate of one hundred liters per day, sufficient for a family of five. SONO has made larger filters to clean a hundred liters an hour for community and semi-commercial use; smaller tabletop units are also under development. **CS**

A. Children get clean drinking water from the SONO water filter, Naltona, Barguna district, Bangladesh.
B. Woman pours groundwater into the SONO, Naltona.
C. Schematic diagram of the two-bucket filter.
D. Distribution of the SONO, Paurashava, Kushtia district, Bangladesh.

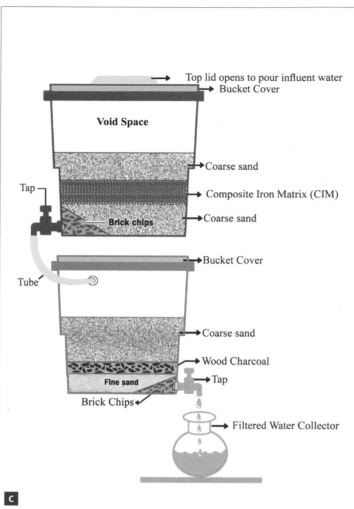

Top lid opens to pour influent water
Bucket Cover

Void Space

Coarse sand

Composite Iron Matrix (CIM)

Coarse sand

Brick chips

Tap

Bucket Cover

Tube

Coarse sand

Wood Charcoal

Fine sand

Brick Chips

Tap

Filtered Water Collector

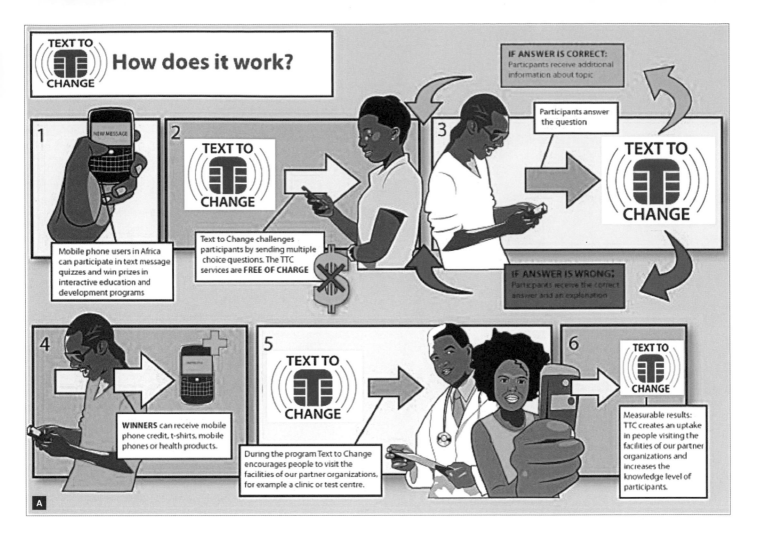

How does it work?

1 Mobile phone users in Africa can participate in text message quizzes and win prizes in interactive education and development programs

2 Text to Change challenges participants by sending multiple choice questions. The TTC services are FREE OF CHARGE

3 Participants answer the question

IF ANSWER IS CORRECT: Participants receive additional information about topic

IF ANSWER IS WRONG: Participants receive the correct answer and an explanation

4 WINNERS can receive mobile phone credit, t-shirts, mobile phones or health products.

5 During the program Text to Change encourages people to visit the facilities of our partner organizations, for example a clinic or test centre.

6 Measurable results: TTC creates an uptake in people visiting the facilities of our partner organizations and increases the knowledge level of participants.

A

Text to Change

Founders: Bas Hoefman, Hajo van Beijma. Uganda, 2007. SMS Behavioral Change campaign designers: Bas Hoefman, Hajo van Beijma. Partners: Aids Information Center, Airtel Uganda. Mbarara, Uganda, 2008

People in Africa often lack access to basic healthcare information, and while nongovernmental organizations organize media campaigns to increase visits to health facilities, they fall short. Since over 70% of the world's five billion mobile-phone users live in emerging and developing countries, Dutch communication and technology specialists Bas Hoefman and Hajo van Beijma, cofounders of the nonprofit Text to Change, realized mobile phones could provide an easy and low-cost method for health communication and data collection. They launched SMS Behavioral Change, the first large-scale, interactive educational text-message campaign in Africa.

SMS Behavioral Change, an incentive-based mHealth (or mobile health) education program, focused on AIDS awareness in Mbarara, Uganda, in 2008. Inspired by a documentary on the growth of mobile-phone use in Africa and aware of the HIV/AIDS pandemic on the continent—370 people are infected every day in Uganda alone—Hoefman partnered with a Dutch epidemiologist and the African mobile-service provider Airtel (formerly

Celtel), which sent messages at reduced rates, to increase voluntary counseling and testing at Uganda's AIDS Information Centers (AIC). Participants received via free text message a multiple-choice HIV/AIDS awareness quiz on their mobile phone; if they answered correctly, they were sent more information about the topic. The quiz winner received a mobile phone, phone credit, or other incentives and was encouraged to visit a clinic or test center. After the first campaign reached 15,000 participants, AIC experienced a 40% increase in visits for testing, and it was repeated in 2009 in the city of Arua.

Text to Change partners with national governments, United Nations agencies, mobile-communication providers, for-profit companies, and NGOs to design free, accessible health, education, economic-development, and transparency programs that aim to effect change through customized information and services. Their numerous projects have also addressed child trafficking in Uganda, Kenya, Tanzania, Cameroon, Namibia, and Bolivia, expanding to twelve more countries in 2011. **CS**

A. Poster of Text to Change mobile health text-message campaign.
B–D. Mobile phone kiosks throughout urban Uganda.
E. Text to Change quiz on mobile phone.

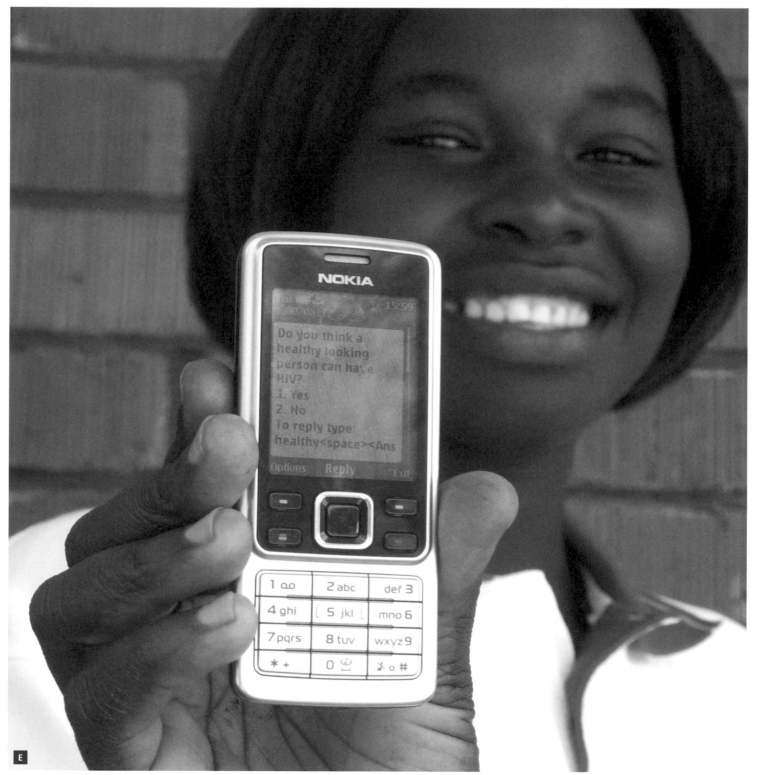

MAPPING PUBLIC TOILETS *in* DIEPSLOOT TOWNSHIP

TOILET CONDITION KEY

💧	✚	◑	⊗	●
leaking	*structural issues*	*one of two toilets is working*	*neither toilet is working*	*upgraded toilet or drain*

B

JOHANNESBURG

C

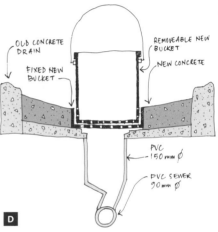

OLD CONCRETE DRAIN
REMOVEABLE NEW BUCKET
FIXED NEW BUCKET
NEW CONCRETE
PVC ·150 mm ∅
PVC SEWER 90 mm ∅

D

WASSUP (Water, Amenities and Sanitation Services Upgrade Project)

Initiated by Anna Rubbo, Global Studio–University of Sydney, with Jennifer van den Bussche, Ida Breed, Anne Fitchett, Daniel Griffin, Minna Ninova, Samuel Sikhosana, Mark Tyrrell, and Diepsloot settlement community. Collaborators: Sticky Situations, Johannesburg Department of Planning, University of the Witwatersrand. Diepsloot, Johannesburg, South Africa, 2007–present. Bucket drain: cement, sand, buckets; tap and toilet upgrades: plastic taps, plastic cisterns, ceramic pans, other plumbing parts, tools, paint, brushes, plastic or cardboard stencils

Global Studio, spearheaded in 2004 by the UN Millennium Project Task Force on Improving the Lives of Slum Dwellers and developed by the University of Sydney, Columbia University, and the University of Rome, serves as a model for community development and urban design, with five hundred participants from sixty-six universities in thirty-six countries since 2005. WASSUP emerged in 2007 from a collaboration between Global Studio and Diepsloot residents in the city of Johannesburg, the University of the Witwatersrand, the Johannesburg Department of Planning, and local community developers Sticky Situations.

Diepsloot was established in 1994 as a relocation site for families removed from other informal settlements, many of them immigrants from other African countries. Over 60% of the 150,000–170,000 residents are under- or unemployed. Over 70% live in shacks, under the poverty line, and share prefabricated toilet facilities and water

standpipes. Despite challenging conditions, a 2007 survey showed that 98% of Diepsloot's residents did not want to move away from its vibrant informal economy and energetic culture.

Focusing on environmental upgrades, public health, and safety measures, the designers and residents used GIS technology to map and fix toilets; developed a system to fix leaking drains; and piloted a new rubbish-collection system. WASSUP grew out of these efforts. Easy solutions such as stenciled instructions and the design of a new bucket drain system began to address the problems. A new artist network and local children celebrated by painting the forty-six newly upgraded toilets. The branding of WASSUP, now a business cooperative, created further local recognition, encouraged community involvement, and reduced vandalism. **CS**

A. Local children paint an upgraded toilet facility, Diepsloot, Johannesburg, South Africa.
B. GIS map locating every toilet facility and its condition, Diepsloot.
C. Blocked drain and leaking toilet prior to upgrade.
D. Section diagram of bucket drain system.

A

Water for Low-income Communities (*Tubig Para sa Barangay*) Program

Designers: Manila Water Company, with Manila-area informal settlement community. Metro East Zone, Manila, Philippines, 1998–present. High-density polyethylene and steel pipes, small- and large-diameter valves, brass and galvanized-iron fittings, bolts, nuts, bollards, board-ups, pumps, motors, water meters, generator sets

In the Philippines, over half of its citizens live on less than two dollars a day. In Manila, 90% have difficulty making ends meet. In 1997, only 26% had access to affordable and clean tap water; others were left to pay high prices to water vendors, queue for hours at public faucets and community wells, or tap illegal connections. Those in informal settlements were unable to apply for regular water connections because they lacked proof of land ownership.

Manila Water, a private utility, designed the innovative *Tubig Para Sa Barangay* service, which enables marginalized households to connect to a piped-in water supply. To accommodate the ill-defined streets and dense makeshift housing, an underground water pipe was brought to the settlement and connected to a cluster of meters. Inhabitants made their own connections and were given thirty-six months to pay a subsidized fee to cover the cost

of their household's pipes and individual meter. Water costs were one-fifth of what they paid before, and reduced contamination resulted in an 80% drop in diarrhea cases.

To ensure that the most marginalized could continue to afford water, Manila Water promoted health and sanitation programs and formed partnerships with community cooperatives to manufacture materials for the water supply. The water utility built strong partnerships, the "*ka-sangga*" (partner) system: the local government eased land-title requirements; community leaders assisted with connection applications and explained the project to other residents, who in turn protected the new infrastructure; and investors and lenders provided financial assistance for sustained delivery of this basic need. **CS**

A. Clustered meters, Manila, Philippines.
B. Unsanitary conditions prior to upgrading, Barangay Pag-asa informal settlement, Binangonan, Rizal province, Philippines.
C. Laying pipes, Binangonan.
D. A boy showers with water from an individual house pipe, Baybay Sapa informal settlement, Antipolo City, Rizal province.
E. A clustered metering diagram shows the current system design. Official household meters are clustered on the street, and low-income residents are individually billed, making consumption easier to monitor.

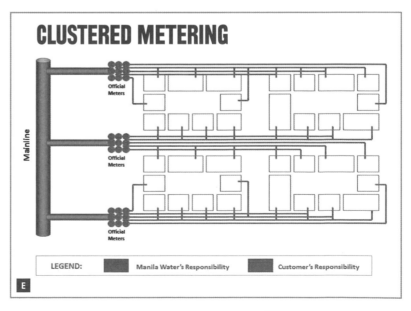

CLUSTERED METERING

Mainline

Official Meters

Official Meters

Official Meters

LEGEND: Manila Water's Responsibility   Customer's Responsibility

For more information on *Design with the Other 90%: CITIES* and to contribute to the Design Other 90 Network, visit www.cooperhewitt.org/other90.

SELECTED BIBLIOGRAPHY

Bicknell, Jane, David Dodman, and David Satterthwaite, eds. *Adapting Cities to Climate Change: Understanding and Addressing the Development Challenges*. London: Earthscan, 2009.

Bornstein, David. *How to Change the World: Social Entrepreneurs and the Power of New Ideas*. Oxford: Oxford University Press, 2004.

Brand, Stewart. *Whole Earth Discipline: An Ecopragmatist Manifesto*. New York: Viking, 2009.

Brillembourg, Alfredo, Kristin Reireiss, and Hubert Klumpner. *Informal City: Caracas Case*. Munich: Prestel, 2005.

Brugmann, Jeb. *Welcome to the Urban Revolution: How Cities Are Changing the World*. New York: Bloomsbury Press, 2009.

Burdett, Ricky, and Deyan Sudjic, eds. *The Endless City*. London: Phaidon Press, 2007.

———, eds. *Living in the Endless City: The Urban Age Project by the London School of Economics and Deutsche Bank's Alfred Herrhausen Society*. London: Phaidon Press, 2011.

Charlesworth, Esther, ed. *Cityedge: Case Studies in Contemporary Urbanism*. Burlington: Architectural Press, 2005.

Correa, Charles. *Housing & Urbanisation*. Bombay: Urban Design Research Institute, 1999.

Davis, Mike. *Planet of Slums*. London: Verso, 2007.

Dobson, Richard, Corline Skinner, and Jillian Nicholson. *Working in Warwick: Including Street Traders in Urban Plans*. Durban: School of Development Studies, University of KwaZulu-Natal, 2009.

Douala in Translation: A View of the City and Its Creative Transformative Potentials. Rotterdam: Episode Publishers, 2007.

Eriksson, Hans. *Evaluations of Urban Observatories in Francophone Africa*. Dakar: ENDA, 2006.

Ernsten, Christian, Tess Broekmans, Sjoerd Feenstra, and Gert Urhahn, eds. *The Spontaneous City*. Amsterdam: BIS Publishers, 2010.

Faris, Stephan. *Forecast: The Surprising—and Immediate—Consequences of Climate Change*. New York: Holt Paperbacks, 2009.

Farmer, Paul, and Amartya Sen. *Pathologies of Power: Health, Human Rights, and the New War on the Poor*. Berkeley: University of California Press, 2005.

Garau, Pietro, Elliott D. Sclar, and Gabriella Y. Carolina. *A Home in the City: UN Millennium Project, Task Force on Improving the Lives of Slum Dwellers*. London: Earthscan, 2005.

Glaeser, Edward. *Triumph of the City: How Our Greatest Invention Makes Us Richer, Smarter, Greener, Healthier, and Happier*. New York: Penguin Press, 2011.

Informal Toolbox: Slum Lab Paraisópolis. São Paulo: Prefeitura da Cidade de São Paulo, 2008.

Jégou, François, and Ezio Manzini. *Collaborative Services: Social Innovation and Design for Sustainability*. Milan: POLI.design, 2009.

Lantz, Maria, and Jonatan Habib Engqvist, eds. *Dharavi: Documenting Informalities*. Stockholm: Royal University College of Fine Art, 2008.

Levine, Ruth, et al. *Millions Saved: Proven Successes in Global Health*. Washington, D.C.: Center for Global Development, 2004.

Managing Asian Cities: Sustainable and Inclusive Urban Solutions. Philippines: Asian Development Bank, 2008.

Meadows, Donella, Jorgen Randers, and Dennis Meadows. *Limits to Growth: The 30 Year Update*. Vermont: Chelsea Green, 2004.

Meyer, Han, Dale Morris, and David Waggonner, eds. *Dutch Dialogues: New Orleans/Netherlands: Common Challenges in Urbanized Deltas*. Amsterdam: SUN, 2009

Moreno, Eduardo López. *UN-Habitat: State of the World's Cities 2008/2009: Harmonious Cities*. London: Earthscan, 2008.

Moreno, Eduardo López, Oyebanji Oyeyinka, and Gora Mboup. *UN-Habitat: State of the World's Cities 2010/2011: Bridging the Urban Divide*. London: Earthscan, 2008.

Moyo, Dambisa. *Dead Aid: Why Aid Is Not Working and How There Is a Better Way for Africa*. New York: Farrar, Straus and Giroux, 2009.

Neuwirth, Robert. *Shadow Cities: A Billion Squatters, a New Urban World*. New York: Routledge, 2006.

Nierenberg, Danielle, Molly O'Meara Sheehan, and Linda Starke. *State of the World: Our Urban Future: A Worldwatch Institute Report on Progress Toward a Sustainable Society*. New York: Worldwatch Institute and W. W. Norton, 2007.

Otter, Steve. *Khayelitsha: uMlungu in a Township*. South Africa: Penguin, 2007.

Peirce, Neal R., Curtis W. Johnson, and Farley M. Peters. *Century of the City: No Time to Lose*. New York: Rockefeller Foundation, 2008.

Pieterse, Edgar, ed. *Counter-Currents: Experiments in Sustainability in the Cape Town Region*. Auckland Park: Jacana Media and African Centre for Cities, University of Cape Town, 2010.

A Place to Be Free: A Case Study of the Freedom Park Informal Settlement Upgrade. Cape Town: Development Action Group, 2009.

Prahalad, C. K. *The Fortune at the Bottom of the Pyramid: Eradicating Poverty Through Profits*. Upper Saddle River, NJ: Wharton School Publishing, 2005.

PUKAR, ed. *Mumbai's Barefoot Researchers*. Mumbai: Partners for Urban Knowledge, Action, and Research, 2009.

Rieniets, Tim, Jennifer Sigler, and Kees Christiaanse, eds. *Open City: Designing Coexistence*. Amsterdam: SUN, 2009.

Sassen, Saskia. *Cities in a World Economy*, 4th ed. Newbury Park, CA: Sage, 2011.

Satterthwaite, David, and Gordon McGranahan, eds. *UN-Habitat: Meeting Development Goals in Small Urban Centres: Water and Sanitation in the World's Cities*. London: Earthscan, 2006.

Sen, Amartya. *Development as Freedom*. New York: Alfred A. Knopf, 1999.

Smillie, Ian. *Freedom from Want: The Remarkable Success Story of BRAC, the Global Grassroots Organization that's Winning the Fight Against Poverty*. Sterling, VA: Kumerian Press, 2009.

Werthmann, Christian, ed. *Tactical Operations in the Informal City: The Case of Cantinho Do Céu*. São Paulo: Secretaria Municipal de Habitação, 2009.

Yunus, Muhammed. *Banker to the Poor: Micro-lending and the Battle Against World Poverty*. New York: Public Affairs, 1999.

SELECTED INDEX

Bold denotes project names.

10x10 Sandbag House, 124–25
28 Millimetres: Women Are Heroes, 140–41
Abalimi Bezekhaya, 94–99, 186–87
Adeya, Arthur, 170
AIDS Information Centers (Uganda), 216
Airtel Uganda, 216
Ali, Zehra, 135
Angélil, Marc, 138
Angola, 108
Aravena, Alejandro, 118
Archer, James Howard, 164–65
Argentina, 108
    Buenos Aires, 22–23, 26, 54–59, 108, 122–23, 160–61
Arputham, Jockin, 32–39, 108
Art Center College of Design, 210–11
Asian Coalition for Housing Rights (ACHR), 61, 70
Asrilant, Viviana, 122
Babajob.com, 176–77
Bamboo (*Tacuara*) Loofah Panels, 132–33
Baandhani Federation, 150
Bang Bua Canal Community Upgrading, 114–15
Bangladesh, 4, 22, 154–55, 202–3, 214–15
    Dhaka, 15, 16, 21, 24, 84, 172–73, 202–3
Base ECTA, 132
Becerra, Liliana, 211
bePRO Motor-taxi Helmet, 188–89
Bekinschtein, Eduardo, 160
Bicycle Phone Charger, 190–91
BioCentre, 27, 192–93
Black, Jacqueline, 211
Blagsvedt, Sean Olin, 176
Bolivia, 108–9, 216
Bolnick, Joel, 108
Boonyabancha, Somsook, 60–71
Boye, Marianne Godding, 188
BRAC, 21, 172, 202
Brazil, 15, 19, 21, 22, 28, 29, 38, 49, 108, 200
    Diadema, 8, 16, 49, 166–67

Rio de Janeiro, 8, 21, 140–41, 148–49, 179
São Paulo, 8, 19, 27–28, 49, 80, 138–39
Brillembourg, Alfredo, 174
Bussche, Jennifer van den, 219
Calcagno, Lucía E., 160
Cambodia, 22, 108
Cambridge, Grant, 196
Cantagallo, *see* Lima, Peru
Caracas Mejoramiento de Barrios, 156
CID Consulting, 18, 113
Center for Future Civic Media, 142
Center for Urban and Regional Excellence (CURE), 17, 18, 130
Chazali, Syammahfuz, 134
Chennai City Connect, 194
Chennai Sustainable Transportation Network, 194–95
Chile, 4, 22, 26, 43
    Iquique, 44, 118–19
    Santiago, 210–11
Chimalhuacan Municipality, *see* Mexico City, Mexico
China, 4, 21, 41, 200
    Guangzhou, 28, 200–1
Cho, K. C., 211
Colombia, 19, 108
    Bogotá, 49, 80, 86, 200
    Medellín, 17, 42–43, 49, 50, 80, 81, 82, 86, 204–5
Community Cooker (*Jiko ya Jamii*), 23, 25, 29, 164–65
Community Organizations Development Institute (CODI), 29, 67, 69, 114
Community Organization Resource Centre (CORC), 111
COOPA-ROCA collective, 29, 179
Cristal de Luz, 178–79
Dala, 184
d'Cruz, Celine, 108
Filippi, José de, Jr., 166
Design Home Solutions, 120
Design Indaba, 124
Design With Africa: Bicycle Modules, 26, 116–17
Design Without Borders, 188

DesignSpace Africa, 124
Diadema Reurbanization, 166–67
Diepsloot informal settlement, *see* Johannesburg, South Africa
Digital Drum, 100–5, 196–97
Dipankar, Aditya, 176
Dobson, Richard, 180
Door Step School, 212
Dot Dot Dot Ex Why Zed (...XYZ) Design, 26, 116
DRC (Democratic Republic of the Congo), 108
East Timor, 108
EcoFaeBrick, 134
Ecuador, 22, 206–7
    Quito, 206–7
Egypt, 108, 182
    Cairo, 18, 113
Elemental, 26, 43, 118–19
Environment and Development Action (ENDA), 29, 162
ETH Zürich, 138
eThekwini Municipality, *see* Durban, South Africa
Fabricant, Robert, 208
Federation of the Urban and Rural Poor (FEDUP), 111
Ferrario, Marco, 120
Floating Community Lifeboats, 6, 154–55
Freedom Park, *see* Cape Town, South Africa
Frog, 208
Garden-in-a-Sack, 198–99
George Mason University, 214
Ghana, 102, 108
Ghonsla Insulation Panels, 135
Global Cycle Solutions, 190
Global Studio, 219
Gómez-Márquez, José F., 206
Gottlieb, Dan, 211
Grassroots Mapping, 142–43
GroundTruth Initiative, 24, 146
Guangzhou Bus Rapid Transit System, 28, 200–1
Gupta, Nandita, 130
Gwiba, Moses, 184–85
Haas&Hahn, 21, 22, 148

Hagen, Erica, 146
Haiti, 76, 85, 108, 170
Harvard Graduate School of Design, 79, 86, 144
Health Volunteer (*Shasthya Shebika*) Kit, 202–3
Hehl, Rainer, 138
Heliópolis, *see* São Paulo, Brazil
Hernandez, Stella, 210, 211
Herr, Seth, 196
Herscovitch, Penny, 211
Hoefman, Bas, 216
Homeless People's Federation, 110
Honduras, 108
Hussam, Abul, 214
Incremental Housing, 4, 43–44, 118–19
India, 19, 21, 22, 33, 36, 38, 108, 112, 120, 134, 135,
    150, 176, 182, 190, 212, 214
    Ahmedabad, 28
    Bangalore, 38, 176
    Chennai, 28, 194–95
    Delhi, 17, 18, 120
    Kolkata, 84
    Mumbai, 17, 19, 25, 32, 34
    New Delhi, 120–21, 130–31
    Pune, 25, 34, 52, 112, 212–13
    Sangli, 150
    Surat City, 16
Indira Nagar, *see* Sangli, India
Indonesia, 23, 70, 108, 134
Informal Settlement World Map, 144–45
Innovations in International Health, MIT, 206
Institute for Transportation and Development Policy,
    194, 200
Integral Urban Project, 42, 50, 204
Interlocking Stabilized Soil Blocks (ISSB), 136–37
International Design Development Summit (IDDS),
    190
iTeach, 208
iTRUMP: Warwick Junction, 40, 47, 48, 180–81
Jahangeer, Doung Anwar, 184
Jamii Bora Trust, 26, 168
Jamil, Eleena, 158

Japan, 22, 152
JR, 53, 140–41
Kaba, Christina, 94–99, 186
Kabir, Khondaker Hasibul, 172
Kaputiei New Town, 12, 26, 168–69
Kenya, 4, 6, 22, 24, 182–83, 192–93
    Kisaju, 12, 26, 168–69
    Nairobi, 4, 23–27, 47, 53, 74, 75, 76, 100, 141, 146–
    47, 164–65, 168, 170–71, 183, 192–93, 198–99
Khayelitsha informal settlement, *see* Cape Town,
    South Africa
Khosla, Renu, 130
Kibera informal settlement, *see* Nairobi, Kenya
Kibera Public Space Project, 170–71
Kiwia, Bernard, 190–91
Klumpner, Hubert, 174
Koolhaas, Jeroen, *see* Haas&Hahn
Korail, *see* Dhaka, Bangladesh
Kounkuey Design Initiative, 170
KwaZulu Natal settlement, 208–9
Leal, Maria Teresa Tetê, 179
Lefébure, Jean-Marc, 196
Liberia, 108, 202
Lipps, Andrea, 4, 120, 124, 128, 132, 134, 136, 141, 142,
    144, 160, 162, 166, 168, 176, 179, 206, 208, 211, 212
Luhrmann, Fiona, 144
Mahila Milan, 25, 32–33, 34, 36, 39, 52, 69–70, 108,
    112
Make a House Intelligent, 126–27
Makerere University, 188
Malawi, 76, 108
Mangolpuri slum resettlement colony, *see* New Delhi,
    India
Manila Water Company, 220–21
Map Kibera, 24, 75, 146–47
Maron, Mikel, 146
Massachusetts Institute of Technology (MIT), 19, 77,
    142, 190, 206
Mathare informal settlement, *see* Nairobi, Kenya
**Medellín Metrocable and Northeast Integral Urban
    Project**, 204–5

MEDIKits, 206–7
Mehra, Rakhi, 120
Mercado, Nubia, 211
micro Home Solutions, 120–21
Millennium School Bamboo Project, 17, 158–59
Miraculous Hills Community Resettlement, 25, 110
Modular Homeless Shelter, 120–21
Moladi, 128
Morro da Providência, *see* Rio de Janeiro, Brazil
Mozambique, 108, 128
M-PESA Money-transfer System, 6, 73, 182–83
Mpahlwa, Luyanda, 124
Mpahlwa, Uli, 124
Mulder, Roelf, *see* Dot Dot Dot Ex Why Zed Design
Munir, Abul K. M., 214
Munyanya, Mohammed K., 168
Musaazi, Moses Kizza, 136–37
Musuva, Mumo, 164
My Shelter Foundation, 16, 158
Namibia, 108, 128, 216
National Slum Dwellers' Federation (NSDF), 32–39,
    112
Nepal, 23, 108, 214
Nicaragua, 206–7
Nigeria, 73, 108
Odbert, Chelina, 170
Olsen, Kristoffer Leivestad, 188
Omotto, Josiah, 192
Oxfam, 192
Packages, 135
Pakistan, 23, 108, 135, 202
    Karachi, 70
    Lahore, 135
Paraguay, 132–33
Patel, Sheela, 7, 32–39, 108
Patron, Domingo Pablo Risso, 160
Payatas Scavenger's Homeowner Association, 24, 110
Philippi Township, *see* Cape Town, South Africa
Philippine Action for Community-led Shelter
    Initiatives, 110
Philippines, 16, 19, 70, 108, 110, 158–59, 220

Camarines-Sur, 17, 158–59
Manila, 4, 6, 24, 26, 220–21
Quezon City, 110
Pieterse, Edgar, 6, 40–53
Planning Systems Services, 164
Plastic Formwork System, 128–29
Platform of Hope (*Ashar Macha*), 20, 21, 172–73
Pocket Reconstruction, 130–31
Praça Cantão, Favela Painting Project, 148–49
Prasanna Desai Architects, 112
Project Masiluleke, 208–9
Proyecto Rehabitar, 160–61
Proyectos Arqui5 C.A, 16, 156
Qually, Byron, *see* Dot Dot Dot Ex Why Zed Design
Randall, Elizabeth, 144
Reali, Mario Wilson Pedreira, 166
Relay for Participatory Urban Development, 162
Restrepo, Alejandro Echeverri, 204
Rezwan, Mohammed, 154
Rocinha, *see* Rio de Janeiro, Brazil
Rolón, Elsa María Zaldivar, 132
Rotich, Juliana, 72–77
Rubbo, Anna, 219
Safaricom, 73, 182
Safe Agua Water System, 210–11
Sangli Inclusive Planning, 150–51
San Rafael-Barrio Unido sector, La Vega settlement,
    see Caracas, Venezuela
Santa Marta, *see* Rio de Janeiro, Brazil
São Paulo Municipal Housing Secretariat (SEHAB), 19,
    80, 138
Sapra, Sharad, 100–5, 196
Savda Ghevra resettlement colony, *see* New Delhi,
    India
School on Wheels, 212–13
Secretary of Housing and Urban Development of
    Argentina, 160
Senegal, 29, 162–63
Dakar, 13–14, 162–63
Shack/Slum Dwellers International (SDI), 18, 24, 25,
    32–39, 108–112

Sheffield Road Upgrade: Community Mapping, 32,
    36, 111
Shelter Associates, 150
Shidhulai Swanirvar Sangstha, 154
Shuawa Arts Organization, 142
Shukla, Sukant, 130
Sierra Leone, 108, 202
Sitio Bangkal, Barangay San Isidro, *see* Philippines
Small, Robert, 94–99
Solidarités International, 198
SONO Water Filter, 214–15
Soonets, Silvia, 156
Sorda, Gabriela, 54–59
South Africa, 12, 19, 23, 24, 26, 34, 48, 76, 95, 99, 108,
    116, 128–29, 182, 196, 208–9
Cape Town, 4, 8, 19, 22, 24, 32, 41, 94–95, 97, 98, 99,
    111, 116, 124–25, 186–87
Durban, 41, 47, 48, 180–81, 184–85
Johannesburg, 128, 200, 218–19
Rustenburg, 116
SPARC (Society for Promotion of Area Resource
    Centres), 33, 34, 36, 112
Spaza-de-Move-on, 184–85
Sri Lanka, 23, 108, 202
Steinbru, Vanja, 188
Sticky Situations, 219
Struck, Arturo Ortiz, 126–27
Sultanpuri, slum resettlement colony, *see* Delhi, India
Sustainable Mobility & Accessibility Research &
    Transformation (SMART), 28, 194
SuryaHurricane solar lamps, 154–55
Swaziland, 108
Takemura, Shinichi, 152–53
Taller Territorial de México, 126
Tangible Earth, 152–53
Tanzania, 108, 182, 202, 216
Arusha, 190
Technology for Tomorrow, 136
Un Techo Para mi País Social Innovation Center, 59,
    211
Text to Change, 216–17

Thailand, 23, 29, 60–71, 108, 114
Bangkok, 13, 14, 60–71, 114–15
Toy, Jennifer, 170
Uganda, 100–6, 108, 190, 202, 216–17
Kampala, 27, 136–37, 188–89, 196–97
Mbarara, 216
Umande Trust, 27, 192
UN-Habitat, 15, 17, 19, 26, 41, 44, 135, 144, 192
UNICEF, 27, 100–5, 196
University of Buenos Aires, 26, 55, 122, 160
University of Sydney, 219
***Urbanism Manual for Precarious Settlements (Manual
    de Urbanismo para Asentamientos Precarios)***, 26,
    54–59, 122–23
Urban Mining, 138–39
Urban Think Tank, 19, 29, 47, 174
Urhahn, Dre, *see* Haas&Hahn
Ushahidi, 72–77, 146
Vale, Márcio Luiz, 166
Venezuela, 19, 23, 24, 108
Caracas, 16, 46, 156–57, 174–75
Vertical Gym (*Gimnasio Vertical*), 29, 46, 47, 174–75
Vietnam, 23, 108
Voice of Kibera, 146–47
Warren, Jeff, 142
Warwick Junction, *see* Durban, South Africa
**WASSUP (Water, Amenities, and Sanitation Services
    Upgrade Project)**, 218–19
**Water for Low-income Communities (*Tubig Para sa
    Barangay*) Program**, 6, 220–21
Wei, Diane Jie, 211
Werthmann, Christian, 78–93, 144–45
Wyk, Westley van, 124
Yerwada Slum Upgrade, 34, 37, 38, 52, 108, 112
Yoff, *see* Dakar, Senegal
Yoff Sustainable Wastewater System, 162–63
Zabaleen Waste Recycling, 18, 113
Zambia, 108, 190
Zimbabwe, 108, 109

ACKNOWLEDGMENTS

Cooper-Hewitt, National Design Museum would like to thank the following individuals and organizations for their invaluable help and cooperation during the preparation of the *Design with the Other 90%: CITIES* exhibition, book, and Web sites.

Design with the Other 90%: CITIES Advisory Committee

Benjamin de la Peña, Associate Director, Rockefeller Foundation

Joan Shigekawa, Senior Deputy Chairman, National Endowment for the Arts

Nick Bilton, Lead Writer, Bits Blog, and Design Integration Editor, *New York Times*

Naser Faruqui, Director of Innovation Policy and Science, International Development Research Centre

José de Filippi, Jr., Representative, Brazil, and former Mayor of Diadema, Brazil

Patricia Mechael, Ph.D., MHS, Director of Strategic Application of Mobile Technology, Public Health and Development, Center for Global Health and Economic Development at the Earth Institute, Columbia University

Rakesh Mohan, Vice Chairman (nonexecutive), Indian Institute of Human Settlements, and Global Adviser, McKinsey Global Institute, McKinsey and Company

George Y. Obeng, Research Fellow and Lecturer, Technology Consultancy Centre, Kwame Nkrumah University of Science & Technology

Sheela Patel, Chair, Shack/Slum Dwellers International, and Founding Director, Society for Promotion of Area Resource Centers

Edgar Pieterse, NRF South African Research Chair in Urban Policy and Director, African Centre for Cities, University of Cape Town

Darren Walker, Vice President of Education, Creativity and Free Expression Program, Ford Foundation

Citi: Reginia Brown, Montserrat Garrido, Mark Ingall, Susan Song

Rockefeller Foundation: Anna Brown, Robert Buckley, Brinda Ganguly, Justina Lai, Michele Tall

Deutsche Bank: Alessandra DiGuisto, Gary Hattem, Sam Marks, Arti Trehan

Procter & Gamble: Martha Depenbrock, Philip Duncan

Smithsonian Institution: G. Wayne Clough, Secretary; Richard Kurin, Undersecretary for History, Art, and Culture; William Bohnnet, National Board; Nancy Proctor

At Cooper-Hewitt:

Communications and Marketing: Jennifer Northrop, Laurie Olivieri, Micah Walter

Conservation: Perry C. Choe, Annie Hall

Curatorial: Matilda McQuaid, Bareket Kezwer

Development and External Affairs: Elyse Buxbaum, Deborah Fitzgerald, Kelly Gorman, Kelly Mullaney

Education: Caroline Payson, Shamus Adams, Mei Mah

Exhibitions: Jocelyn Groom, Matthew O'Connor, Mathew Weaver

Membership: Debbie Ahn, Nick Golebiewski

Publications: Chul R. Kim

Registrar: Steven Langehough, Melanie Fox, Larry Silver

Interns: Natalie Balthrop, Lara Huchteman

Formerly of Cooper-Hewitt: Sophia Amaro, Paul W. Thompson

Exhibition design: Moorhead & Moorhead: Granger Moorhead, Robert Moorhead

Exhibition graphics and Web site design: Tsang Seymour Design: Catarina Tsang, Patrick Seymour, Elena Penny, Eva Bochem-Shur, Carlos Abreu, Jillian Hobbs, Minali Chatani

Lighting design: Luce Group

Structural engineering: Gilsanz Murray Steficek

Fabrication: Creative Engineering

Profiles

10x10 Sandbag House: Luyanda Mpahlwa, Ulrike Mpahlwa, Westley Van Wyk

28 Millimetres: Women Are Heroes: Marc Azoulay

Abalimi Bezekhaya: Rob Small, Christina Kaba, Travis Blue, Matt Miller

Babajob.com: Sean Blagsvedt, Vir Kashyap

Bamboo (*Tacuara*) Loofah Panels: Elsa María Zaldivar Rolón

Bang Bua Canal Community Upgrading: Somsook Boonyabancha, Pissinee Chanpreechays, Thomas Kerr, Yanyong Boon-Long, Supreeya Noot

bePRO Motor-taxi Helmet: Vanja Steinbru, Kristoffer Leivestad-Olsen, Marianne Lie Berg

Bicycle Phone Charger: Bernard Kiwia, Jodie Wu, Daniel Mokrauer-Madden

BioCentre: Josiah Omotto, Dyfed Aubrey, Onono Cleophas, Pauline Nyota

Chennai Sustainable Transportation Network: Raj Cherubal, Daniel Robinson

Community Cooker: Jim Archer, James Kibochi, Mumo Musuva

Cristal de Luz: Maria Teresa Tetê Leal

Design With Africa: Bicycle Modules: Roelf Mulder, Byron Qually

Diadema Reurbanization: Mayor Mario Reali, Thiago Silva, Marilene Felinto, Marco Antonio Fialho, Wagner LaMonica

Digital Drum: Sean Blaschke, Terra Weikel

EcoFaeBrick: Syammahfuz Chazali

Floating Community Lifeboats: Abul Hassant Mohammed Rezwan

Garden-in-a-Sack: Winnie Mueni Mbusya, Keith Porter, Margarita Tileva

Ghonsla Insulation Panels: Zehra Ali

Grassroots Mapping: Jeff Warren

Guangzhou Bus Rapid Transit System: Walter Hook, Jessica Morris, Stephanie Lotshaw, Luc Nadal

Health Volunteer (*Shasthya Shebika*) Kit: Tania Zaman, Faisal Rezwan

Incremental Housing: Alejandro Aravena, Victor Oddó

Informal Settlement World Map: Christian Werthmann, Fiona Haran Luhrmann

Integral Urban Project: Silvia Soonets

Interlocking Stabilized Soil Blocks: Moses Kizza Musaazi

iTRUMP: Warwick Junction: Richard Dobson, Tasmi Quazi

Kaputiei New Town: Ingrid Munro, Elector Atieno, Mohammed Munyanya, Esther Ogola

Kibera Public Space Project: Chelina Odbert, Jen Wai-Kwun Toy, Arthur Adeya

Make a House Intelligent: Arturo Ortiz Struck

Map Kibera: Erica Hagen, Mikel Maron

Medellín Metrocable and Northeast Integral Urban Project: Alejandro Echeverri, Laura Gallego, Ximena Covaleda

MEDIKits: José Gómez-Márquez, Anna Young, Emma Tall

micro Home Solutions: Marco Ferrario, Rakhi Mehra

Millennium Bamboo School Project: Illac Diaz, Eleena Jamil

Miraculous Hills Community Resettlement: Rolando Palacio, Jason Rayos, Ruby Haddad

M-PESA Money-transfer System: Pauline Vaughan, Waceke Mbugua, Philibert Julai

Plastic Formwork System: Camalynne Breedt, Hennie Botes

Platform of Hope: Khondaker Hasibul Kabir, Quamrul Hasan

Pocket Reconstruction: Renu Khosla, Nandita Gupta, Sukant Shukla

Praça Cantão, Favela Painting Project: Jeroen Koolhaas, Dre Urhahn

Project Masiluleke: Robert Fabricant, Rachel Regina, Zinhle Thabethe

Proyecto Rehabitar: Eduardo Bekinschtein, Lucia Calcagno, Domingo Risso

Safe Agua Water System: Mariana Amatullo, Elisa Ruffino, Dan Gottlieb, Penny Herscovitch, Liliana Becerra

Sangli Inclusive Planning: Pratima Joshi

School on Wheels: Prachi Gondi, Jayashree Joglekar

Shack/Slum Dwellers International: Jockin Arputham, Wilma Adams, Benjamin Bradlow, Indu Agarwal, Jeremy Bean, Joel Bolnick, Sarah Ibanda, Catherine Nimusiima

Sheffield Road Upgrade: Community mapping: Bunita Kohler, Aditya Kumar

SONO Water Filter: Abul Hussam, Abul K. M. Munir

Spaza-de-Move-on: Doung Anwar Jahangeer

Tangible Earth: Shinichi Takemura

Text to Change: Bas Hoefman, Jan-Willem Loggers

Urbanism Manual for Precarious Settlements: Gabriela Sorda, Giovanni Da Prat

Urban Mining: Rainer Hehl, Maria Teresa Diniz dos Santos

Vertical Gym (*Gimnasio Vertical*): Alfredo Brillembourg, Marielly Casanova, Hubert Klumpner, Allison Schwartz

WASSUP: Anna Rubbo, Jennifer van den Bussche

Water for Low-income Communities (*Tubig Para sa Barangay*) Program: Lia Guerrero, Regina T. Unson

Yerwada Slum Upgrade: Prasanna Desai

Yoff Sustainable Wastewater System: Malick Gaye, Amadou Diallo, Cheikh Seck

Zabaleen Waste Recycling: Laila Iskandar

Research

Acumen Fund: Taylor Ray, Yasmina Zaidman

Laura Berenson

Adélia Borges

Edible Landscape Project: Vikram Bhatt, Marielle Dubbeling, Shuaib Lwasa

Emiliano Gandolfi

FrontlineSMS Medic: Josh Nesbit

Harvard University: John Beardsley, Rahul Mehrotra, Hashim Sarkis, Aylin B. Yildirim

Homeless International: Lucy McFarland

Institute for Transportation & Development Policy: Bernardo Baranda Sepúlveda, Andrés Fingeret, Ulises Navarro

International Development Research Centre: Mark Redwood, Mélanie Robertson

International Institute for Environment and Development: David Dodman, David Satterthwaite

KCAP Architects and Planners: Kees Christiaanse

Kickstart International: Martin Fisher

MIT: Julian Beinart

New School for Social Research: Michael Cohen

Netherlands Architecture Institute: Martine Zoeteman

Rutgers University: Gabriella Carolini

Stanford University: Jenna Davis, Perry L. McCarty

Sustainable Mobility & Accessibility Research & Transformation: Sue Zielinski

Technische Universität Berlin: Jörg Stollmann

TU Delft: Han Meyer, Veronica Zagare

UN-Habitat: Eduardo López Moreno

University of Manchester: Diana Mitlin

University of Pennsylvania: Anuradha Mathur

Voice of America: Jill Moss

World Resource Institute: Nancy Kete

Argentina: Blinder Janches & Co: Flavio Janches; Boldarini Arquitectura e Urbanismo: Marcos Boldarini; Emiliano Espasandin

Bangladesh: BRAC University: Huraera Jabeen, Shakil Ahmad Shimul

Brazil: Center for Digital Inclusion: Dhaval Chadha, Maria Eduarda Mattar; Davis Brody Bond: Anna Dietzsch; Institute for Transportation & Development Policy: Helena Orenstein de Almeida; Projeto Aprendiz: Gilberto Dimenstein; City of Sao Paulo: Elisabete França, Joo Hyun Ha, Vanessa Paida, Pedro Smith; Movimiento Territorial de Liberación: Marisol Cirano, Rosa Batalla; SouthSouthNorth: Thais Corral

India: Center for Environmental Planning and Technology University: Dinesh Mehta, Utpal Sharma, Abhijit Lokre, Dhruv D. Bhavsar; Indian Institute for Human Settlements: Aromar Revi; P. K. Das & Associates: P. K. Das; PUKAR: Anita Patil Deshmukh; SAATH: Rajendra Joshi, Keren Nazareth, Devuben Parmas; Mahila Housing SEWA Trust: Bijal Bhatt, Hansahen R. Dantani; Society for the Promotion of Area Resource Centers: Aditya Sawant; Charles Correa; Rahul Mehrotra

Kenya: Architecture for Humanity: Isaac Mugumbule; Cherie Blair Foundation: Henriette Kolb; Global Alliance for ICT and Development: Ravi Palepu; Hot Sun Foundation: Nathan Collett, Mercy Muriga, Josphat Keya; Maji na Ufanisi: Philip Lentek, Anne Muthoni; New Nairobi Dam Community Group: Ibrahim Maina; University of Nairobi: Elijah Biamah, Peter Ngau; Ushahidi: Erik Hersman, Melissa Tully

Mexico: Carlos Slim Health Institute: Rodrigo Saucedo; Arquitectura 911SC: José Castillo; RVDG arquitectura + urbanismo: Ruysdael Vivanco de Gyves

Philippines: Ayala Foundation: Guillermo M. Bill; Cities Development Initiative for Asia: Michael Lindfield, David Villeneuve, Emiel Wegelin; Homeless People's Federation Philippines: Ofelia Bagotlo, Sonia Cadornigara, Josie Cantoria, Norberto Carcellar, Nonoy Cebu, Celia Tuason, Sandra O. Yu

Senegal: African Institute of Urban Management: Oumar Cissé; Resource Centres on Urban Agriculture and Food Security: Marie Sophie; Tostan: Cody Donahue, Rebecca Tapscott; Université Laval: André Casault, Denise Piché, Émilie Pinard

South Africa: Abahlali Basemjondolo Movement: Mzonke Poni; Cape Peninsula University of Technology: Mugendi K. M'Rithaa; Cell-Life: Peter Benjamin; City of Cape Town: Stanley Visser, Godfrey Domingo, Christopher Hewitt; Community Media Trust: Jack Lewis, Debbie Kroon; Design Indaba: Ravi Naidoo, Nadine Botha, Mike Purdam; Development Action Group: Helen Macgregor; Southern African Housing Federation: John Hopkins; University of Cape Town: Harro von Blottnitz

Thailand: Community Architects for Shelter and Environment: Patama Roonrakwit

Uganda: ACTogethr: Sarah Ibanda, Catherine Nimusiima; GZT: Beatram Okalany; Makerere University: Bernard Kariko-Buhwezi; UN High Commissioner for Refugees Uganda: Needa Jehu-Hoyah, John Kilowoko

Venezuela: Consejo Comunal Santa Lucia: Juan Ugas; Ângela Capasso; Gerardo Rojas

PHOTOGRAPHIC CREDITS

Cover: © Proyectos Arqui5 C.A.; © Oscar Pabón
Back Cover: © Solidarités International

SMITH: 1: © 2006 Acumen Fund. 2, 4, 6, 9–11, 15: Cynthia E. Smith, © Smithsonian Institution. 3: ©Thapphawut Parinyapariwat. Sidebar: © Prefeitura do Município de Diadema. 5: © Eleena Jamil Architect. 7: © Khondaker Hasibul Kabir. 8: © Jeroen Koolhaas and Dre Urhahn. 12: © Shack/Slum Dwellers International (SDI). 13: © ...XYZ Design. 14: © Umande Trust. 16: © Karl Fjellstrom, Institute for Transportation & Development Policy

PATEL/ARPUTHAM (Shack/Slum Dwellers International): 1, 3–4, 6–7, 9: © SDI. 2, 5: © Community Organisation Resource Centre. 8: © SPARC. 10: Cynthia E. Smith, © Smithsonian Institution

PIETERSE: 1: © Dennis Gilbert/Courtesy of Working in Warwick. 2–3, 13: © Derechos de autor pertenecen a: Empresa de Desarrollo Urbano de Medellín EDU, Alcaldía de Medellín, Empresa de Transporte Masivo del Valle de Aburrá Limitada - Metro de Medellín Ltda y el Centro de Estudios Urbanos y Ambientales, urbam Universidad EAFIT. 4: © Elemental. 5, 9, 11–12: Cynthia E. Smith, © Smithsonian Institution. 6: Rendering: Tsang Seymour, © Smithsonian Institution, based on materials provided by the author. 7: © Kounkuey Design Initiative. 8: © Iwan Baan. 10: © Gerald Botha. 14: © Prefeitura do Município de Diadema. 15: © SDI. 16: © JR

SORDA (*Urbanism Manual*): 1–10: © Manual de Urbanismo para Asentamientos Precarios

BOONYABANCHA: 1, 3–5, 7–11: © Asian Coalition for Housing Rights (ACHR). 2, 6: © Chawanad Luansang/openspace

ROTICH (Ushahidi): 1–2: © Ushahidi, Inc. 3–5: Jonathan Shuler, © Ushahidi, Inc. 6: Caleb Bell, © Ushahidi, Inc. 7–8: © 2011 AfriGadget.com

WERTHMANN: 1, 21: © Harvard Graduate School of Design, Katie Powell. 2–3: © Fabio Costa, Prefeitura da Cidade do Rio de Janeiro. 4: © Gareth Doherty. 5: © Alejandro Echeverri, EDU, Municipality of Medellín. 6: © Nelson Kon. 7–8, 13: © Christian Werthmann. 9: © Hans Dieter Temp. 10: © Harvard Graduate School of Design, drawn by: Jonathan Tate, Anne Vaterlaus, and Catherine de Almeida. Map Sources: São Paulo Metrópole. Regina Maria Prosperi Meyer, Marta Dora Grostein and Ciro Biderman. São Paulo: Editora da Universidade de São Paulo, Imprensa Oficial do Estado de São Paulo, 2004, p 63: informal settlements as of 2000. Resolo: Regularização de Loteamentos no Municipio de Sao Pãulo. São Paulo: Portela Boldarini Aquitetura e Urbanismo, 2003, p. 27: irregular settlements. Centro de Estudos da Metrópole: http://www.centrodametropole.org.br/home.html. 11: © São Paulo Housing Agency. 12: © Harvard Graduate School of Design, Cynthia Silvey. 14: © Harvard Graduate School of Design. 15: © Harvard Graduate School of Design, Tomás Amorim. 16–19: © Harvard Graduate School of Design, Andrew ten Brink. 20: © Harvard Graduate School of Design, Rina Salvi. 22–23: © Harvard Graduate School of Design, Joseph Claghorn.

KABA/SMALL (Abalimi Bezekhaya): 1–7: Cynthia E. Smith, © Smithsonian Institution

SAPRA (Digital Drum): 1–3: © UNICEF Uganda/Sean Blaschke. 4: © UNICEF Uganda/Anne Lydia Sekandi. 5: © UNICEF Uganda/Sean Blaschke. 6: © UNICEF Uganda/Terra Weikel. 7: © CSIR/Grant Cambridge. 8: © UNICEF Uganda/Tadej Znidarcic. 9: © UNICEF Uganda/Terra Weikel. 10: © UNICEF Uganda/Anne Lydia Sekandi

EXCHANGE: Shack/Slum Dwellers International: © SDI; © SPARC. Miraculous Hills Community Resettlement: Cynthia E. Smith, © Smithsonian Institution. Sheffield Road Upgrade: Community Mapping: © Community Organisation Resource Centre. Yerwada Slum Upgrade: © SDI; © Prasanna Desai Architects. Zabaleen Waste Recycling: © CID Consulting. Bang Bua Canal Community Upgrading: © ACHR. Design With Africa: Bicycle Modules: © ...XYZ Design. Incremental Housing: © Elemental. micro Home Solutions: © marco ferrario, mHS. *Urbanism Manual for Precarious Settlements*: © Manual de Urbanismo para Asentamientos Precarios. 10x10 Sandbag House: © Wieland Gleich - Archigraphy.com. Make a House Intelligent: © Arturo Ortiz Struck. Plastic Formwork System: © moladi South Africa. Pocket Reconstruction: Cynthia E. Smith, © Smithsonian Institution. Bamboo (*Tacuara*) Loofah Panels: © Elsa Zaldívar/Base ECTA. EcoFaeBrick: © EcoFaeBrick. Ghonsla Insulation Panels: © Ghonsla. Interlocking Stabilized Soil Blocks: Cynthia E. Smith, © Smithsonian Institution; © ISSB mkmusaazi. Urban Mining: © MAS Urban Design ETH Zürich

REVEAL: 28 Millimetres: Women Are Heroes: © JR. Grassroots Mapping: © Jeffrey Warren; © Grassroots Mapping. Informal Settlement World Map: © Christian Werthmann. Map Kibera: © Anufia Pisanec; © Map Kibera Trust. Praça Cantão, Favela Painting Project: © Jeroen Koolhaas and Dre Urhahn; © Haas&Hahn. Sangli Inclusive Planning: © Shelter Associates. Tangible Earth: Bill Moggridge, © Smithsonian Institution.

DESIGN WITH THE OTHER 90%: CITIES
Cynthia E. Smith et al.
© 2011 Smithsonian Institution

Published by
Cooper-Hewitt, National Design Museum
Smithsonian Institution
2 East 91st Street
New York, NY 10128, USA
www.cooperhewitt.org

Published on the occasion of the exhibition
Design with the Other 90%: CITIES
Organized by Cooper-Hewitt, National Design Museum, Smithsonian Institution,
and presented at the United Nations, October 15, 2011–January 9, 2012.

Design with the Other 90%: CITIES is sponsored by

Generous support is provided by ROCKEFELLER FOUNDATION

Additional funding is provided by Procter & Gamble, Deutsche Bank, Smithsonian
2.0 Fund, the Albert Kunstadter Family Foundation, and Smithsonian Institution's
Research Opportunity Fund.

This exhibition is presented at the United Nations in the context of the United
Nations Academic Impact initiative.

This publication is made possible in part by The Andrew W. Mellon Foundation.

Distributed to the trade worldwide by Distributed Art Publishers
155 Sixth Avenue, 2nd floor
New York, NY 10013, USA
www.artbook.com

First edition: October 2011
ISBN: 978-0-910503-83-9

Museum Editor: Chul R. Kim, Director of Publications
Book design: Tsang Seymour Design
Printed in South Korea by Taeshin Inpack Co. Ltd.

Library of Congress Cataloging-in-Publication data available from the publisher.